QUICKBOOKS ONLINE 2023

A STEP BY STEP GUIDE FOR BOTH BEGINNERS AND PRO USERS OF QUICKBOOKS ONLINE

JACOB GODWIN

TABLE OF CONTENTS

INTRODUCTION

QuickBooks is an accounting program created by *Intuit* whose products offer desktop, internet, and cloud-based accounting programs that can process invoices and business payments. The majority of QuickBooks' customers are medium-sized and small enterprises. QuickBooks is well-liked by these consumers due to its simplicity of use and reporting capabilities.

Numerous features from the Web have been incorporated by Intuit into QuickBooks, including:

- ❖ Outsourcing and guidance with remote payroll
- ❖ Reconciliation and online banking
- ❖ Enhanced mail capabilities with Microsoft Outlook
- ❖ Functions of electronic payments
- ❖ Remotely accessible features
- ❖ Map capabilities

Additionally, QuickBooks provides support features and other features including pre-authorization of electronic funds and employee time monitoring alternatives. Intuit also offers QuickBooks Online, a cloud-based service that enables users to access the program through a secure logon by subscribing for a fee. Intuit frequently updates and upgrades its QuickBooks software.

QuickBooks is typically regarded as being simple to use and comprehend, even for business owners and users who lack financial or accounting knowledge. The accessibility of ready-to-use templates for the creation of graphs, company plans, invoices, and spreadsheets is another advantage of QuickBooks. By automating business owners' signatures on business checks (which are scanned and uploaded for usage), it can also help them save time and effort. Another key benefit of QuickBooks is its integration with other programs. It can walk people through each of its capabilities and has an intuitive user interface.

Accounting software like QuickBooks is used to monitor revenue and expenses. Many owners of small and medium-sized businesses utilize QuickBooks. There were 3.3 million QuickBooks Online subscribers as of 2019, and 40% of them were small companies. There are different subscription tiers made available for QuickBooks Online. Multi-currency functionality are available on the majority of QuickBooks Online subscription tiers. Businesses who work with overseas clients and suppliers will find this handy.

PART 1: GETTING STARTED WITH QUICKBOOKS ONLINE

CHAPTER ONE

WELCOME TO QUICKBOOKS ONLINE

What Is QuickBooks Online?

QuickBooks is actually the most common small business accounting software that businesses use to manage income and spending and keep track of their company's financial health. It can be used to bill clients, pay invoices, generate reports, and prepare taxes. QuickBooks offers numerous solutions that are suitable for everybody, from a freelancer to a medium-sized enterprise.

QuickBooks has numerous options, but QuickBooks Online is recommended for the majority of new businesses. QuickBooks Online offers a free 30-day trial that does not require a credit card.

How does QuickBooks operate?

QuickBooks Online supports both monthly and annual plans. After you join up, you'll be able to use services tailored to your sort of business. There are additional desktop versions available. The features are intended toward freelancers, small and medium-sized business owners, and entrepreneurs.

QuickBooks Online works with other Intuit products. TurboTax (for preparing personal income tax returns) and ProConnect (tax software for accounting professionals). It also interfaces with a wide range of other software and apps. These include, to name a few, those that manage charitable donations, scheduling, time tracking, document management, payment processing, and inventory management.

Users can manage and automate a wide range of business operations with these integrations and compatible technologies. There is a free 30-day trial option available before you have to part with your money. This is an excellent opportunity to learn about QuickBooks Online.

While there are numerous options available, you are not required to sign up for all QuickBooks services at once. You can begin with a single program, such as accounting or payroll software, and add others as your business grows. If you outgrow a service, you can select whether to eliminate or upgrade it.

A typical QuickBooks setup would look something like this: you sign up for the accounting software, then install QuickBooks Live to assist fully customize your setup. As your company expands, you hire full-time workers, contractors, and freelancers. After that, you may sign up for QuickBooks Payroll to automate monthly payments and QuickBooks Time to track billable hours.

What's the distinction between Quicken and QuickBooks?

People sometimes draw similarities between Quicken and QuickBooks since they are both popular finance programs. They do not, however, fulfill the same function.

- ❖ **QuickBooks** is accounting software for small businesses.
- ❖ **Quicken** is personal finance software designed for individuals and families that want to keep track of their finances.

Versions of QuickBooks

QuickBooks is compatible with a large number of devices, but each version has minor peculiarities that you should be aware of. Check to see if the software is compatible with your operating system and device before making a decision.

1. QuickBooks for the Mac

   for Mac is a Mac-specific version of the accounting software. It differs from the Desktop and Online editions in that some features are optimized for the Mac platform. The Mac 2021 version is available for $399.99 one-time payment.

2. QuickBooks Desktop

QuickBooks Desktop is intended for use with Windows. It includes many of the main functions of accounting software. Users can select from three distinct bundles. The most comprehensive bundle includes additional features such as more granular user permissions and automatic data encrypted backups.

3. QuickBooks Online

Online is intended to be user-friendly, as it can be accessed by web browser or mobile device.

The QuickBooks Multicurrency capability is actually one of the most notable features of QuickBooks Online. This function is useful if you are to carry out foreign commerce. The Essentials, Plus, and Advanced subscriptions all have multicurrency support.

QuickBooks Desktop vs. QuickBooks Online

- ❖ QuickBooks Online, at its most basic, is the cloud-based version of QuickBooks. All of your data is saved in QuickBooks' cloud, and you can access it from any device, at any time. QuickBooks Desktop, on the other side, is installed locally and has a licensing mechanism.
- ❖ QuickBooks Online offers a monthly price system; you select the appropriate package and then pay for the service each month. QuickBooks Desktop, on the other hand, offers a three-year license or you can pay for annual updates.
- ❖ QuickBooks Online's most expensive plans support up to 25 users. However, QuickBooks Desktop Pro charges $299 for each extra user, up to a maximum of three. Meanwhile, Desktop Premier and Enterprise support up to five and thirty users, respectively.

❖ When using QuickBooks Online, QuickBooks handles your security. However, because QuickBooks Desktop is installed locally, you are to take care of your own data security.

❖ QuickBooks Online also has additional automation tools, which may suit small businesses better - the more duties you can outsource to the program, the more effective your business is expected to be. QuickBooks Desktop also equipped a more antiquated and difficult-to-use user interface than QuickBooks Online.

QuickBooks Software Options

1. **Payroll:** Payroll processing is an essential function for any business. The payroll add-on calculates payroll as frequently as you specify. Three options provide your firm with the scalability it requires to build and add features as required. The Core plan covers everything a small to medium-sized business requires to get started, while the Premium and Elite plans include services such as same-day direct deposit and expert setup support.

2. **Online Transactions:** You realize the significance of sustaining a steady positive cash flow as a business owner. QuickBooks Payments allows you to accept online payments when you issue invoices from the app. If you have a large number of global locations, QuickBooks enables you to accept payments in local currencies. Of course, it's best to begin by checking to see if QuickBooks accepts payments in the currency you're dealing with. All transactions are done automatically as they take place.

3. **Invoicing:** Invoicing is an important operation for many businesses, especially those that supply services or depend on freelancers. Invoices can be generated from scratch or using an estimate in QuickBooks. To receive recurring payments, you can even construct an invoice. The invoice can then be mailed to clients or printed and delivered in paper form. It allows you to easily run and view reports including the number of unpaid invoices, total amount owed by clients, and invoice details (paid or due).

4. **Tracking Employee Time and Expenses:** Using QuickBooks, it is very easy to keep track of the time and billable expenses incurred through employees or subcontractors. Either they may submit it manually and have a bookkeeper on your end enter the information in the app, or they can enter it themselves using the QuickBooks mobile app.

5. **Tracking of Bills and Expenses:** While QuickBooks is being installed, your bank and credit card accounts can be linked. Your bills and expenses will then be tracked automatically by QuickBooks. However, manual bill tracking is always an option if you choose. A manual transaction, perhaps one involving cash or a check, can be immediately recorded. Once more, QuickBooks provides a wide range of reports for reviewing your expenses and bills. You can easily track upcoming payments to make sure you pay your bills on timely if you maintain track of your bills.

How QuickBooks Can Benefit Your Company

Signing up for QuickBooks increases the probability that other platforms your business may use, such as customer relationship management (CRM) software, may interface with it and streamline processes. QuickBooks is one of the well-known names in the accounting software industry. Right now, QuickBooks is offering two promotions: sign up and receive a 50% reduction on the first three months, or try it out for free for 30 days.

Here are some other ways QuickBooks might help your business.

1. **Financial Reports at Your Disposal:** All common financial statements, such as the cash flow statements, balance sheet, and taxes paid, are readily available to you. You can either print these off and provide them to your accountant when you file your taxes, or you can invite them to see these statements online without the need for a login name or password.

2. **Uncomplicated Inventory Management:** It can be highly time-consuming to manually track inventory when you sell it, record the

information in the appropriate expense account, and determine your taxable income at the end of the fiscal year. QuickBooks simplifies things by carrying out every task automatically. Any time you get payment for an item from your inventory, the appropriate expense account is updated and automatically reflected in your taxable income.

3. **Simple Taxation**: Tax season is challenging and unpleasant for many reasons. It is easier for your business since QuickBooks automatically calculates the income and costs as they happen. Every cycle, taxes are calculated automatically, even for payroll, which has a substantial tax obligation. Print everything your accountant needs to finish the returns fast, then mail it to them. The QuickBooks mobile app makes it simple to scan and submit receipts in real-time, so you don't have to scramble to gather them when it's time to file your taxes. You might also invite them to see the reports on their own and download any files they require.

Checking On QuickBooks Pricing

If you're looking for an accounting solution, first decide whether you want online, cloud-based software or a desktop application that keeps your data locally. QuickBooks pricing varies greatly based on whatever product you select and how many people you require.

While price is an essential aspect, it should not be the only thing to consider when assessing accounting software solutions. Before making a final decision, consider the simplicity of use and essential features of each edition.

QuickBooks subscription pricing
1. Quickbooks Online

Products for QuickBooks Online are available with a monthly subscription. One of the company's most well-liked options for small-business owners in terms of accounting software is the cloud-based offering. The first few months of service for new customers of QuickBooks Online are often discounted or offered as a free 30-day trial. Users are not required to pay termination fees if they change plans or cancel.

Plan name	Price	Features
Simple start	$30 per month	Basic accounting tools on a single user license
Essentials	$55 per month	Up to 3 users can use the basic start features for bill administration and time monitoring.
Plus	$85 per month	Up to 5 users can utilize all important functions, including project monitoring and inventory tracking.
Advanced	$200 per month	Up to 25 users can use all of the services, plus a dedicated account team, extensive business analytics, batch invoicing for employee expenditures, workflow automation, and more.

2. Self-Employed QuickBooks

Specifically created for independent contractors, freelancers, and business owners, QuickBooks Self-Employed is a "lite" version of the Online software. It helps you distinguish between personal and corporate funds and is perfect for people who receive income from a variety of sources.

Plan name	Price	Features
Self-employed	$30 per month	Quarterly tax projections, methods for separating personal

		and corporate costs, and mileage tracking.
Self-employed tax bundle	$25 per month	All Self-Employed capabilities, as well as the capacity to use QuickBooks to pay quarterly anticipated taxes online and upload data to TurboTax.
Self-employed live tax bundle	$35 per month	Access to CPAs as well as all Self-Employed Tax Bundle features

3. QuickBooks Desktop Pro Plus

The ease of use of QuickBooks Desktop Pro Plus will appeal to small business owners who want to operate with locally installed software. There are plans that can accommodate up to three users, and payroll may be added for an additional $500 per year plus $2 per employee each month.

Plan name	Price	Features
Pro plus	Start at $349.99 per year for 1 user.	Basic bookkeeping tools that are locally installed

4. QuickBooks Desktop Premier Plus

This edition of QuickBooks Desktop is more capable than Pro Plus and will work well for companies that need to project future revenue and expenses. Industry-specific reports are also available to Premier subscribers. Plans are available for up to five users, and payroll can be added for an additional $500 per year plus $2 per employee each month

Plan name	Price	Features
Premier plus	Start at $549.99 per year for 1 user.	All Pro Plus features, as well as customized inventory reports, industry-specific reports, forecasting tools, and more.

5. QuickBooks Desktop Enterprise

QuickBooks Desktop Enterprise, one of Intuit's most effective business accounting products, offers a number of additional features like accessibility to even more than 200 report templates and special customer support. There are many levels of cloud access that business owners can purchase, and plans accommodate up to 40 users.

Note: Only local access plans are covered by the rates stated below; cloud access and increased user counts result in higher annual prices.

Plan name	Price	Features
Silver	Starts at $1,340 per year for 1 user	Inventory management, advanced reporting, task costing, priority customer support, and other features are available in industry-specific editions.
Gold	Starts at $1,740 per year for 1 user.	Payroll features plus all Silver features.
Platinum	Starts at $2,140 per year for 1 user.	Advanced inventory, advanced pricing rules, and workflow approvals in addition to all Gold features.
Diamond	Starts at $4,200 per	All Platinum features,

year for 1user (only offered as a monthly subscription).	plus $1 per employee every pay period for Assisted Payroll to handle filings for federal and state payroll taxes. Users can additionally add a QuickBooks Time Elite connector for $5 per employee per month and a Salesforce CRM connector for $150 per month.

6. QuickBooks Mac Plus

As the name would suggest, this version of QuickBooks is specifically designed for business owners that prefer locally installed accounting software and utilize Apple computers. Plans allow for a maximum of three users, and business owners could add payroll services at an extra cost.

Plan name	Price	Features
Mac plus	Starts at $349.99 per 1 user.	Basic bookkeeping tools, plus data recovery services.

Payroll

QuickBooks Payroll has three plans: Core, Premium, and Elite, each with greater functionality than the one before it. Their prices and features are as follows:

1. Core - $45 per month, plus $5 per employee per month. This strategy covers the essentials: It processes payroll automatically, files payroll taxes, and provides employee benefits like as health insurance and workers' compensation.

2. Premium - $75 per month plus $5 each for each employee. This plan offers automatic time tracking, same-day direct deposit, and role-based access for more detailed but automated management over payouts.

3. Elite - $125/month plus $10 per employee per month. This service provides tax penalty protection as well as hands-on assistance with setup and troubleshooting from an expert.

Comparing Quickbooks Features And How to Navigate Through Each

The best cloud-based accounting software for small business owners and entrepreneurs is QuickBooks Online. By automating your bookkeeping, tracking your sales tax and payroll tax, and utilizing the reporting tools offered by the various plans, you may save time. To better monitor your cash flow and make financial decisions for your company, you will have access to the most recent information.

This guide will assist you in determining which QuickBooks Online plan is ideal for your small business in order to help you make that decision.

Self-employed plan

The Self-Employed plan comes last. This accommodates just one user and costs only $15 per month.

This strategy is intended for independent contractors who record their income as sole proprietors on an IRS Schedule C form.

QuickBooks Online Easy Start Plan or Simple Start plan

If you use a debit or credit card to pay for your expenses and have straightforward invoicing requirements for your clients and customers, QuickBooks Online's Simple Start or Easy Start Plan is the best option. This is a fantastic place to start if you're a consultant or contractor that has to keep track of expenses as they occur, send invoices and receive payment, monitor mileage, and run basic reports!

The Simple Start or Easy Start Plan for QuickBooks Online will keep track of all the data you require to submit sales tax returns, prepare your income tax returns at the end of the year, and run reports to monitor the performance of your company all year long.

QuickBooks Simple Start Plan Price

QuickBooks Online Simple Start Plan costs

- ❖ $30 per month in the United States,
- ❖ $22 per month in Canada and Australia, and
- ❖ £15.00 per month in the United Kingdom.

Features of QuickBooks Simple Start

To examine the features available in the various QuickBooks Online plans, let's start with the Simple Start Plan. These are the fundamental features of QuickBooks Online, and they are all available in both the Essentials and Plus plans.

1. **Connect Your Credit Card and Bank Accounts:** QuickBooks Online allows you to connect your bank and credit card accounts and import bank transactions directly. This is where QuickBooks Online's magic begins! You will be able to automate many of your transactions and save hours of manual entry bookkeeping by using artificial intelligence based on your earlier entries and bank rules you define.

2. **Capture Expenses Using the App:** You won't have to worry about misplacing receipts or being unable to claim expenses on your taxes, and you'll have easy access to those receipts under "attachments" if you're audited or need to retrieve a receipt for any reason.

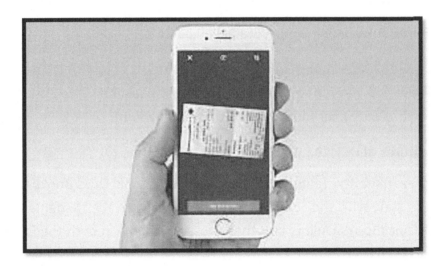

3. **Mileage tracking:** You can use the app to track your miles in order to quantify car travel, claim expenditures, and receive assistance if you are audited.

4. **Track and Report Sales Tax:** There will be no more guessing or adding up invoices and losing out on tax credits. Sales tax is calculated on all transactions recorded in QuickBooks Online.

5. **Account Reconciliation:** It is critical to reconcile your bank and credit card accounts on a regular basis to ensure that your records are comprehensive and accurate. QuickBooks Online makes reconciliation simple, and any problems are immediately identified for fast rectification!

6. **Invoice Your Customers and Receive Payments on the Go:** You may create an invoice right away using QuickBooks Online by logging in on your laptop, using the app on your phone or tablet, or both. You can email your client instantly, and ideally you can also get paid there and then!

7. **Create fundamental accounting reports:** This package includes all the reports you'll need to understand how your business is doing. To assist you in running your firm, create an income or profit and loss statement and a balance sheet. To monitor your cash flow, you may also run an accounts receivable report to find out who owes you money.

8. **Send Estimates to your Customers**: Send an estimate to your prospective customer and obtain approval for your quote ahead of time. When the task is finished, this is readily converted to an invoice. Saving time after a project is completed and it is time to relax after a long day of work!

9. **Progress Invoicing:** Improve your cash flow management. Rather than waiting until the finish, you can send an invoice halfway

through the process. This is similarly simple to create using your estimate.

Quickbooks online Essentials

The QuickBooks Online Essentials Plan is a good alternative when your business expands and you have credit with your suppliers and contractors and pay them after the items and services have been delivered to your small business.

It also allows you to manage and bill time, customize invoices further, and automate more operations. This is the most popular plan; it has more features than the Simple Start Plan and is a terrific bargain.

QuickBooks Essentials Plan Price

The QuickBooks Online Essentials Plan is priced at:

- ❖ $55 per month in the United States
- ❖ $44 per month in Canada, $37 per month in Australia,
- ❖ and £22 per month in the United Kingdom.

QuickBooks Online Essentials Plan allows for up to three users.

Features of the QuickBooks Essentials Plan

To compare the features available in the various QuickBooks Online plans, the additional options available if you upgrade to an Essentials Plan are as follows. You can also learn about what's available to this plan via the Simple Start and Easy Start Plans, as well as what's available if you upgrade to the Plus Plan.

1. **Enter and Pay Bills:** When you buy products and services and plan to pay for them later, you enter the total cost as a "Bill" in QuickBooks. By doing so, you capture the expense - the cost of what you are acquiring - at the time of purchase while also recording an amount owed. You may examine your entire spending

at any time in order to monitor your profitability, as well as how much you owe in order to manage your cash.

2. **Record Time Activity as Billable to a Customer:** Capturing time activities and marking some as billable to a customer allows you to manage your time and the time of your employees, and guarantees that you don't forget to charge for your valuable time when you invoice your customer. If you record your time as you do the activity, there is less likelihood that you will forget to record it at the end of the day or week. By labeling it billable, you will be notified when you create an invoice that there is time to add to that invoice, and you will have the option of adding it to the current invoice or keeping it until the next invoice you send. In either case, you are considerably less likely to forget to bill your customer for time that they should be paying for.

3. **Weekly Timesheet:** You can use the weekly timesheet option in addition to entering single time activities. All individual time actions flow into the weekly timesheet, and inputs can also be submitted directly to the timesheet. If you have employees who work on the same customer multiple times each week, this is an excellent alternative to logging individual activities. The customer being worked on, the service performed, and whether or not it is billable can all be entered. You can also input information that will be copied to the invoice when it is time to bill the client.

4. **Recurring transactions:** Recurring transactions are a fantastic time saver. I use them in my business, and when combined with automated payment processing, I receive and record monthly subscriptions automatically! Recurring transactions can be accessed by clicking the gear icon in the upper right corner. You can set up recurring transactions for bills you pay on a regular basis, especially if they have several lines and would be difficult or time-consuming to categorize from the bank feed.

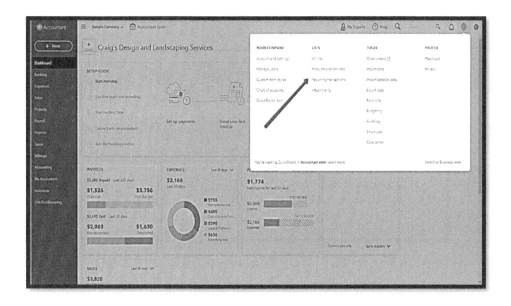

Recurring transactions can be utilized to prevent you from having to input all of the categories or rows each time you make a major entry. Daily sales are an outstanding example of this. You can keep a transaction as "unscheduled" and use it anytime you need it by creating one. Not all recurring transactions must be recorded automatically!

On the bottom black bar of most transactions, there is an option to "Make recurring."

5. **Delayed Credits and Charges:** Delayed credits and charges are referred to as "non posting" transactions, which implies they are not immediately recorded to your records and must be used by you. A delayed charge would be if you have a monthly subscription for your clients and you don't want to create an invoice or a sales receipt yet, but you want to include it when you do invoice them.

A delayed credit is a sum you want to subtract from your customer's invoice. When someone makes a deposit in advance, I use delayed credits. I want to make sure I record the amount transferred to the bank and don't forget to deduct it when I send an invoice to my client. I avoid the awkwardness of submitting an invoice without the prepaid amount subtracted by arranging a delayed credit!

You can set up a delayed charge or a delayed credit as a recurring transaction to guarantee that you don't forget to charge for those regular sums that aren't paid for right away!

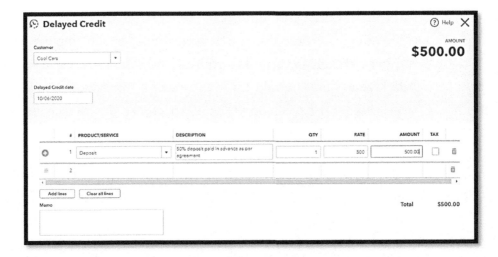

6. **Multicurrency:** If you buy or sell products in a different currency, being able to track those items in the relevant currency will offer you far more precise results and, once set up, will save you a lot of time and confusion! You can enable multicurrency by clicking the gear icon under accounts and settings. You will be warned that this cannot be undone; the only disadvantage of having multi currency enabled is that extra columns will appear in your reports. These are readily removed.

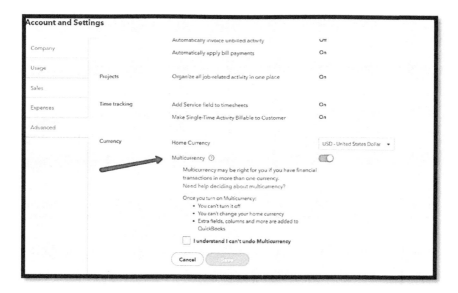

QuickBooks Online calculates any exchange differences automatically, and it does an excellent job at it! I wouldn't bother with this option if you don't use foreign currencies or have only a few charges on your credit card, for example. I would recommend using the multi currency function if you have customers who bill in other currencies or bills that you record now and pay later in other currencies.

7. **Pay Down Credit Card:** A fantastic new feature that allows you to easily enter a credit card payment without duplicate recording it or mucking it up from the bank feed.

23

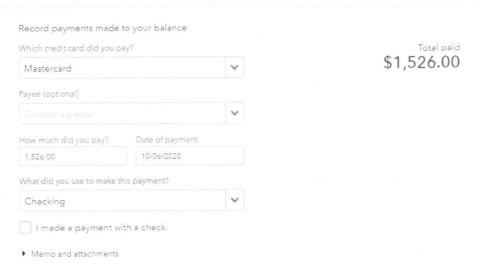

The fields are then displayed on your invoice.

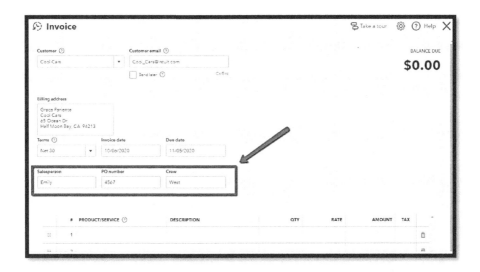

You may also filter reports to include custom fields, which could be beneficial for assessing staff sales for commission purposes or managing an area without having to subscribe to the plus plan for location monitoring.

9. **Gratuities and Tips:** A relatively recent function allows you to track consumer tips and subsequently pay them out to your staff or workforce. This feature must be enabled in Accounts and Settings.

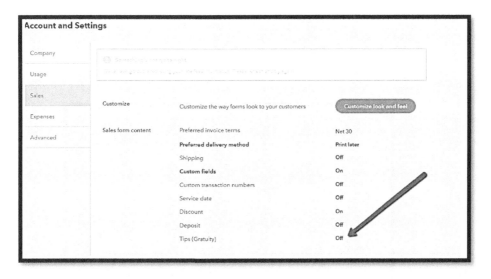

When you enable the tips option, you can include a tips box on your sales receipts:

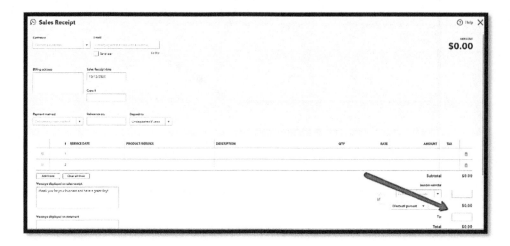

Any tips collected are then stored in a new "Tips" account created in the chart of accounts, where they may be tracked and distributed to your employees and workers. Any unpaid tips will be straightforward to track, and you can verify the worth of undistributed tips at any moment. A fantastic new function!

10. **Account for Shipping:** The shipping charge is another new field you may add to your invoices. If you charge to ship goods to clients and want to track them individually, you can enable this feature under Accounts and Settings.

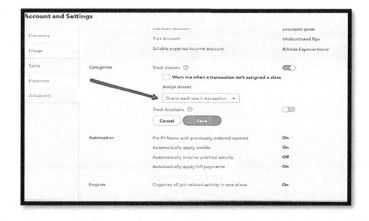

When enabled, a new field shows in your invoice:

Any shipping amounts input will be tracked separately, allowing you to readily see what you have gathered for shipping. You can thus be certain to either recuperate or properly track your shipping expenditures in order to manage your business decisions around shipping and shipping rates to your consumers. With correct information on how much you charged for shipping, you may either recuperate your shipping costs or properly track them in order to manage your business decisions regarding shipping and shipping charges to your consumers.

QuickBooks Online Plus

You can take your business to the next level with the QuickBooks Online Plus subscription. The additional reporting choices provided by the class and location features allow you to see the results of your small business using characteristics that are relevant to you. The QuickBooks Online Plus

Plan is required if you track and sell inventory. You can appropriately account for the cost of things sold, issue purchase orders to your suppliers, and keep track of the inventory on hand.

Budgeting and project management tools help you keep on schedule and manage your cash flow and business success. The QuickBooks Online Plus plan provides you with all of the information you need to make sound business decisions in real time.

The price of the QuickBooks Online Plus Plan

- ❖ In the US, $85 per month,
- ❖ In Canada, $66 per month,
- ❖ In Australian $52 per month,
- ❖ In UK, £32 per month,

Up to five users may use QuickBooks Online Plus.

Features of the QuickBooks Plus Plan

The following extra options are accessible if you upgrade to a Plus Plan in order to evaluate the features offered in the various QuickBooks Online plans. Additionally, you can read about the features that are included only in the Essentials Plan, the Simple Start Plan, and the Easy Start Plan.

1. **Class Tracking:** One of my favorite aspects of QuickBooks Online is this one. You can run a variety of reports by class by class-tagging each line of a transaction. The possibilities are truly endless when it comes to creating reports for different parts of your company, various departments, and sales divisions.

   Classes are enabled in Accounts and Settings:

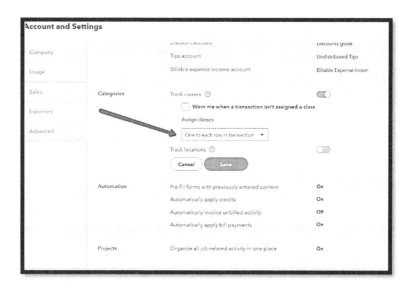

If you want to make sure that every transaction is included in a class, whether it be a division or a sector of your organization, you would switch this on. You then have the option to receive a warning if a transaction is not allocated a class. You can still find any items overlooked when you record them by running a class report and looking at unspecified items; more on that below; don't worry if you don't choose this.

Another choice is to apply a class to every row in a transaction or to the transaction as a whole. In order to split a bill between many classes, I would advise choosing the first choice, which is only accessible for complete transactions when we look at locations next. For instance, if you receive a bill for numerous goods from various divisions, such as a huge stationery order or an expense report from a traveling salesperson.

Here is an easy illustration:

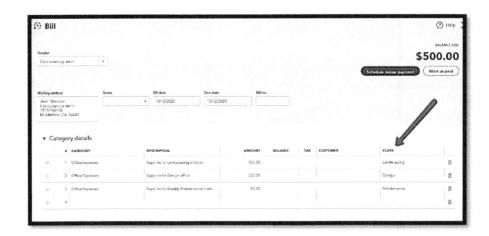

Now let us take a look at the reporting

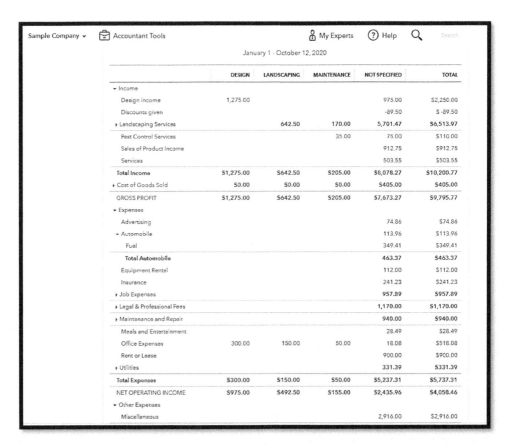

January 1 - October 12, 2020

	DESIGN	LANDSCAPING	MAINTENANCE	NOT SPECIFIED	TOTAL
▾ Income					
Design income	1,275.00			975.00	$2,250.00
Discounts given				-89.50	$ -89.50
▸ Landscaping Services		642.50	170.00	5,701.47	$6,513.97
Pest Control Services			35.00	75.00	$110.00
Sales of Product Income				912.75	$912.75
Services				503.55	$503.55
Total Income	$1,275.00	$642.50	$205.00	$8,078.27	$10,200.77
▸ Cost of Goods Sold	$0.00	$0.00	$0.00	$405.00	$405.00
GROSS PROFIT	$1,275.00	$642.50	$205.00	$7,673.27	$9,795.77
▾ Expenses					
Advertising				74.86	$74.86
▾ Automobile				113.96	$113.96
Fuel				349.41	$349.41
Total Automobile				463.37	$463.37
Equipment Rental				112.00	$112.00
Insurance				241.23	$241.23
▸ Job Expenses				957.89	$957.89
▸ Legal & Professional Fees				1,170.00	$1,170.00
▸ Maintenance and Repair				940.00	$940.00
Meals and Entertainment				28.49	$28.49
Office Expenses	300.00	150.00	50.00	18.08	$518.08
Rent or Lease				900.00	$900.00
▸ Utilities				331.39	$331.39
Total Expenses	$300.00	$150.00	$50.00	$5,237.31	$5,737.31
NET OPERATING INCOME	$975.00	$492.50	$155.00	$2,435.96	$4,058.46
▾ Other Expenses					
Miscellaneous				2,916.00	$2,916.00

The various groups share portion of the money as well as the bill we divided above. The classless items display as "Not Specified". The profitability of each division would be clear to observe if every item had a class assigned to it. A class called "Admin" can potentially be appropriate for all of your administrative expenses. A fantastic alternative is to generate unique reports for each class. You can do this by giving a report on profitability to each division's manager.

2. **Location Tracking:** As was already said, location tracking enables you to add a new component to your transactions and reporting, giving you more alternatives for information and reporting.

   Additionally, you can decide on a field's name:

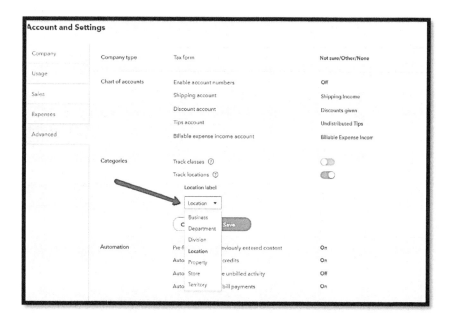

Let's choose Territory for this activity. Location tracking is distinct from class tracking in that it can only be used for a full transaction. As you can see, Territory shows in the "location" field at the top of the invoice. This invoice will be classified in that Territory for all products. The same holds true for any bills you keep track of.

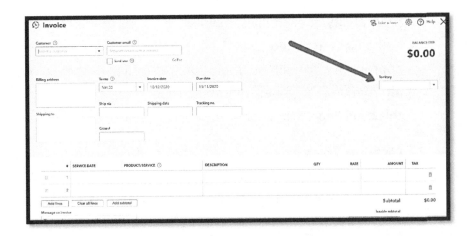

To see the outcomes of the regions you have allocated your transactions to, you can run reports by "Territory."

3. **Inventory:** For your basic inventory requirements, QuickBooks Online's inventory feature is quite effective.

The things you want to sell to your consumers can be set up and categorized:

You have the choice to enter the cost and sales price, and QuickBooks will record the quantity on hand. You can choose how you want the sales revenue to be classified when you set up your products.

4. **Purchase Orders:** You must enable the feature in Account and Settings under the Expenses page if you want to send purchase orders to your vendors.

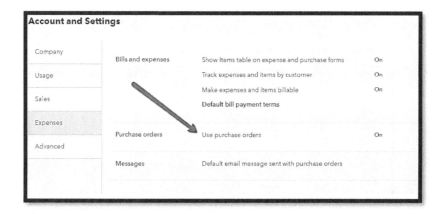

The costs you established when you generated the inventory items will already be prefilled for the goods you choose when creating the order. You can choose to apply the charges to any classes or locations you've established for your company, and if the purchase is directly related to a certain work, you can designate a customer.

Before sending the purchase order, you can add any note you would like to include for the vendor.

You can utilize the purchase order to copy the products immediately to a bill after you've received the goods.

Alternatively, you can open a bill and choose to include the purchase order in that transaction.

5. **Make Expenses and Items Billable to a Customer:** The fantastic function of "tagging" an expense or item chargeable when you register an expense is only accessible with the QuickBooks Online Plus package. You are more likely to recoup all costs associated with your consumers if you bill an expense or item as soon as you incur it. You can add a new field to your bills by enabling the "make expenses and items billable" function in Account and Settings.

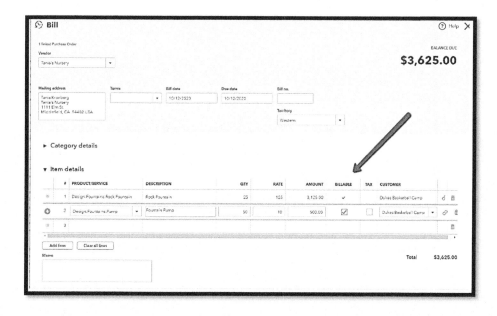

By designating these costs as chargeable, they will show up on our customer's invoice as follows:

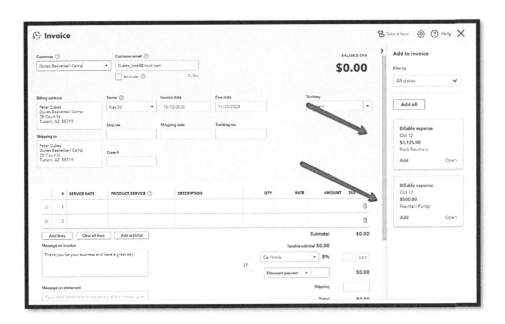

The invoice with the increased chargeable expense for the above-mentioned rock fountain:

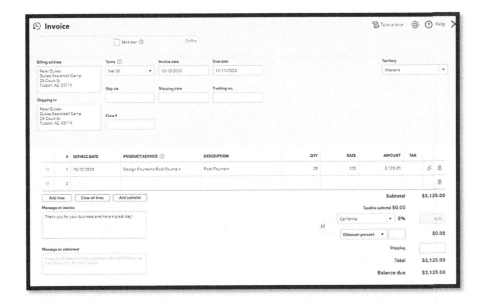

If you tag your invoices and have this nice reminder when you create an invoice for your customer, you are far less likely to forget to include charges to your invoices. Before sending the invoice, you can also manually adjust the amount that is charged. A further feature allows you to establish a default markup percentage:

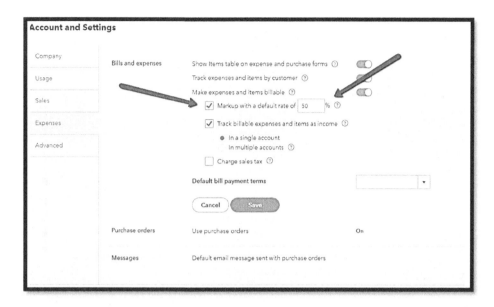

The default markup rate and amount are displayed on the bill when you enter a bill after activating the markup option. If you want to charge your customer more or less than the default, you can easily alter this percentage

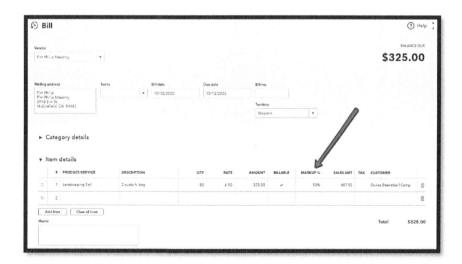

6. **Budgeting:** QuickBooks Online includes an extremely rudimentary budgeting option that is also extremely manual. If you have a simple budget against which you want to track your results, you can input it in the budget feature:

You can divide your budget into months or quarters, or enter annual figures. You may also divide your budget by customer, class, or region, allowing you to construct budgets for each of your divisions or departments.

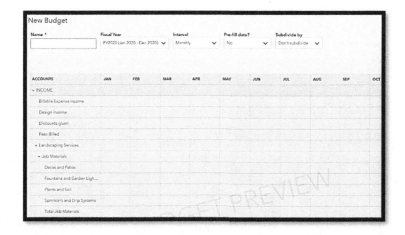

Budget reports are offered to help you compare your progress to actual figures.

7. **Projects:** When you enable the projects feature in the QuickBooks Online Plus Plan, you can control expenditures and assess the profitability of any projects you are working on right away. To establish a project, add the project's name, the customer it pertains to, and any other information pertinent to your job, with plenty of room for notes!

As previously discussed, you can input many types of transactions when entering them. You can now tag them to the project to which they pertain:

All transactions pertaining to a project will be gathered under the projects page.

You can see what projects you are currently working on, what you have invoiced, and what costs you have allocated all at a glance. This could be especially useful in tracking when you should be invoicing to reclaim costs for your cashflow or to guarantee that you finish the task on time and within budget. It is also an excellent tool if you have a large number of projects for a single customer. You can divide the projects and manage them individually, then invoice the customer and define the project to which the invoice and costs pertain.

8. **Use items table on expense and purchase forms and track expenses and items by customer and purchase forms:** This function is beneficial if your company has inventory. When you buy stuff (products), you can record those purchases in your transactions. For instance, expenses and bills. This allows you to maintain your inventory up to date and correct.

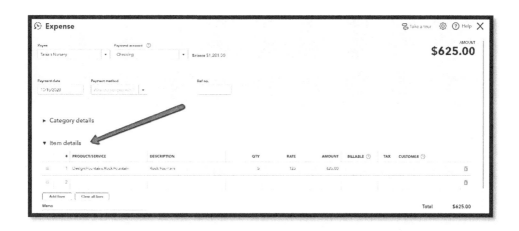

If you purchase products rather than categories, the expenses will be added to inventories on your balance sheet. These things will be kept in inventory until they are sold, at which point they will be added to your cost of goods sold and sales figures. You can watch this video to see how it works. It leads you through the process of using the forms and explains how these transactions affect your financial statements.

QuickBooks Online advanced plan

The QuickBooks Online advanced plan is far more powerful, with advanced reporting and add-ons not available in any other plan. It enables you to batch invoices and expenses, change user roles, automate your workflows further, and back up and restore your corporate data.

QuickBooks Advanced Plan Price

The QuickBooks Online Plus Plan is priced at:

- ❖ $200 in the United States and
- ❖ $140 in Canada.
- ❖ In the United Kingdom and Australia, the QuickBooks Online Advanced Plan is not accessible.

It can accommodate up to 25 users.

Features of the QuickBooks Advanced Plan

With many QuickBooks Online businesses being forced to upgrade to the new Advanced Plan due to changes in user limits, I thought it was time to investigate what additional features are available in order to assist my clients in making the best use of them and justifying the increase in monthly subscription price from $85 for a QuickBooks Online Plus Plan to $200 for a QuickBooks Online Advanced Plan.

This option has been accessible in the United States for some time and is now available in Canada.

The extra features are as follows:

- ❖ Backing up and restoring your QuickBooks Online file
- ❖ Extra custom reporting fields
- ❖ Expenses for employee's features
- ❖ Classes and locations are limitless.
- ❖ Customized user access

1. **Employee Expenses:** The expense capturing functionality used by QuickBooks Online Advanced has been improved so that employees may access it from their mobile devices. Limiting the categories that your employees can choose from and giving them a "nickname"—a label that makes sense to them but may not match the category or account name used in your chart of accounts—are both fantastic features. This lessens the likelihood that the spending will be classified incorrectly, which would inevitably lead to erroneous books.

2. **Custom Reporting Fields:** An effective tool to help you get the data that is crucial for your business is more robust reporting fields. You can better measure your KPIs and metrics to manage your business by filtering and sorting your reports based on the fields you choose. You can have up to 12 custom fields with the QuickBooks Online Advanced Plan. Access to custom fields can be found under lists in the gear icon.

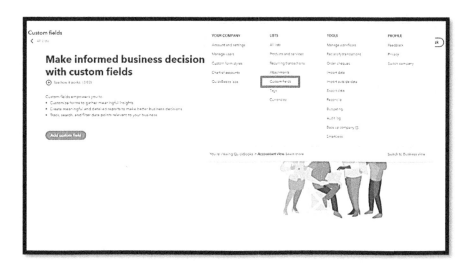

The option to have a dropdown list for each field and to define the kind of information to be included in each field is what I love most about this enhanced feature.

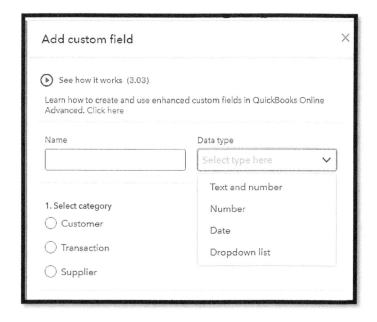

Then, you can choose which forms each custom field should show on, as well as whether you want it to be on a published form or only be viewable to QuickBooks Online users in your company.

Consider any additional data that your company would want to track, and then consider where that data might be gathered. Use the Salesperson field on estimates and run a report filtering for it if you want to see who is producing the most estimates. You could like to see a specific subcategory of expense listed on your bills. There are countless choices, so get in touch if you need help configuring any of these features. I enjoy producing fresh reports and making sure companies have the data they require to prosper and expand.

3. **Customized User Access**: A weakness between QuickBooks Online and QuickBooks Desktop is addressed by the option to control what your QuickBooks Online users can access. A "role" can now be created that restricts a user's access to the resources they require to perform their job.

You can choose which forms the "role" can access in each of the categories Sales, Expenses, Banking, Inventory, and Workers, as well as whether they have the ability to merely view, create, modify, or delete records, or a combination of these.

As you can restrict who can make changes and view sections that may not be necessary for their position, this is a far more effective way to grant access while also increasing security.

4. **Back Up and Restore Data:** Your QuickBooks Online file is unlikely to be unavailable or corrupted because it is continuously backed up in the cloud. But there are circumstances in which having a backup and the option to "roll back" to an earlier version of your QuickBooks Online file will be useful. From the gear icon on the top right, you can enable this option.

You should then see a list of your QuickBooks Online file with the option to back up or restore to a previous time.

CHAPTER TWO

CREATING A QUICKBOOKS ONLINE COMPANY

Sign Up For Quickbooks Online

Find out how to set up a brand-new Intuit account.

To manage settings for all of your QuickBooks Online products, log into your Intuit account. Everything is linked to a single email account. Any time you wish to join up for a new QuickBooks Online product, use this account.

1. Visit the website for Intuit accounts. (https://accounts.intuit.com/signup)
2. Select the link to "Create an account."
3. Please provide your phone number and email address. It's possible that you already have an account if you get the notice "This user ID is already taken." Enter your email address after clicking the Sign in or Recover your account links.
4. Create a password.
5. Select Create Account when you're prepared.

You'll get an email with a link and directions on how to confirm your email address. then you are set.

Exploring Your New Company

Welcome! Let give you the tools you will actually need in managing your business effectively and easily while also enabling you to constantly monitor its performance. But you might be thinking, "Where do I begin?"

Please follow along as I demonstrate how to log into your QuickBooks account.

Enter your company's details.

Gear Icon > Account and Settings > Company

The first step is to add your company's information. Since this data automatically populates on the sales forms and invoices you give your clients, accuracy is crucial. Check the following in your Accounts and Settings menu:

❖ Company/Business Name
❖ Business Address (if your legal business address is already listed in QuickBooks, you may also put a PO Box as the "Customer Facing" address)
❖ Contact Email
❖ Website
❖ Mobile Number

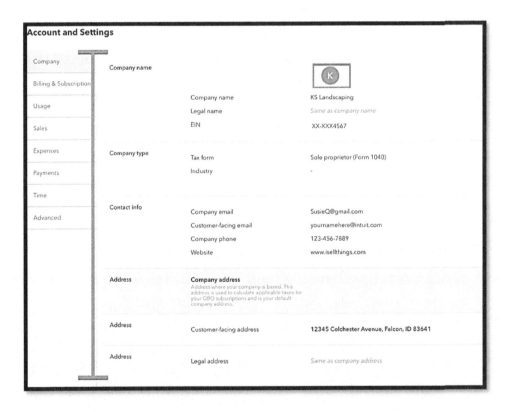

Click the pencil icon in the corner to make changes, then click Save when finished.

Next, make sure the tax form you intend to submit at the end of the fiscal year and the specified company type are accurate.

It is necessary to have an Employer Identification Number (EIN) or Social Security Number. Contact your accountant or the IRS for assistance if you need it in deciding which of these is necessary for your company.

Designate your fiscal year start date

Gear Icon > Account and Settings > Advanced > Accounting

Inform QuickBooks of the start and finish dates of your company's fiscal year. Similar to the beginning of the tax year, January is often the first month of the fiscal year for most firms. You should be aware of your tax year schedule as the company owner.

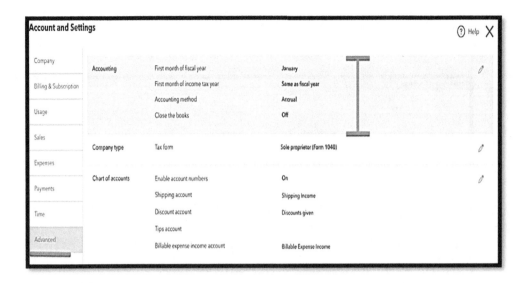

While you're here, you may also decide on a date to "close the books" on the fiscal year, which is 12 months from your start date. While you are getting ready to file your taxes, this function prevents anyone from altering or modifying your QuickBooks data. However, you may turn it off at any time.

Choose between cash and accrual accounting.

Gear > Account and Settings > Advanced > Accounting

Tell QuickBooks whether your company will report income using the cash or accrual method from the same menu. Many new enterprises prefer cash accounting. The cash technique is perhaps easier because you simply track revenue and costs when they are received and paid, but both methods have merits.

Note: To learn more about a term, click on any of the? mark symbols in your settings.

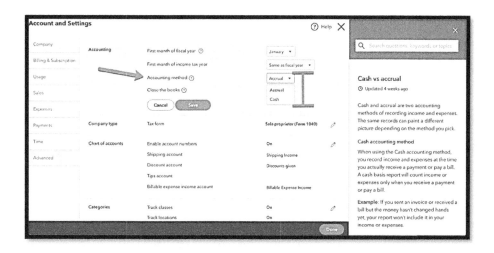

Choose your accounting currency.

Gear Icon > Account and Settings > Advanced > Currency

This is the final phase in our Settings adventure. Multicurrency allows you to track transactions in foreign currencies, but only if you have bank accounts, clients, or vendors who do not accept your native currency.

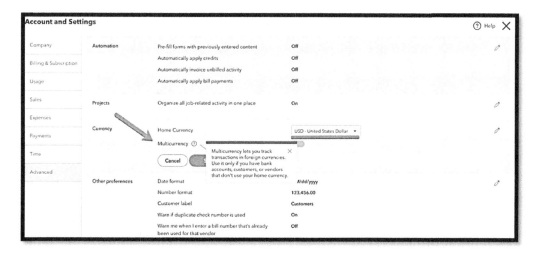

Check that the home currency you've chosen is the one you intend to accept from consumers.

Note: If you intend to use the Multicurrency option, first choose your home currency. You cannot disable or alter your home currency after you have enabled the Multicurrency option.

Choose a logo for your company/business.

Gear Icon > Account and Setting> Company Name

Now that you've completed all of the administrative tasks, you can begin personalizing your QuickBooks experience.

Your logo is your visual brand, and it appears on all invoices, estimates, and sales receipts sent to consumers. Here are some pointers to help you properly upload your eye-catching logo:

❖ The file format should be.gif,.bmp,.png,.jpg,.jpe, or.jpeg.
❖ It must be less than 1MB.
❖ Use the RGB color space standard with a bit depth (or color depth) of 24-bit or fewer.
❖ Square logos (or circular logos that can fit within a square) work best. Rectangular logos will expand.
❖ Make use of a white background to blend in with the sales form.

Set your default "Net Payment" invoice terms

Gear icon > Account and Settings > Sales > Sales Form content

Your first invoice will be sent soon, so get ready. Let's make sure your clients are aware of when they must make a payment. In the Account & Settings tab, which you've already noticed is actually where you make the majority of general changes to your account, you may adjust your default net payment invoice terms.

Choose Due on receipt from the dropdown menu if you want payment immediately now. If not, choose a suitable time period from the dropdown. The drop-down menu will actually allow you to add new custom payment terms by clicking + Add New.

Although you may always modify the terms for specific Invoices directly on the form, the net payment terms you select in this option will serve as the default.

Set up Sales Tax

Left Menu > Taxes tab

If you sell things, you have to collect sales tax (in most states). When you initially set up your account and choose the Tax Tab, you will be guided through a setup module where questions regarding where you sell your items will be asked. Before continue, ensure your accounting system is configured (cash or accrual). The Sales Tax Liability Report will reveal how much you owe once your setup is complete.

Receiving Payments and the "Undeposited Funds" Account

Learn about crucial accounting phrases by visiting The QuickBooks Encyclopedia. So to differentiate between two commonly used terms: sales receipts and invoices.

❖ Invoices: invoices are used when you sell a product or service and expect to be paid later. Once the invoice is paid and the money is received (through QuickBooks Payments or another method), the payment is recorded in QuickBooks.

❖ Sales receipts: anytime you sell a good or service and get paid right away, you use sales receipts. You have already received payment after you provide the sales receipt. The payment will be entered into QuickBooks and accounted for. This implies that the receive payment stage is not required to be finished.

When an invoice payment is received, handle it by selecting +New, then Receive Payment. Your Undeposited Funds account will then be credited with the payments made in response to the invoice. The Receive Payments feature's default "deposit to" account is this one. Using the Bank Deposit feature, you must record these payments to the appropriate account in QuickBooks when you receive the payment into the Undeposited Funds account.

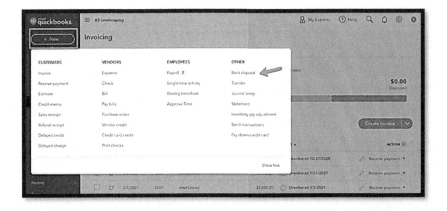

Decide if you want to track inventory

Gear Icon > Account and Settings > Sales

We feel that planning ahead of time is critical for your business. If you intend to track inventory quantities, enable Track quantity on hand now. We go over the entire inventory setup procedure here. If you wish to begin tracking, it is advisable to begin with the Inventory function. Going back to re-edit your whole product list, not to mention the associated vendor and expenditure accounts, is time consuming. Instead, save time by creating a Products and Services list for inventory tracking.

Create an Invoice in QuickBooks Test Drive

+New > Invoices or Invoicing > Invoices tab

It can be intimidating to work with real data and transactions when you're unfamiliar with a product. We have the perfect answer! Discover the various invoicing tools by using the QuickBooks Test Drive. Be ready to use Test Drive often and to learn the ins and outs of QuickBooks Online during your initial few weeks of use.

Please keep in mind that Test Drive simulates QuickBooks Online Plus. Click the +New icon once you're in Test Drive. The bulk of QuickBooks transactions are initiated through this option.

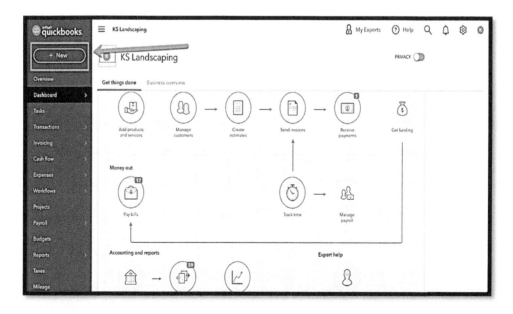

Examine each of the highlighted portions below, as well as the data types that go into each data field.

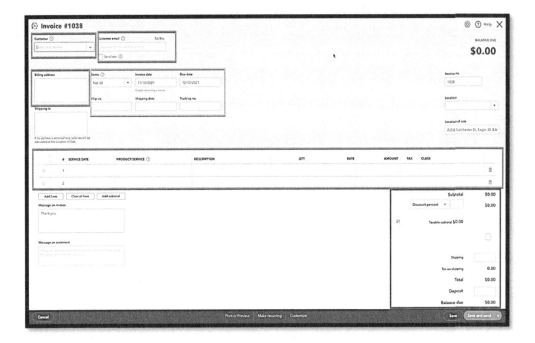

Reviewing The Quickbooks Interface

The QuickBooks screen has a lot going on, so let's start by taking a tour to get acquainted with the user interface! We're looking at the QuickBooks Home screen, which appears when you initially log in.

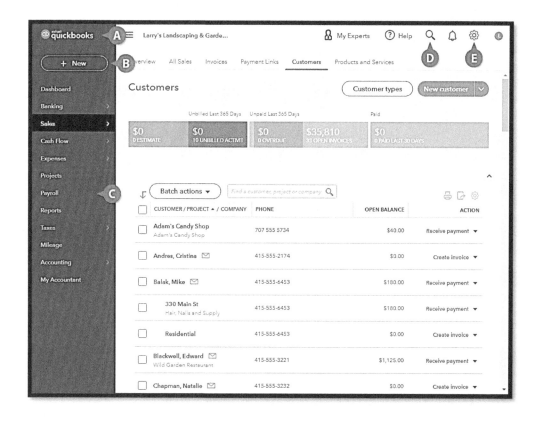

A. **Home (QuickBooks logo):** To return to the home screen, simply click the QuickBooks logo.

B. **New button:** The New button is located directly beneath the QuickBooks logo and is used to create new invoices, cheques, and other transactions.

C. **The Navigation Bar:** The Navigation Bar is located beneath the New button and allows you to access other areas of QuickBooks.

D. **Search (Magnifying glass):** In QuickBooks, the magnifying glass is used to search for transactions.

E. **Settings (Gear):** Use the gear icon to access QuickBooks settings, see lists (including your company's Chart of Accounts), and manage other users.

SetUp A Chart Of Account In Quickbooks Online

In this section, you'll learn how to delete, add, and alter accounts in the QuickBooks Online Chart of Accounts. In addition, you will know how you can import a chart of accounts from an Excel spreadsheet or from comma-separated values (CSV) file.

How To Add an Account to the Chart of Accounts List

Step 1: Go to the Chart of Accounts.

To begin, click the gear icon in the upper right-hand corner of your QuickBooks dashboard, and then pick Chart of accounts from pop-up window that appears, as shown below.

Step 2: Finish the Account Setup Screen.

The account setup window of your new account will then open after you click the green New button in the top right corner of the screen.

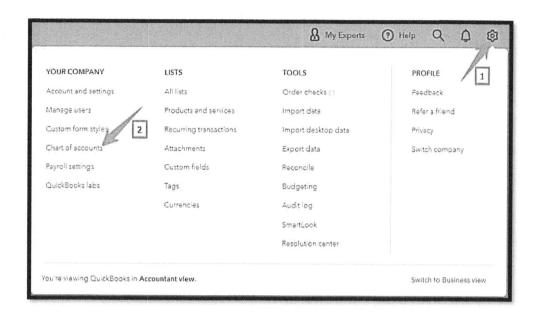

The following fields are available on the account setup screen:

A. Account Type: From drop-down menu, select an account type.

B. Detail Type: From drop-down menu, choose a detail type. The available detail types will differ depending on the account type. The gray box underneath the detail type explains the detail type you've chosen.

C. Account name: Give your account a name that will help you recognize it when selecting accounts to submit transactions to. For example, instead of "Checking Account," include the bank name and the final four digits of the account number, such as "US Bank Checking x1234."

D. Number: It is optional to provide a number for your account. If you want to use account numbers and this field isn't available, follow the steps in How To Set Up Advanced Settings to enable account numbers.

E. Account Description: You may provide an optional account description.

F. Is sub-account: You can structure your accounts by creating parent and sub-accounts. For example, you could create a parent account called "Utilities Expense" and then subaccounts called "Electric Expense" and "Gas Expense." Tick the box next to Is subaccount if this is a subaccount. Then, from the drop-down box, select the parent account.

Step 3: Save Your New Chart of Account

When you are satisfied with your answers, select Save and New by using the drop-down arrow next to the green Save and Close button to add another account.

How to Edit an Account in the Chart of Accounts List

To edit an existing account, locate it in the Chart of Accounts screen and click drop-down arrow beside the View register. After clicking Edit, the account setup screen will appear.

Click the green Save and Close button after making the necessary changes to the account.

NUMBER	NAME	TYPE ▲	DETAIL TYPE	CURRENCY	QUICKBOOKS B/	BANK BALANC	ACTION
☐ 1110	1110 Company Checking Acco	Bank	Checking	USD	121,499.76		View register ▾
☐ 1120	1120 Company Savings Accoun	Bank	Checking	USD	25,824.05		View registe ⊙
☐ 112720	112720 Checking Account - Ba	Bank	Checking	USD	600.00	Connect bank	
						Edit	
☐ 112730	112730 Money Market - First N:	Bank	Money Market	USD	0.00	Make inactive (won't reduce usage)	
☐ 1140	1140 Petty Cash Account	Bank	Cash on hand	USD	2,241.00	Run report	
☐ 1160	1160 Payroll Clearing (owner's	Bank	Checking	USD	0.00		View register ▾
☐ 1170	1170 Bank of America Checkin;	Bank	Checking	USD	10,138.02		View register ▾
☐ 1180	1180 Chase Checking Account	Bank	Checking	USD	3,783.65		View register ▾
☐	Cash on hand	Bank	Cash on hand	USD	0.00		View register ▾
☐	Checking	Bank	Checking	USD	0.00		View register ▾

How to Delete an Account in the Chart of Accounts List

Instead of deleting accounts, you must declare them inactive in QuickBooks Online. If an account has never been used in a transaction, it will no longer count toward your allocated number of accounts. If the account has been used previously for a transaction, the history will be saved and the transaction would still count toward your maximum.

Click drop-down arrow beside View register for that account you want to render inactive from the Chart of Accounts page. Choose Make inactive from drop-down list after that.

How to View and Print Your Accounts Chart

Navigate to the chart of accounts screen and click on Run Report icon in the upper right corner of the screen to get a copy of your chart of accounts. After clicking Run Report, a duplicate of the chart of accounts appears. The chart of accounts can then be printed or sent via email after being exported to an Excel file, if necessary.

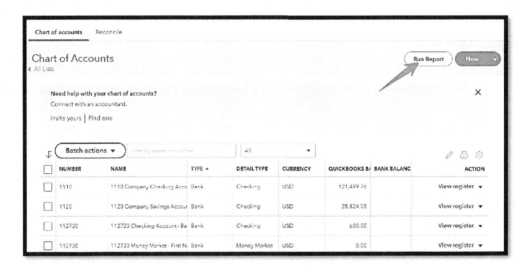

How To Import Accounts to the Chart of Accounts List

If you're moving your books from another bookkeeping application, you might well be able to export your chart of accounts from the old software into an Excel spreadsheet or CSV file, that can then be loaded into QuickBooks Online. Imported accounts will not replace your current chart of accounts; rather, they will add to it.

Note: Avoid creating duplicate accounts: If an account already exists with the same name in your chart of accounts or import file, QuickBooks Online won't let you import it. QuickBooks Online will provide you a list of the accounts that didn't load because of duplicates once you've imported your accounts.

Step 1: Prepare Your Spreadsheet

The columns for account type, account name, and detail type must all be present in your spreadsheet. If you'd like, you can additionally include a column for account numbers. Additional columns may be included in the spreadsheet, but they won't be imported into QBO Each column's label, which need not be the same as the field name in QBO, should appear on the first line of the spreadsheet.

Step 2. Import Your Spreadsheet

Click drop-down arrow beside to the green New button on your Chart of Accounts screen, then choose Import.

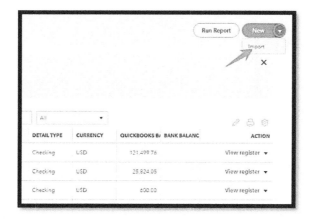

Next, select the spreadsheet you have prepared for importation by clicking the Browse option.

After selecting your spreadsheet, click the green Next button in the lower right corner of the screen (not shown).

Step 3: Map Your Spreadsheet for QuickBooks Import

On the following screen, you must map the data in your spreadsheet to that four fields imported by QBO. Choose the column in your spreadsheet that holds the data for each QBO Field.

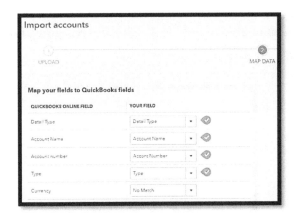

Step 4: Double-check and Import Your Data

When you're finished mapping, click the green Next button. The final screen before importing allows you to edit any account details or deselect any accounts you do not want to import.

How QuickBooks Creates and Classifies Accounts

QuickBooks Online creates a default chart of accounts selection based on the industry you selected when you set up your QuickBooks firm. We recommend reviewing this default chart of accounts to see whether account should be added, updated, or eliminated.

QuickBooks Online requires detailed information for each account, including an Detail Type and Account Type. Accounting accounts must be properly classified in order for QBO to perform successfully. For example, your Accounts Receivable account must have the Account Type "Accounts Receivable" mentioned. If a new client invoice is submitted, QuickBooks Online will not know to raise this account.

After double-checking the information, click on the green Import button to finish the importing procedure. Your chart of accounts should now incorporate the new accounts. Similarly, the Detail Type of your inventory account must be "Inventory" so that QuickBooks Online understands which account to raise when you acquire things.

Reviewing company settings

Customize QuickBooks Online to perform exactly how you want it to. Here's how to adjust your settings and enable and disable features.

Modify the settings

1. Navigate to Settings.
2. Choose Account and settings.
3. Choose a tab.

   Note: If you wish to learn about the settings you can alter, see the section Settings you can change below.

4. In a section, click Edit.
5. Choose an item to be updated. When you select an area, fields will display, and a question mark will tell you what they are for. Make your changes, then click Save.

6. To save your settings, click Done.

The settings you can change

Here's a quick rundown of the settings and functions available to you.

Company preferences

From the home screen, pick the Gear Menu and then the Company Settings tab under the column heading "Settings."

You can change the company logo that appears on sales forms and purchase orders, the company name that appears on sales forms and purchase orders, the legal name that appears on forms, and the EIN/SSN that appears on tax forms. You can also change the company type, industry, and contact information. Here you can also change your communication choices with Intuit.

Subscription and billing preferences

As your firm expands, you can adjust your subscription level here. You can also use TSheets for time tracking, order checks and supplies, join up for QuickBooks Online Payments, QuickBooks Live Bookkeeping, or begin using QuickBooks Payroll.

Usage preferences

This tab displays your usage and limits based on your membership package. This covers how many billable, how many charts of accounts, and how many tag groups

Sales preferences.

Click on the pencil symbol in the top right corner of the "Sales form content" sub-menu after selecting the Sales bar. You can put your own sales information here. In the "Messages" section, you can additionally personalize and edit messages to your clients. Make sure to click Save when you've completed modifying your Sales options before continuing.

This is where you may make modifications to your sales form, such as the design and form fields. You can determine when reminder emails are sent to clients and whether or not to display past statements at the bottom of an invoice.

Expenses preferences.

From the Settings Navigator, choose the Expenses tab. To modify, select "Edit" from the drop-down menu next to the "Bills and Expenses" sub-menu.

Editing your expense settings is possible here.

You can select numerous spending settings here, such as whether to use purchase orders or make charges chargeable.

Payments preferences.

If you have previously subscribed to QuickBooks Payments, you can gain access to it through Payments.

Time preferences

The Time tab allows you to set the first day of the work week, track the services your team provided while working for a client, and decide whether employees and suppliers may see how much you charge clients for their work.

Advanced preferences.

This menu contains a plethora of additional choices for configuring your account. Choose accounting options such as the fiscal year's first month and accounting method. Set the level of automation for tasks like applying credits, billing unbilled activity, and applying bill payments. You can also configure regional settings such as the home currency and date format.

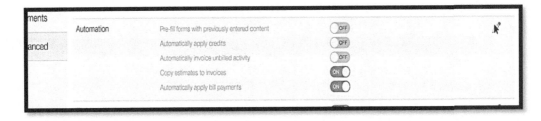

The settings in this section will provide you with everything you need to set up your basic corporation in QuickBooks Online. You don't have to fill out everything right away because we'll go through it all later.

Quickbooks Labs

As part of the QuickBooks Online update, Intuit published QuickBooks Labs in September 2014. This QuickBooks feature is categorized as an experimental plug-in. These have QuickBooks integration. You might want to run the plug-in with a phony company file first in order to safeguard your QuickBooks data.

What is Quickbooks Labs

Testing for upcoming features and upgrades to QuickBooks Online is done in the QuickBooks Labs. They refer to it as a high-tech playground for our early adopters and new media. They claim that some plug-in features malfunction or vanish.

At this time, the QuickBooks Labs provide the following experimental plug-ins:

Redesigned Reports

Company Templates for Accountants

Commerce Network

PayByCoin

Autocomplete Widget

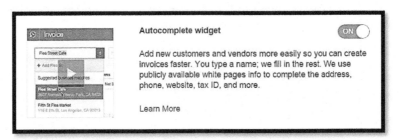

Collapsible Left Navigation

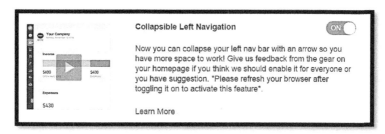

Collapsible Left Navigation   ON

Now you can collapse your left nav bar with an arrow so you have more space to work! Give us feedback from the gear on your homepage if you think we should enable it for everyone or you have suggestion. "Please refresh your browser after toggling it on to activate this feature".

Learn More

CHAPTER THREE

IMPORTING FROM QUICKBOOKS DESKTOP AND SAGE 50

Using An Online Service To Migrate Sage 50 To Quickbooks Online

Do you wish to transfer your Sage 50 accounting data to QuickBooks Online? To move your data automatically, use the Dataswitcher wizard conversion. Any business must take a huge step before switching accounting software. To make the transition from Sage 50 to QuickBooks Online simpler, Dataswitcher, a company that specializes in accounting software conversions, has partnered with Quickbooks. Only the accrual-basis accounting system is supported by the converter. All you need to know regarding this process is covered in this section.

Time to convert your Sage 50 data to QuickBooks Online

This depend on the size and format of your Sage 50 file, processing timeframes may vary. From the time your data is put into the Dataswitcher conversion wizard, it typically takes up to 72 hours. Please be aware that this does not account for the time you will need to prepare and review your data before to or following the conversion. For more information, you can contact the QuickBooks Online support if your data file has not been converted after 72 hours.

Data from Sage 50 that won't be converted

Data types that cannot be transformed include:

- ❖ Budgets
- ❖ Attachments
- ❖ Non-posting entries (estimates)

- ❖ Partially closed or closed estimates and purchase orders
- ❖ Deleted transactions
- ❖ Memorized transactions
- ❖ Invoice template
- ❖ Jobs that are not been attached to transactions
- ❖ Reversed journal entries
- ❖ Bank reconciliation history
- ❖ Fixed Assets
- ❖ Sales orders (unsupported in QBO)
- ❖ Work tickets (unsupported in QBO)

Sage 50 pre-conversion checklist items

There are some actions you must do and others that are basically optional before sending that your Sage 50 file to Dataswitcher for the conversion. Although optional chores don't apply to everyone, we nonetheless advise that you evaluate them in case they do.

1. Finish the current tax period before the conversion (Optional)

It is not advise changing your Sage 50 file in the middle of a tax season. Planning the conversion for the conclusion of your current period or a subsequent period is advised. You should always file your taxes based on information in your Sage 50 file at the end of each tax period before beginning a new period in QuickBooks Online.

2. Verify the consistency of the Sage 50 file

Poor data conversion will lead to problems with QuickBooks Online later. You must verify the integrity of that your Sage 50 file to lessen the likelihood of this occurring. By doing the actions listed below,

- ❖ Click Help on the main menu.
- ❖ Opt for Support Utilities.
- ❖ Integrity Check is chosen.

Before you start the conversion, any discrepancies that Sage 50 reveals must be fixed.

3. Examine the ranges of account numbers

Sage 50's account numbers are ranges (called Account IDs in Sage 50). Verify that all account numbers are inside your chart of accounts' acceptable range. If they are not, Dataswitcher won't be able to tell, you are converting your file to QBO whatever account type the account number always belongs to (such as Profit & Loss or Balance Sheet).

Make sure the account number that you will use to reconcile your profit and loss accounts at year's end has not actually been altered from its default setting. If you don't, when those entries are converted in QuickBooks Online, they will be duplicated, which will throw your accounts out of balance.

4. Aged AP and AR

Check the balances in your general ledger on the conversion date by running your Aged AR & Aged AP reports. If not, take care of any errors and, if necessary, file integrity check in Sage 50.

5. Sync up your financial accounts

Sage 50 requires a complete reconciliation of your bank accounts. Otherwise, it will be challenging to determine whether the conversion was successful.

6. Adjust your tax accounts.

Sage 50 requires a complete reconciliation of your tax accounts. Otherwise, it will be challenging to determine whether the conversion was successful.

7. The reports that will be examined following the conversion.

You are in charge of reviewing the outcomes once your conversion is complete. Before your conversion, you must run the following reports in Sage 50 and you must download a copy of them.

- ❖ Aged receivables up to the conversion date
- ❖ Aged payables up to the conversion date
- ❖ Balance sheet report up to conversion date
- ❖ Bank Account balances up to conversion date
- ❖ Income statement
- ❖ Trial Balance up to the conversion date
- ❖ Taxable / Exempt Sales (if you collect sales tax)

Dataswitcher will actually convert everything to your local currency if the option to display foreign currencies is enabled while you are extracting the trial balance.

8. Make backup for your Sage 50 file

Making a backup for your Sage 50 file is advised. It is advise renaming this backup file PRE CONVERSION.PTB if you haven't yet cleaned up your Sage 50 file. It is advised to use the file name PRE CONVERSION.001 if your Sage 50 file has already been cleaned up.

You should make a copy of the following documents and preserve them securely for auditing purposes:

- ❖ Sales tax report
- ❖ Purchase tax report
- ❖ Account transactions

Pre-conversion checklist tasks in QuickBooks

There are some activities in QuickBook Online that you must finish before you can submit your Sage 50 file to Dataswitcher and others that are actually optional. Even if optional tasks may not be applicable to you, it is advice that you make review on them.

1. Delete your data from QuickBooks Online.

Once you start the conversion process, it's critical that there are actually no previous transactions in your QuickBooks Online file. If your firm does have data, you must remove it from QuickBooks Online before forwarding your Sage 50 file to Dataswitcher.

2. Sales Tax

Before to your conversion, QuickBooks Online shouldn't have had Sales Tax activated. There will be need to remove your QuickBooks Online data if it has actually been activated.

3. Bank & Credit card accounts

It's possible that QuickBooks Online will ask you to link your credit card and bank accounts when you first log in. Please wait until the post-conversion checklist instructs you to do this before you perform it.

Getting started converting your Sage 50 data to QuickBooks Online

When you have finished all required pre-conversion checklist tasks for Sage 50 and QBO, you will get a file with the name DS CONVERSION.001 (not PRE CONVERSION.001). You should email Dataswitcher this file.

You must fill out the website's online form to allow you send your file to Dataswitcher. You will then be directed to the Dataswitcher conversion wizard by this. The next stages will be guided by the Dataswitcher conversion wizard:

Step 1: Things you must understand

You will be prompted to: on the Dataswitcher wizard's conversion initial screen.

- ❖ Take a look at the conversion check list.
- ❖ Reset the password for QuickBooks Online.

❖ Till the conversion is finished, refrain from using QuickBooks Online.

Select Let's do it when you're prepared.

Step 2. Contact information

You must supply the following details:

❖ Business name.
❖ Email address of the conversion-related employee in your company.

Next or sign in using your Intuit ID are available.

Step 3: Things you would you like to move?

Select Continue after choosing the Pro plan.

Step 4: Examine your decision.

Data that will be converted by default is shown in Dataswitcher along with additional additions that are optional. Choose the appropriate option if you want to add any optional extras to your conversion. You can temporarily waive some of these fees by using the coupon code JVWCX-TTV4J-8TUTR.

To continue, click Confirm.

Step 5: Prepare your data

Check the boxes to show that you have finished all pre-conversion requirements, such as:

❖ In Sage 50, all accounts were reconciled.
❖ Finished filing taxes in Sage 50.
❖ Extracted from Sage 50 all open invoices and credits.
❖ As stated in the pre-conversion procedures, you extracted all necessary reports from Sage 50.
❖ I checked to make sure you're utilizing accrual accounting.

❖ Online QuickBooks has been reset.

❖ Read and comprehend the Sage 50 conversion procedure restrictions.

By clicking Browse on your computer, choosing your Sage 50 file, and then selecting open when all check boxes have been checked, you can upload your Sage 50 file.

For your file to upload, click Confirm.

Step six: Data file checks

In order to make sure that QuickBooks Online is prepared to accept the converted data, Dataswitcher will start reviewing your account settings right away. Please wait; this typically takes a few minutes. Do not shut off your browser during this time.

Select Start to begin sending your Sage 50 file to Dataswitcher after this is finished.

Step 7: Move your data

Dataswitcher verifies that they have started the conversion process for your data, and they will give you a URL that you can type into your browser at any moment to check the conversion's progress.

Additionally, you'll get an email confirming that you got your Sage 50 data file. You can equally examine the progress of the conversion at any time by clicking a link that will take you back to the Dataswitcher conversion wizard.

Reminder: Avoid using QuickBooks Online during this time. This might prevent the conversion from happening.

Post-conversion checklist tasks in QuickBooks Online

You must check and approve the conversion before utilizing QuickBook Online. Some of the tasks that are required and optional for reviewing your file are listed below. Although optional chores don't apply to everyone, it is advise that you evaluate them in case they do.

1. Review and approve your conversion

When your data has been converted, Dataswitcher will send you an email with that subject "Your conversion is ready to review." You have 72 hours to do a review and approve the conversion from the date and time of receipt. Dataswitcher assumes clearance after 72 hours.

2. Do not link your credit card or bank accounts.

Mark up the transactions in QBO as reconciled to reflect the bank reconciliation performed in Sage 50 prior to conversion before integrating your bank or credit card accounts. Connecting your bank or credit card accounts is discussed later; don't do it now.

3. Enter or update the details of your business.

You had the choice to ask Dataswitcher to convert your company's contact information (email, address, phone, etc.) for you when you uploaded your file. You just need to check it for accuracy if you chose this. If not, you must do so right away.

To input the details of your business:

1. Select Account and Settings from the Settings menu.
2. Enter your company's name and contact details after choosing Company.
3. In order to conduct customer communications and billing communications properly, update or check the email addresses.
4. In the Company email field, provide the email address where you want Intuit to send you monthly invoices for your QuickBooks Online membership.

5. Input the email address you want your clients to identify with your company in Customer-facing email box if you do not want them to reach you at the Company email address.
6. Choose Save.

4. Set the Fiscal Start Month

- ❖ Choose Advanced.
- ❖ Choose the first month of your fiscal year in Accounting.
- ❖ Pick Save, then click Done.

5. Compare reports from Sage 50 with QuickBooks Online to verify your data.

Compare the reports you previously exported from Sage 50 to the ones you run in QBO by "This Fiscal Year or This Year." It is important to note that QuickBooks Online reports on individual days, but Sage 50 reports on periods. While checking the conversion in QuickBooks Online, use the end-of-period dates provided by Sage 50.

6. Indicating transactions as reconciled

Important: Before integrating your bank and credit card accounts with QuickBooks Online, it's imperative that you do this step.

It is requested that you balance the transactions in Sage 50 before transferring the data to Dataswitcher in the pre-conversion checklist for Sage 50. There is no record of that reconciliation in the QBO file. To correct this, you must mark all transactions that occurred before the conversion date as reconciled so that only subsequent transactions will be taken into account.

To accomplish this, launch QuickBooks Online's bank reconciliation process, and when prompted, follow these steps:

- ❖ Next to the option Deposit (USD), select blank check.
- ❖ Select Yes, and select all.

❖ Close to Save for later, select dropdown and then select Finish Now.

Start using your QuickBooks Online

You can start using QuickBooks Online as soon as you've reviewed, checked off, and authorized your conversion on the post-conversion checklist.

If you have not utilized QuickBooks Online before, there is need to read the content below to obtain a better understanding of your new accounting program.

Transfer From QuickBooks Desktop To QuickBooks Online

Moving your QuickBooks Desktop file to QuickBooks Online? Here's a step-by-step guide to assist you. To begin, ensure that your data is clean and ready for transfer to QuickBooks Online

Step 1: Before converting your file, review some important details.

❖ Only data from QuickBooks Desktop can be imported within the first 60 days of your QuickBooks Online company's launch. When you import, your Desktop file will erase any existing information in your Online file.

❖ We recommend that you keep your data file on QuickBooks Desktop and keep your transactions on both sets of books until you establish that QuickBooks Online is the best fit for your company.

❖ When you relocate your file, some information may be lost.

❖ Check out the import restrictions and feature changes between QuickBooks Desktop and QuickBooks Online.

❖ If you are using an earlier version of QuickBooks Desktop than 2016, download and install an updated trial, restore your company file, and then use it for conversion

❖ Both your QuickBooks Desktop file and your QuickBooks Online account must be logged in as the administrator.

❖ Begin the conversion from the QuickBooks Desktop company file rather than QuickBooks Online.

❖ The QuickBooks file should not exceed the target limit 350, 000 in order to be converted properly. To verify, press Ctrl+1 right on your keyboard and look for Total Targets. When exporting, if the file exceeds the desired limit, you will only be offered the choice to import your listings and/or balances. Your file can be condense in order to lower the total number of targets.

❖ Don't try to convert the file if you've already enabled Payroll in QBO.

❖ Before relocating, ensure that all of the sales tax filings are up to date. After conversion, there may be need to make adjustments to the sales tax filings.

Step 2: Export the data from your QuickBooks Desktop company.

Files for QuickBooks Desktop Pro/Premier

1. Open the file to be exported.
2. Navigate to Company > QuickBooks Online Export Company File.
3. To have access connect to QuickBooks Online, simply follow the directions.

If you didn't see the option to export? Update your QuickBooks Desktop. Follow these steps:

1. Navigate to Help > QuickBooks Update.
2. Right In the "Update Now" window, choose all updates, then Get Updates.
3. When the changes are finished, click Close, then File > Exit.
4. When prompted, restart QuickBooks and continue installing the updates. Depending on the time when QuickBooks was last updated, these upgrades may take up to 15 minutes to install.

Step 3: Log in to QuickBooks Online and begin importing your data.

1. Input your QuickBooks Online login (typically that same email address you used to sign up), agree to the Terms of Service, and then click Sign in.

2. You will have access to this screen if you have inventory in the file and are importing from QuickBooks Desktop 2016 or later; otherwise, go to step 3.

Bringing in inventory? QuickBooks Online Advanced or Plus will be required. Inventory tracking is not available in Simple Start or Essentials. If you have a large inventory, you can track the quantity of your product items on hand in Plus or Advanced.

3. Choose the QuickBooks Online company into which you wish to import your data, or establish a new one.

Have you already set up a QuickBooks Online business? Don't start a new business. Simply select the one you generated from the drop-down menu.

4. Click OK, I get it.

Once the import is complete, you will receive a confirmation email. It should be noted this can take up to 24 hours.

Step 4: Connect your QuickBooks Online account to HCP and then import data

Move Your Books To Quickbooks Online With An Online Tool

Don't worry if your QuickBooks Desktop is outdated or you don't have access to it. You can move your books with the aid of an online application.

Using this tool is permitted if

❖ QuickBooks Pro, Premier, Enterprise, or QuickBooks for Mac files are available. If you save a backup for Windows, the utility will transport data from QuickBooks company files (.QBW), portable files (.QBM), backup files (.QBB), and QuickBooks for Mac files (.qbb).

❖ Since you don't have QuickBooks Desktop, you want to assist your client in switching to QuickBooks Online.

❖ You wish to transfer a QuickBooks Desktop file to QuickBooks Online even though you did not have QuickBooks Desktop.

Step 1: Open the online tool

1. Click on the link for the QuickBooks version you use:

   a. QuickBooks Pro/Premier

      i. You can also access QuickBooks Mac files saved as Windows files using this link.

   b. QuickBooks Enterprise

2. Choose Get Started and log in using your Intuit Account.

Step 2: Add your company's file.

In order to upload your company file, follow these procedures.

1. Choose Temporary Files after choosing the file icon.
2. Click Upload Files and then navigate to the company file (.QBW) that you wish to move.
3. After uploading your company file, close the pop-up window.
4. To view your uploaded company file, choose Refresh.

Uploading your company file

Step 1:
Select the file icon from the menu bar on the top left corner.

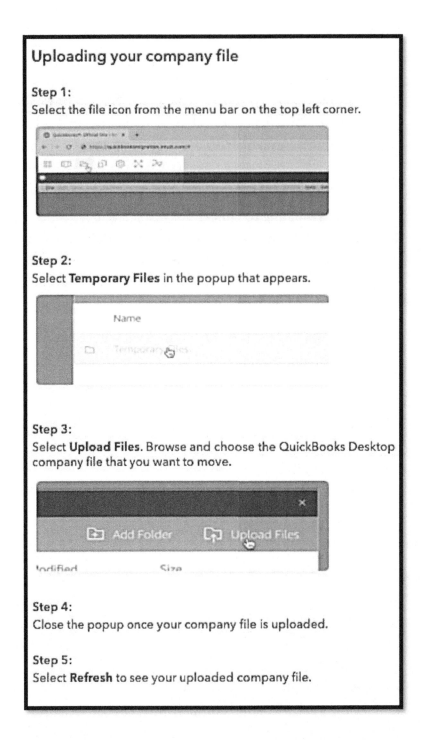

Step 2:
Select **Temporary Files** in the popup that appears.

Step 3:
Select **Upload Files**. Browse and choose the QuickBooks Desktop company file that you want to move.

Step 4:
Close the popup once your company file is uploaded.

Step 5:
Select **Refresh** to see your uploaded company file.

Step 3: Auto-update your file and move it to QuickBooks Online

Once your file has been uploaded, we will automatically update it to the most recent version of QuickBooks Desktop. Following that, you'll have an opportunity to switch to QuickBooks Online.

Follow the on-screen prompts to complete the transition to QuickBooks Online. Contact customer service if your books do not update to QuickBooks Desktop or transfer to QuickBooks Online.

PART 2: MANAGING YOUR BOOK

CHAPTER FOUR

SETTING UP CUSTOMERS, VENDORS AND EMPLOYEE LISTS

Setup Your Customers In QuickBooks

Step 1: Select Customer Center from the Customers menu.

Step 2: Click New Customer & Job in the upper left corner of the new screen, then pick New Customer from the drop-down menu.

Step 3: Enter your customer's name in the Company Name box, the date you want them to start in the As of Date area, and the amount they owe you as of the date you want them to start in the Opening Balance field. (You do not need to input any information in the Customer Name box; whatever name you enter in the "Company Name" area will be automatically populated in the "Customer Name" and "Invoice/Bill To" fields. If your fiscal year begins in January and you decide to begin using QuickBooks in May, I recommend that you begin your company in QuickBooks on January 1 (your current year) and enter all transactions (individually) on January 1, rather than bulking them in opening balances and general journal entries. This allows you in keeping track of everything for the entire year and provide valuable, thorough reports. Customers will be able to receive meaningful statements of accounts as well as copies of partially paid invoices.

Step 4: Enter all additional relevant information, including the address, on that screen. Fill in the Customer address below the Customer's name that is already there in the Invoice/Bill To field. If you will be shipping to a different address for this customer, click the Ship To drop-down menu and then Add New. Complete the fields in the new window, and click Ok.

Step 5: After you've done entering your customer's address information, select Payment Settings on the left side of the New Customer window.

Step 6: Fill out all essential fields to configure how you will engage with this consumer regarding payments. If an option is not available in a drop-down menu, click Add New, enter the necessary information, and then click Ok to return to the New Customer screen. (Add Online Payment Link To Invoices is an option that allows your clients to pay you using Intuit's "Payment Network" and you to receive the funds in QuickBooks) (additional fees apply). It is a highly useful feature that enables for quicker funding and greater convenience. Visit the "Payment Network" page on Intuit's website to learn more about this feature. If you decide to use it, you can modify the customer accounts that will be affected and change this choice

NOTE: Intuit's Payment Network was discontinued on June 30, 2016.

Step 7: Navigate to Sales Tax Settings. You can completely avoid this step if you will not be collecting taxes from your customers. If you will be and did not say yes at the first setup interview, you must now enable sales tax.

Step 8: Select Additional Info and input the customer type in the Customer Type area, as well as the customer's representative in the Rep field.

Step 9: If you are presently working on or have a job pending for this customer, enter the job information in the Job Info boxes. If you have multiple jobs in progress for this customer, you can input them once you finish setting up the customer.

Step 10: Click OK button. You should see the new customer in your list of customers.

Setup Your Vendors Account On Quickbooks

Step 1: Select Vendor Center from the Vendors menu.

Step 2: In the top left corner of the new screen, click New Vendor, then select New Vendor from drop-down menu.

Step 3: Enter your vendor's name in the Company Name area, the date you want them to start in the As of Date field, and the amount you owe them as of the date you want them to start in the Opening Balance field. (You do not need to input any information in the Vendor Name area; whatever name you enter in the "Company Name" box will be automatically populated in the "Vendor Name" and "Billed From" fields.

Step 4: Fill out the rest of the form, including the address information. Fill in the Vendor address below the Vendor's name that is already there in the Billed From box.

Step 5: Once you've done entering your vendor's address information, click on Payment Settings on the left side of the New Vendor page.

Step 6: Fill out all required fields to configure how your vendor interacts with you regarding payments. If an option is not available in a drop-down menu, click Add New and add the necessary information before returning to the New Vendor screen.

Step 7: Go to Tax Settings. In the Vendor Tax ID area, enter your vendor's tax ID number. (If you work with unincorporated vendors, such as outside consultants or subcontractors, you must send a 1099-MISC form to anyone who is paid more than a certain amount per year. Check the box that says "Vendor qualified for 1099."

Step 8: Select Account Settings. (Accounts selected here will appear in the accounts area when you enter a bill for this vendor.) Bills from your power company, for example, will appear in your utilities account if you allocate it to utilities. Spending a little time correctly setting up your accounts will save you a lot of time later.

Step 9: Select Additional Info and input the vendor type in the Vendor Type area.

Step 10: Click the OK button. The vendor you just created should appear in your list of vendors.

Setup Your Employees Files In Quickbooks

Step 1: Select Employee Center from the Employees menu.

Step 2: Click New Employee in the upper left corner of the new screen. On the page, click the Turn on Payroll link. It should bring you to the interface seen in the screenshot below:

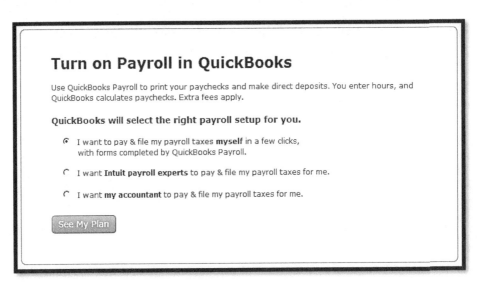

Make your choice and then click See My Plans. Then, choose the plan you want and pay for it. When you're finished, close that window to return to the previous one and conclude the employee setup. After enabling payroll and creating employee files, you will be able to produce your payroll at any time. Now, let's get back to making employee files:

Step 3. In the New Employee window, click Personal, and then enter your employee's name, social security number, gender, and date of birth into the fields provided.

Step 4: Next, choose Address & Contact and provide your employee's address and phone number.

Step 5: If you use special numbers to identify your employees, click More Info and enter this employee's number in the provided field.

Step 6: Select Payroll Info to configure your payroll schedules, payroll item(s), taxes, and tax withholding information. To add a payroll schedule, select the drop-down icon in the Payroll Schedule column, then click Add New. Answer the questions in the new box to tell QuickBooks how to calculate and schedule your payroll, then click Ok. (The Pay Frequency field is automatically filled in with the info you entered).

Step 7: In the "Earnings" Item Name field, click the drop-down icon. In the new window, choose how you want QuickBooks to track your payroll item (hourly, annual, commission, or bonus) and click Next. The next screen you see will be determined by the last choice you made; enter all information. You can add as many items as you want to indicate each employee's various items (normal pay, commission, bonus, etc.). When you're finished, click Finish.

Step 8: If you have a pension plan, 401K, or other type of plan to enter, select the drop-down icon in the "Additions, Decuctions, and Company Contributions" Item Name area and enter it.

Step 9: Select Sick/Vacation, fill out the forms, and click OK.

Step 10: Select Employment Information and provide your employee's hire date and type.

Step 11: Press the OK button. You should see the newly created employee in your employee list. You can always edit your employees' information afterwards.

Adding New Records To A List

Using customers types
Make customer types.

1. You may quickly create types for your consumers.
2. Go to Get paid & pay or Sales, then select Customers
3. From Customers screen, select Customer types.
4. Select New customer type.
5. Enter a name for the customer type, then Save

Assigning customers type

Let's establish the retail customer/business customer kinds and then assign each one to the right customer.

1. Go to the Sales menu on the left side to select Customers.
2. This will bring up a list of all your clients.
3. Tap the Customer types menu in the upper right to select the New customer type button.
4. Fill in the name in the New customer type form, then click Save. For instance, a retail or business customer.
5. Repeat the process to add another client type.

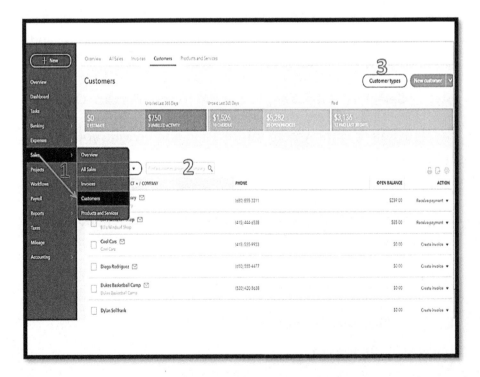

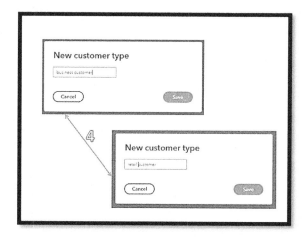

After you've added them, assign each type to the proper client. Here's how it's done:

1. Select Customers from the Sales menu on the left panel.
2. Click on the client's name in the list to see additional information.
3. To open Customer information window, then click the Edit button.
4. Select the Additional details tab and then the Customer Type drop-down to select the relevant type.
5. To keep the modifications, click Save.

Please keep in mind that the Customer type is only available in the Plus or Advanced versions. If you are currently using QUICKBOOKS ONLINE Essentials, you should consider upgrading to one of the versions listed above to take advantage of the feature.

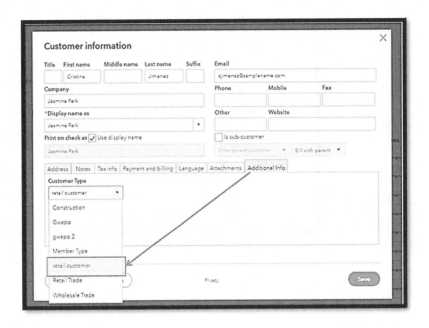

Customize your Customers page

Customize your Customers page to see which customer types you assigned.

1. Select Customers from the Get paid & pay or Sales menus.
2. Right above the Action column, click the Gear symbol.
3. Mark the Customer Type box with a checkmark. This will create a new column.

Run a report

Run one out of these reports to get a snapshot of the customer types.

1. Go to Business Overview, then Reports, or Reports.
2. Navigate to the section Sales and Customers. Select one of the following:
   a. Detail report on sales by customer type
   b. Report on Sales by Customer Detail by Customer Type

Working With Records

How to record expenses in quickbooks

1. Open expenses

Navigate to the Create (+) Menu and select Expense under Suppliers.

2. Select a Payee

If you're adding a new payee, enter their name then click Add.

You can add additional information by clicking Details or by saving and returning later.

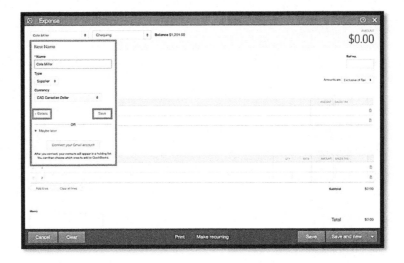

3. Select an Account

Select the account from which the funds for this purchase were drawn. have in mind that even if your debit card contains a Visa or MasterCard logo, you must select a Chequing Account.

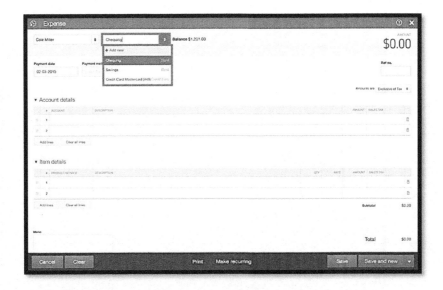

4. Fill in the Date

Input the date you purchased this item.

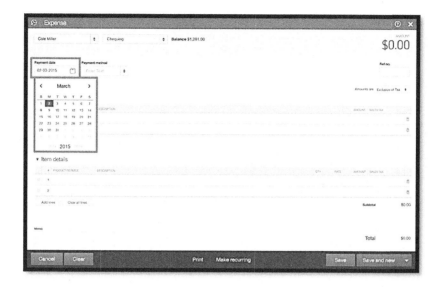

5. Select a Payment Method

What method did you use to pay for this purchase? Choose from cash, check, and credit card.

6.Select a Category

Select an right category for that item or service you paid for under Account.

If you bought things or services from several categories with this one particular cheque, put each category and the actual amount you spent on all these items on separate lines by clicking Add lines.

7.Insert a Description

Fill in the blanks with information about this purchase.

8. Enter Amount

Fill in the amount for those purchases in the amount field. Fill in the Sales Tax field with the right sales tax.

9. Saving

Save and New if you want to save this and start a new one, or Save and Close if you're done.

Using Attachments in QuickBook

There are many tricks and tips that can help you use attachments in QuickBooks better. Using this feature to its fullest not only makes it more easier to keep good records, but it also makes it easier to talk to customers.

What's the point of using attachments?

Attachments can be used in QuickBooks in three ways:

1. Attaching pictures, contracts, or drawings to invoices or estimates
2. Attaching bills or copies of checks to expense forms helps keep track of payments.
3. To include receipts for money spent on travel, restaurants, shopping, etc.

When and how to start using attachments

You must first upload the files before you can use attachments in QuickBooks. You can upload documents in PDF format, or you can upload images of paper bills, receipts, contracts, and so on. First, you must transfer the required data to your computer. Following this, you'll need to transfer the necessary data to QuickBooks by uploading the files. In two ways you can accomplish this:

1. The page, titled "Attachments," is where you can quickly and simply download any relevant files. When you need to attach multiple files to a single transaction and then reference them individually, this is the best choice.
2. It is also possible to upload attachments separately and associate them with the appropriate transaction later.

How to use the Attachments page to upload attachments

1. Launch QuickBooks, then choose Gear, then Attachments. Then you may drag and drop files into the attachments queue to upload them. Additionally, you will have the choice to paper clip the chosen files.
2. The new attachments can now be used to make an invoice or expense, be exported as a zip file, or be selected together with other attachments.
3. A list of all attachments can then be printed.
4. The rows and columns you want to display can be selected.
5. Then down load the attachment.
6. Additionally, you are with the option to update, add a new invoice or expense, remove an attachment, or change one attachment in many ways.

The column that displays which attachments are connected to particular expense or invoice transactions will then be visible to you.

Some basic tips

Arranging attachments according to transaction value: This can be done by selecting Edit for a particular attachment, then inserting the necessary information in the Notes or File Name area. To enable sorting by quantity, return to the main Attachments page and click the Note or Name header.

You can scroll through the attachment preview box as well: Again, select Edit for a particular attachment, launch the Preview window, and then scroll the mouse either horizontally or vertically through the attachment. You can also zoom in to focus on particular details. You can also use the Right, Left, Up, and Down arrow keys.

Upload new attachments while you are creating a new transaction

When you are in the middle of establishing a new expense or invoice transaction, QuickBooks also allows you to upload new attachments. You can accomplish this by:

1. Create a new transaction by clicking Create, then the "+" symbol. For example, you may make a new estimate by selecting Create + Estimate.
2. Scroll down the page to the Attachments area of the estimate form.
3. You can then drag and drop a new file or select Show Existing to see a list of previously uploaded attachments.
4. Another tip is to email an attachment and the form to which it is attached by selecting Attach to email, then Save and Send.

Additional tips about attachments

❖ Columns in the Attachments list can be resized and sorted.
❖ You can also include receipts obtained via email. For example, if you purchased a product from Amazon and received an email receipt, you can save the emailed receipt as a PDF, upload it to QuickBooks, and then complete the standard upload steps.

Searching Quickbooks Online Lists For People

There are several uses for the Vendors, Customers, and Employees pages in QuickBooks Online (QuickBooks Online). Compared to the other pages, the Contractors page has more restrictions; you can use it to look up contractors and generate 1099s. From the Customers, Vendors, or Employees pages that list every person in those categories, you can sort the people inside the list, export the list to Excel, and take actions on a particular group of people in the list.

On each list page, you can print a straightforward report by using the Print button (located directly just above Action column).

How to Work with a Specific Person in QuickBooks Online

You can view the transactions linked with a certain customer, vendor, or employee, as well as the individual's details, and you can attach files to the person. You will be working with customers here.

To find a specific person, enter some characters that match the person's or company's name in the Search box above the list of people.

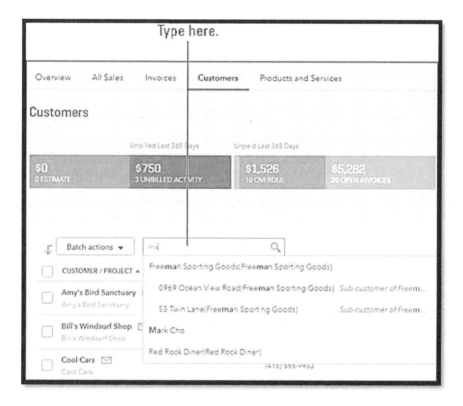

To find a specific individual on a list, utilize the Search box above the names on the list.

When you choose a person in the list, QuickBooks online takes you to the page that is particularly related with that person. The page has two tabs; in the example below, you can actually see the Transaction List tab and the Customer Details tab. If you have activated the Projects function in your company, QuickBooks online will display a third tab named Projects, which will list any projects you have established in your QuickBooks Online company.

The Transaction List tab displays all QuickBooks Online transactions linked with the selected person.

To modify that person's details, select the Edit button from either tab. To add a transaction associated with that person, select the New Transaction button. Track important financial data by adding files to a person's profile page. For instance, you may link the 1099 form from a vendor, the contract from a client, or the receipts from an employee. You are not limited to text documents; images are also acceptable. Simply drag and drop this item into the Attachments box located at the bottom left of the relevant information page. Alternatively, you can click the box to open the standard Windows Open dialog box and select the document you want to attach.

Each attachment can only be 25MB in size. To examine documents that you've already linked to a person, click on the Show Existing link underneath the Attachments box, and QuickBooks Online displays the associated attachments in a pane on the right side of your screen.

Additionally, you can add files to a transaction. To view transactions with attachments, add the Attachments column to such table that appears on the user's Transaction List page. Click the table gear button just above Action column to show the Transaction List page for the person. When a list shows, select Show More. A check box for Attachments appears when you choose Show More Modifications to Display Less; select it to include the Attachments column in the table grid. You can recognize it as the column heading with a paper clip. When you display the Attachments column for one individual, it also displays for all individuals of that kind in the Transaction List table. If any given transaction has attachments, the number of attachments will be displayed in the column. Clicking the number displays the attachments for the transaction; clicking an attachment in the list opens that item.

Attachments are added to transactions when they are created; only attachments related with transactions display on the various Transaction List pages, while attachments associated with people appear on the relevant person's profile.

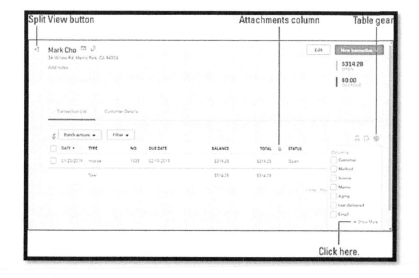

Adding the Attachments column to the Transaction List table.

When you're through with one person in a list, you may easily move to another by using the list's Split View list pane. You can display a pane listing the persons stored in the list by clicking the Split View icon (seen in the preceding image) (take a look at the following image).

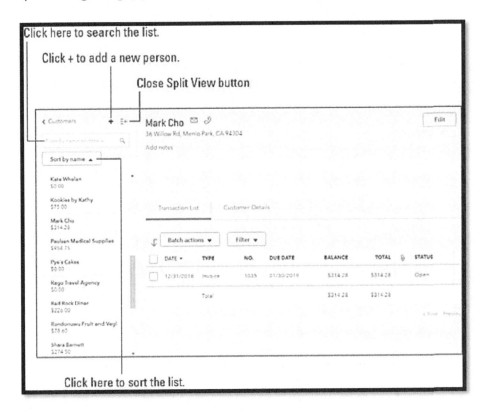

Displaying the Split View of a list.

To find a person, navigate down the list in the Split View pane or enter a few letters of the person's or organization's name into to the Search box at the top of the list. The list can also be sorted by name or open balance. Go to a person's page by clicking on their name. Click the plus (+) icon at the top of the list in the Split View window to add a new person to the list. Customers can be reached by either clicking Sales in the Navigation bar, followed by clicking Customers, or by clicking Customers at the head of the Split View list. To close Split View, click the Close Split View button.

Sorting a list in QuickBooks Online

You can sort the listings on the Customers and Vendors page by name or open balance, in addition to sorting in Split View. Quickbooks online organizes the entries on these pages alphabetically by name in ascending order by default. Employees can be sorted alphabetically and reverse alphabetically, by pay type, or by status (active or inactive). Contractors cannot be sorted; Quickbooks online sorts them alphabetically by default.

To modify the sort order of the Customers or Vendors lists, click Sales or Expenses in the Navigation bar, followed by Customers or Vendors to reveal the appropriate page; in this example, we are using the Customers page. Then, click the heading for the column you wish to sort by. When you click the Customer/Company column heading, Quickbooks Online sorts the customers alphabetically. When you click the Open Balance column header, Quickbooks Online arranges the list from lowest to highest in Open Balance order.

Exporting Quickbooks Online list to Excel

You can export your client or vendor list to Excel. If you don't have a copy of Excel on your PC, you can actually download and utilize the free Excel mobile app.

Click the relevant link in the Navigation bar (Sales or Expenses) so as to display either the Vendors page or the Customers page; in this example, the Vendors page is used. Three buttons show on the right side of the page, directly ontop the Action column. When you click the middle button, Quickbooks Online exports the list to an Excel file; a file button displays at the bottom of the screen in Chrome.

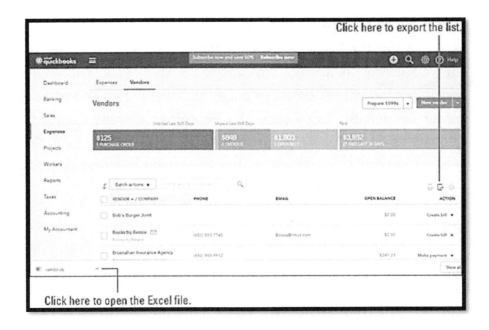

Click here to export the list.

Click here to open the Excel file.

When you press the button at the bottom of the screen, Excel opens the file. You can edit the file by selecting the Activate Editing button in the window's yellow bar at the top. If you are using Excel mobile, you must sign into it with your Microsoft account in order to make changes to the file.

How to work with a batch of people in Quickbooks Online

When working with customers or vendors, one can carry out specific tasks simultaneously for a number of people. When using the Bill.com add-on with Quickbooks Online Essentials, Plus, or Advanced, you may choose specific vendors by selecting the check box next to their name and sending the same email to them. You can even deactivate the chosen vendors.

The Bill.com add-on for Quickbooks Online allows you to pay bills online; there is a full-service Bill.com app, but Now I'm referring to the add-on for Quickbooks Online here. The Bill.com app is available in the Intuit App Center. To access the store, select Apps from the Navigation pane. Bill.com does not charge a monthly subscription cost, however there is a per transaction fee for each payment you handle. You can create and send statements to customers in addition to emails, add the chosen customers

110

to a customer category (which you use to group customers), and make the chosen consumers inactive. Click the Sales or Expenses link in the Navigation bar, then the appropriate list page to see the associated page, to use one of these activities for a group of people. Check the names you want to be part of your action, and then select Batch Actions from the menu. Select the action you want to perform, then carry it out by adhering to the on-screen instructions.

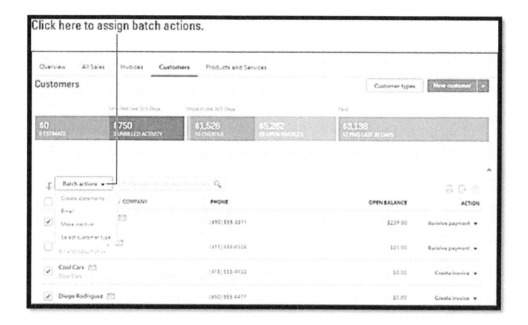

Introducing spreadsheet sync

You may sync Excel with your QuickBooks Online Advanced account using Spreadsheet Sync, enabling you to:

❖ Pull data into an Excel spreadsheet, edit, and then you can post back to QuickBooks Online Advanced.
❖ Using Spreadsheet Sync's list templates, create fresh data to publish to QuickBooks Online Advanced.
❖ Create a custom reports and update them with the most recent QuickBooks Online Advanced data.

Note:

- ❖ Spreadsheet Sync can only be opened and managed by QuickBooks Online Advanced admin users.
- ❖ Spreadsheet Sync is compatible with Excel Office 365. It will not work with earlier versions of Excel.
- ❖ Upgrade to Microsoft Edge if your computer's integrated browser is Internet Explorer 11.

Installing the spreadsheet sync

Use one of the following prompts to launch Spreadsheet Sync from within QuickBooks Online Advanced:

- ❖ Select the Dashboard tab.
1. Select Dashboard from the left navigation panel.
2. In the dashboard pane, scroll down to the Setting up Guide section and thenselect Sync your spreadsheets.
- ❖ Select the Reports tab.
1. Select Reports from the left menu panel.
2. Click the arrow next to Create new report and choose in spreadsheet from the selection menu.
- ❖ Select the Tasks tab.
1. Select Tasks from the left menu panel.
2. Navigate to Setup Spreadsheet Sync and click Launch Spreadsheet Sync.
- ❖ From the Settings menu, Choose Spreadsheet Sync, then allow the Spreadsheet Sync add-in to run:
1. Click Let's Go in the pop-up box.
2. Select Open Link in the following pop-up box.
3. Once Spreadsheet Sync has downloaded, it will prompt you to access Office 365. Choose Trust this add-in.
4. Click Sign in.
5. Type in your QuickBooks user ID and click Sign in.
6. Enter your password and press the Continue button.

Accessing Spreadsheet Sync from QuickBooks Online Advanced or Excel

There are two ways to launch Spreadsheet Sync from QuickBooks Online Advanced.

1. Click the Settings icon.

   From the dropdown option, choose Spreadsheet Sync.

2. Select Reports from the side navigation menu.

   In the upper right, click the caret next to Create new report, then click in spreadsheet.

   Launch Spreadsheet Sync.

Using Excel to launch Spreadsheet Sync

1. In the Excel navigation bar, pick Launch Add-In Spreadsheet Sync.
2. Click Sign in.
3. In the task panel, input your QuickBooks Online user ID and click Sign in.
4. Input your password and press the Continue button.

Signing in again to spreadsheet sync after been signed out automatically

If the Spreadsheet Sync toolbar in Excel is not present, this indicates that you have opted out of Spreadsheet Sync.

   ❖ In the task pane, enter your sign-in credentials again.
   ❖ Before you sign back, therey may need to close and reopen Spreadsheet Sync.

Sign out of Spreadsheet Sync

   ❖ In the toolbar, click the Sign Out button.

CHAPTER FIVE

MANAGING SALES TAX, SERVICES AND INVENTORY

Setting Up Sale Tax

Nobody enjoys thinking about taxes. They can be perplexing because they differ depending on place. Although taxes may appear to be an intimidating chore, setting up the sales tax in QuickBooks Online may be pretty simple.

First, we'll define sales taxes and go through some key phrases associated with them. Then, we'll go over how to set up sales tax in QuickBooks Online and get our customers and items to accept sales tax. We'll also look at filing sales taxes and receiving sales tax reports.

What Exactly Is a Sales Tax?

Let us begin by defining a sales tax. A sales tax is a tax levied by the government on the purchase of products and services. These taxes are paid at the time of sale. The merchant collects the tax and pays it to the government. These taxes are levied against the customers who get the finished goods. Because of supply chains in the modern economy, not every product transaction necessitates the imposition of a sales tax.

With sales taxes, three more concepts to be understood: nexus, excise tax, and value-added tax.

1. **Nexus** - A nexus is a physical presence in a jurisdiction that requires you to pay sales taxes there. This is especially significant in online sales, since customers can be located anywhere in the world.
2. **Excise Taxes** - While certain commodities are exempted from the sales tax because they are food or clothing, others are subject to additional taxes because they are deemed vices. This is true for cigarette and alcohol taxes.

3. **Value-added Tax (VAT)** - A tax levied on products in a supply chain anytime they gain value. This form of tax is widespread in the European Union but not in the United States.

Setting up a Sales Tax

Now that you have a basic understanding of sales taxes, let's look at how you might implement them. QuickBooks Online features wizards that will assist you in setting up sales tax. It will inquire for your residence and state, among other things. Then you must configure sales taxes for your inventory products.

To begin setting up sales tax, ensure that your accounting basis is set to the accrual approach. Let's take a quick look at the differences between an accrual basis and a cash basis for accounting.

Cash Basis and Accrual Basis

You should be familiar with the terms accrual basis accounting and cash basis accounting. Although both systems differ in the order in which transactions are recorded, they produce results that are almost identical over time.

❖ **Accrual Basis** - In this accounting method, transactions and income are recorded when they are earned, while expenses are recorded when they are incurred.
❖ **Cash Basis Accounting** - In this accounting method, transactions and revenue are recorded when cash is received from the client, and expenses are recorded when cash is paid.

The cash basis method is the simplest to implement of the two. This is because it does not necessitate complex accounting procedures such as accruals or deferrals. However, in the United States, cash basis can only be utilized by businesses with less than $5 million in annual sales. Because the timing of getting and spending income varies, there may appear to be high and low profit periods.

The accrual basis approach is used by businesses with sales more than $5 million USD. Because they are not waiting for cash to come in or go out, this strategy makes it easy to see revenues and expenses over time.

QuickBooks Online can automatically track and report sales tax if the accounting is set to accrual. It also automatically calculates sales taxes on purchases. If you are already operating on a cash basis, you should move to accrual before establishing sales taxes, and then you can now switch back.

Setting up an Accounting Basis

Ascertain that the accounting method is set to accrual. This is done by clicking on the gear-shaped Settings icon in the header, followed by Account and Settings in Your Company. The Accounting area is located at the top of the Advanced tab.

To begin altering the parameters, click the pencil symbol. Check that the Accounting Method is set to Accrual before clicking the Save button.

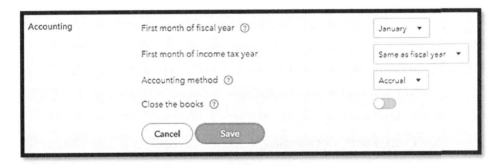

You can do the setting up your sales tax after ensuring that your accounting system is accrual. Begin by configuring the taxes by clicking the Taxes option in the left-side Navigation Pane. You will be directed to the Sales Tax Center, where a wizard promises to set up your taxes in two steps. Click Get Started button to launch the process.

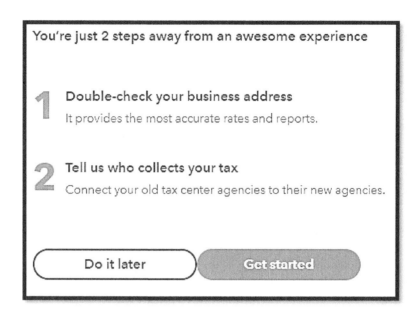

You're just 2 steps away from an awesome experience

1 **Double-check your business address**
It provides the most accurate rates and reports.

2 **Tell us who collects your tax**
Connect your old tax center agencies to their new agencies.

[Do it later] [Get started]

Your address will be displayed, and you can edit it by clicking the pencil-shaped icon. When you've input everything rightly, then click the Next button.

Set up your sales tax center

Double-check your address to make sure it's right.

Here's the address we have for you
We use your physical business address to calculate your sales tax rate.

Business address ✎

123 Sierra Way
San Pablo CA 87999

Then you'll be asked who collects your sales taxes. You must determine whether you must charge sales tax outside of your native state. You must match the name of the tax rate with the name of the official agency from each selection. If you need assistance filling out this information for your business, contact your accountant.

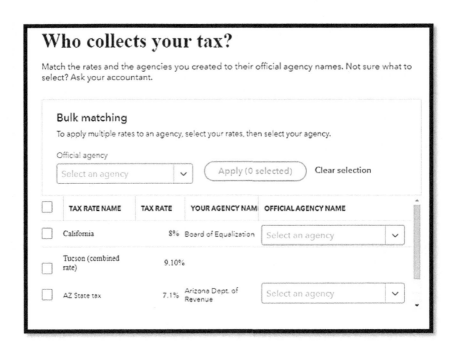

Who collects your tax?

Match the rates and the agencies you created to their official agency names. Not sure what to select? Ask your accountant.

Bulk matching

To apply multiple rates to an agency, select your rates, then select your agency.

Official agency

| Select an agency ⌄ | Apply (0 selected) | Clear selection |

	TAX RATE NAME	TAX RATE	YOUR AGENCY NAM	OFFICIAL AGENCY NAME
☐	California	8%	Board of Equalization	Select an agency ⌄
☐	Tucson (combined rate)	9.10%		
☐	AZ State tax	7.1%	Arizona Dept. of Revenue	Select an agency ⌄

After clicking the Next button, then you will have one more opportunity to evaluate your information before concluding the process. For you to exit the wizard, click on the Continue button.

When you conclude the setup, it will create tax-paying entities for all of your customers. However, not all of your clients may be required to pay taxes. They may be excluded if they are a charity, school, or government entity. In that scenario, you can update their profile accordingly. In the left-side Navigation Pane, navigate to Sales and then to the Customers tab.

Find the customer you want in the list then click on their name to go to their details page. To modify their profile, go to the details page and click the Edit button. Find the Tax Info section on their profile and check the box that says This Customer Is Tax Exempt.

Enter the ID from their exemption certificate as well as information on why they are tax exempt. In the Attachments tab, you may include a copy of their certificate.

Create and Edit Agencies and Rates

The sales tax settings can be modified and new rates added. Click the Sales Tax Settings link in the top-right corner to do this. You will be directed to a website where you can modify the tax settings in a number of ways.

You can add a tax agency using the Add Agency button. In the panel that appears on the right side of the screen, you can enter the agency, the frequency of filing, and the commencement date. Click Save once you have done adding the agency.

A special rate can also be added by choosing the Add Rate button. When adding a rate, you can choose between adding a single rate and a combination rate.

If you only pay taxes to one organization, you can pick a single rate. If you are managing sales tax for several agencies, set up a combined tax rate. When you choose a combined rate, your customers will only see one tax rate on their sales forms. The Sales Tax Center, however, continues to keep track of this and splits the total into amounts that are appropriate for each agency.

The combined tax rate should be given a name, and then the different sales tax obligations should be entered. Click the Add Another Rate link to add other rates. When finished, click the Save button at the bottom of the window.

Additionally, rates and agencies are editable. In the Action column for the agency or rate, click the Edit option.

Each editable item will cause an edit screen to appear on the right side. To save your adjustments, click the Save button.

Clicking Inactive in the Action column will likewise make an agency or rate inactive. Click the gear-shaped icon above the table and select Include Inactive to bring back the list of inactive items.

Adding Sales Tax to Sales Transactions

Sales tax can be added to bills, receipts for purchases, estimations, and credit notes. Let's test it out on a fresh invoice to see how it performs. In the Navigation Pane on the left, select New, then select Invoice under the Customers heading.

Include a taxable item in the invoice. To confirm that the goods is subject to tax, check the box in the Tax columns.

Select the proper sales tax in the bottom-right corner of the invoice. To add a custom rate, select Add Rate from the drop-down menu at the bottom.

Click the Save button once you've completed setting the tax rate.

Making Sales Tax Changes in Sales and Credits

You can go back and combine sales tax with credits and purchases. Start by selecting Sales from the Navigation Pane on the left. Next, select All Sales.

In the list, look for a charge or credit memo. Clicking on it will reveal it. Select the checkbox next to the word "Sales Tax" in the Tax column to add or delete the sales tax.

When you're done, press the Save and Close button.

Changing an Unbilled Expense's Taxable Status

Unbilled expenses can also have their tax status changed. Navigate to the Sales link in the Navigation Pane on the left. Navigate to All Sales from there. Locate and open a chargeable expense charge.

To view the bill, select the Bill link in the header.

Sales tax reporting and payment

Either you or an accountant can take care of your sales tax management. In the left-side Navigation Pane, select Taxes, followed by Sales Tax. You are currently within the Sales Tax Center.

Then, you can view all of the unfiled sales tax returns. Additionally, you'll find those that are past due.

Click the View Return button next to the return you want to file on the right side of the page to file and pay a return.

Your sales tax will then be displayed for you to review.

Mark the checkbox to make the product taxable in the bill's Tax column. Or, to make it nontaxable, uncheck the box.

You can now include a sales tax adjustment. A panel will show up on the right side of the screen if you click the Add an Adjustment option.

You must first include a justification for the modification. Credit, prior payments, and pre-payments are all included as possible reasons for an adjustment in the selection menu. Another option is Other, which can be used for fines, interest, or rounding errors.

Choose an income account if the justification is because of a credit or earlier payment. Choose an expense account if the cause is a fine, penalty, or interest that is owed. If a rounding error caused it, choose an expense account for positive errors or an income account for negative ones.

Then, input the adjustment's amount. To complete the adjustment, click on the Add button.

To get back to the page where you can review your sales taxes, click Record Payment.

After that, QuickBooks Online computes and displays the amount owed to the tax authority. Here, you'll be able to confirm or modify it. By selecting the Report link and then selecting Download Your Full Report, you may also view details. Your taxes are broken down there under the Sales Tax Liability.

Last but not least, specify a payment date and the bank account that will be used. To complete the procedure, press the Record Payment button.

Sales Tax Report

You can get several sales tax reports using QuickBooks Online. Click on Reports in the left-side Navigation Pane to go to the Reports page.

Start typing "sales" into the search field on the reports page. The Sales Tax Liability Report will be displayed. To access the report, click the title. This report details the sales tax you've collected and the amount you still owe to taxing authorities.

The settings can be modified at the page's top. Click the Run Report button to update the report after setting the Report Period to All Dates and the Tax agency to All.

To view the Transaction Report, click the amount. The report includes the transaction type. You can view the invoice's taxable amount, tax rate, and tax amount by clicking on the invoice there.

The Taxable Sales Detail report is another helpful one. By entering this into the search box on the Reports page, you can also find it there. The sales of taxable goods and services are shown in this report. It contains the date, transaction type, client, amount, balance, rate, and quantity.

Categories for Sales Tax Assigning

State-by-state variations exist about whether or not something is taxable. For tax purposes, you might want to classify the things you sell. Clothing, sales tax holidays, food for home use, meals tax, medical products, things with fees, and computer products & services are a few examples of such products.

You can designate sales tax categories after checking your area's tax laws. Select Products and Services from the left-side Navigation Pane's Sales section. Click the New button or, if an existing item has an Edit button in the Action column.

Select Choose a particular category from the Sales Tax Category option once you've located it.

When you click on Choose a Special Category, a popup window containing a variety of automatically produced categories for the item will appear. When finished, click Save and Close to go back to the list of products and services.

Incorporating TurboTax

Tax-focused software is available separately from Intuit. Currently, you are unable to export data from QuickBooks Online to TurboTax from Intuit. The Chart of Accounts likewise does not support tax line mapping. Use detail accounts instead, which you can then assign tax lines to.

However, accountants can use the Book to Tax feature of QuickBooks Online Account. It can now integrate with Intuit Tax Online thanks to that.

Adding Sales Tax to QuickBooks Online from QuickBooks Desktop

One element that does not transfer fully from QuickBooks Desktop to QuickBooks Online is sales tax. You'll see that certain taxes import merely the list and balances, while others convert as journal entries.

On the Chart of Accounting page, there will now be accounts for sales tax payable. Each Sales Tax Agency Payable account in QuickBooks Desktop and each Sales Tax Payable account in QuickBooks Online will have one.

Working With Products And Services

The Items list from the QuickBooks Desktop product is the equivalent of the Products and Services list in QuickBooks Online (QBO). By selecting Gear > Products and Services, the Products and Services list is displayed. The compacted form of the list is displayed in the following illustration so that you can see more products; to access it, use the table gear on the right side of the page.

Creating an inventory item

There are a few extra pieces of information you must provide when creating an inventory item.

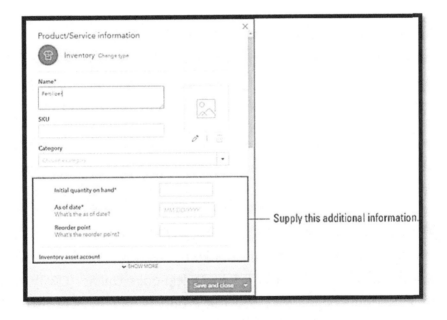

Information on inventory items' supply quantity and inventory asset accounts are provided.

Include the amount you have on hand as well as the date you came to that conclusion. To preserve the item in Quickbooks Online, you must include an As Of date. Make sure to specify an As Of date early enough to accommodate those transactions—typically the start of your fiscal year—if you intend to add previous transactions that employ the item you're putting up.

Keep in mind that you must own some of an item before you may sell it. When you manufacture an item and don't already have any, you'll presumably use an expense transaction to purchase some, which will update your quantities.

You can provide a reorder point if you're using Quickbooks Online Plus. Your minimum quantity that you believe you must always have on hand is your reorder point. When the amount of the item on hand falls to or below the preset reorder point, Quickbooks Online notifies you to place an order for additional. Quickbooks Online uses the reorder point you set to track the quantity of the item in stock.

After you have established an inventory item, you can specify a reorder point by finding it in the Products and Services list and selecting Edit in the Action column. Provide the reorder point after which click Save and Close.

The Products and Services list can also be used to view the products that are low on stock or for which you have set reorder points. To limit the Products and Services list to only showing items for which you have chosen a reorder point and which are also low in stock, click Low Stock at the top of the list, as shown in the following image. To examine items for which you have set a reorder point but don't currently have any, click Out of Stock. You might want to order these items.

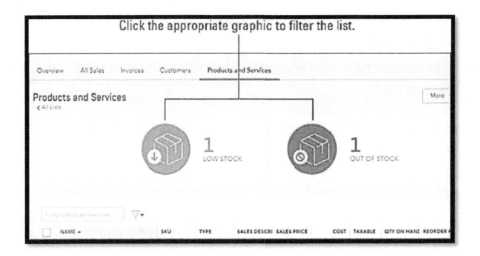

Filtering in QuickBooks Online the Products and Services list can be filtered using these graphics to display just Low Stock or only Out of Stock items for which you have defined a reorder point.

A product for which you've set a reorder point and have one or fewer on hand is considered to be "low stock" by Quickbooks Online.

Click the arrow in the Action column of the low- or out-of-stock item, then select Reorder from the drop-down selection that displays. The details of the item are filled in when a purchase order is created by Quickbooks Online. Send the completed purchase order to the supplier. Remember that Quickbooks Online only generates one purchase order for the chosen items.

Select the items you want to reorder for one vendor, click Batch Actions (which shows above the Action column after you select an item), and then select Reorder to send purchase orders to numerous vendors. Repeat the procedure to order things from a different vendor later.

The filter for Low Stock or Out of Stock goods can be simply removed. When one of these filters is chosen, an X appears in the filter graphic's upper right corner. When you click that X, Quickbooks Online displays the entire list of Products and Services again.

126

How to work with bundles in Quickbooks Online

You can group products that you frequently sell together into bundles if you are using Quickbooks Online Essentials or Quickbooks Online Plus. Consider a bundle as a group item in the desktop product if you use QuickBooks Desktop.

A bundle is not an assembly, and neither does Quickbooks Online monitor a bundle as a separate item with a quantity or a separate cost. Neither does Quickbooks Online construct a bill of materials for a bundle. As a result, Quickbooks Online does not keep track of the quantity of packages on hand.

Consider a bundle as a selection of items—goods and services alike—that a customer purchases from you at the same time, if you weren't using QuickBooks Desktop. Assume, for instance, that you manage a landscaping company that offers lighting, pruning, and fertilization services in addition to the sale of water features.

Normally, if a customer purchases a water feature, you must offer the consumer the water feature itself, the concrete used to install the water feature, and a pump used to circulate water through the water feature. Because you'll need to sell all three at once, you can arrange the three components—the feature, the concrete, and the pump—needed to make a water feature as a package.

The purpose of a bundle is to simplify the selling process by allowing you to add all the things that make up the bundle to a single sales form rather than having to add them individually to several sales forms.

Invoices, Credit Memos, Sales Receipts, Refund Receipts, Delayed Credits, and Delayed Charges are all documents that can use bundles. Documents cannot be purchased in bundles, and bundles cannot be added to price rules.

These steps should be followed to make a bundle:

1. To view the list of products and services, select GearProducts and Services.
2. To see the Select a Type panel, click the New button.
3. Select Bundle

4. Give the bundle a name, an SKU, if necessary, and a description that will appear on sales forms.
5. Select Display Bundle Components under the Products/Services Included in the Bundle section. If you want to list the components contained in the bundle on sales documents, select the When Printing or Sending Transactions check box.
6. To find out which goods are part of the bundle, use the table grid at the bottom of the panel (see the following figure).

   a. To extend the panel and add more goods to the bundle, click Show More.

b. Select one item to be included in the bundle by clicking in the first row of the Product/Service column on Quickbooks Online screen.

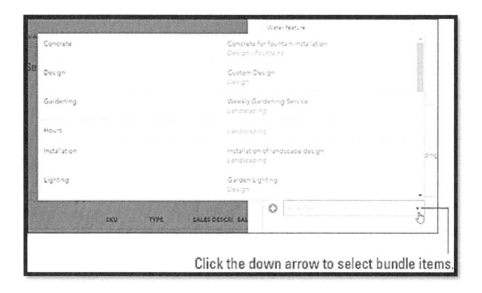

Click the down arrow to select bundle items.

c. Supply a quantity for the item

d. Repeat steps b and c for each item you want to include in the bundle.

Up to 50 items may be included in a bundle. Additionally, you can rearrange the bundle's elements by dragging the graphic that is visible to the left of each one (the one that looks like nine dots).

e. Click Save and Close when you have finished adding things to the bundle.

The bundle is saved by Quickbooks Online, and you may find it at the end of the Products and Services list. To use the bundle, just include it in a sales document similarly to how you would include any other product or service. Additionally, after included a bundle in a sales document, you can alter the bundle's components by adding or removing them as necessary. A bundle's price is equal to the total cost of its parts. Remember that a bundle isn't an assembly; you can discount a bundle but you cannot mark one up or track the quantity on hand for a bundle.

Similar to how you look for any other good or service, you can search for bundles. To search by name or SKU, use the Search box at the top of the Products and Services list.

How to use pricing rules in QuickBooks Online

You can manage product prices by using pricing rules, a feature that is currently in beta testing but is accessible in your Quickbooks Online company if you enable it. You may, for instance,

- ❖ Give select or all consumers a discount.
- ❖ Provide discounts on particular goods.
- ❖ Price increases for the products mentioned.
- ❖ Offer discounted rates for a predetermined amount of time.

Pricing regulations are comparable to price levels for prior users of QuickBooks Desktop; in instance, Quickbooks Online doesn't record a price change as a discount but rather as an override of the sale price.

Bundles cannot be added to price rules, however you can get around this limitation by adding the individual items that make up a bundle. The bundle will then reflect the price rule pricing when you later add it to a sales document.

By selecting Gear—>Account and Features—>Sales and updating the Products and Services section to enable price rules, you may activate the feature.

Although you can create as many price rules as you like, Quickbooks Online performs best with less than 10,000. Select Gear > Lists > All Lists to create a price rule. Click Price rules and then click Create a Rule on the resulting page. The Create a Price Rule page is shown by Quickbooks Online.

To build a pricing rule, use this page.

Enter the rule's name, start and end dates, eligible clients, and the goods or services that Quickbooks Online should apply the rule to on this page.

Decide whether to change the price by a percentage, a fixed sum, or a custom amount. Put a price increase or decrease in the rule's description, and specify how you want Quickbooks Online to handle rounding. Click Save or Save and Close when finished. Quickbooks Online automatically applies any suitable price rules to the transactions when you create a sales transaction.

The best way to create categories in QBO

All subscriptions that utilize sub-items can use categories in place of those items, with the exception of those that switched from QuickBooks Desktop. Using different Products and Services reports, you can use categories to classify the products you sell and, ideally, gain a better understanding of what your customers are purchasing. Transactions cannot be given a category, and classifications have no bearing on your accounting or financial reports.

Classes and/or locations can also be used to further catalog transactions and financial data.

You can add new categories as you add products, or if you'd prefer, you can establish categories beforehand and make them available when you add items by selecting Manage Categories from the More menu on the Products and Services list page. You can perform both, yes.

Clicking the New Category button on the Product Categories page, as shown in the accompanying image, allows you to add a new category. The Category Information panel then displays on the right side of your screen, where you may enter the category name. Check the Is a Sub-Category box and choose the name of the current category if the new category is a subcategory of an existing one. To create a category, click Save at the bottom of the screen.

Up to four levels of subcategories can be created. To put it another way, you could make a category called Clothing and a subcategory of it called Shoes. You can add a Women's Shoes category under the Shoes subcategory, and you can add a Sneakers subcategory under the Women's Shoes category. Sneakers cannot have a subcategory, but you can add a Dress Shoes subcategory under Women's Shoes.

You can change an existing category if necessary by clicking the Edit link next to it in the table on the Product Categories page. The Category Information panel reappears and shows the most recent data for the category. If you want to remove a category, click Remove after making your adjustments.

Whether you remove a category or a subcategory will determine how the removed category affects the items. The items associated to a subcategory are moved up one level by QBO if you remove it. QBO reclassifies the items as uncategorized if you remove a category (without any subcategories).

How To Import Product and Service Items

Instead of using QuickBooks Online's data entry panels, it is significantly faster to enter information about a product or service into a spreadsheet. I advise performing the first few tasks manually as displayed above to get accustomed to the requested fields. If you have a lot of things, it will be quicker to enter the data in an Excel spreadsheet and import it by using these steps.

Step 1: Prepare Your Spreadsheet

For each item of merchandise or services you desire to import, there should be a row in your spreadsheet. A field to be imported into QuickBooks Online is represented by each column. Each column in your spreadsheet needs labels, but these labels don't have to correspond to the field names from QuickBooks Online. During the import process, you can map each column to a specific field in QuickBooks.

The fields for products and services that can be imported are listed below. The section on how to manually enter product and service items contains a more thorough discussion of the fields.

- Type (Inventory, Noninventory, or Service)
- Sales price/rate
- Purchase description
- Purchase cost
- Expense account (must be set up in chart of accounts prior to import)
- Taxable (Yes/No)
- Product/Service name
- Sales description
- SKU
- Income account (must be set up in chart of accounts prior to import)
- Quantity on hand (inventory items only)
- Reorder point (inventory items only)
- Inventory asset account (inventory items only and must be set up in chart of accounts prior to import)
- Quantity as-of date: (inventory items only)

Only the columns you want to import data for must be included. It's acceptable if certain columns are absent. Your spreadsheet should resemble the following:

Product/Service Name	Sales Description	SKU	Type	Sales Price	Purchase Description	Purchase Cost	Quantity on Hand	Reorder Point
Design	Custom landscape design		Service	150 No				
Fountain	Garden rock fountain	341253	Inventory	275 Yes	Rock fountain	150	15	5
Gardening	weekly gardening service		Service	75 No				
Garden Supplies: Rocks	Garden rocks -20 lb. bag	142563	Inventory	75 Yes	Gardem rocks - 20 lb.	50	110	10
Garden Supplies: Soil	Garden soil - 5 lb. bag	1425632	Noninventory	20 Yes	Garden soil - 5lb. Bag	15		
Trimming	Tree and Shrub Trimming		Service	50 No				

Note: Use the first tab In an Excel workbook, only the first worksheet (or tab) will be imported. Make sure your worksheet is in the lower-left corner of your Excel file, on the first tab.

Step 2: Upload Your Excel or CSV File From the Products and Services screen, pick Import from the drop-down menu next to New in the top right corner.

Choose Import on QuickBooks Online's Products and Services screen.

QuickBooks Online's Products and Services screen will prompt you to choose Import.

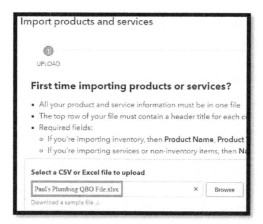

Choosing the file for QuickBooks Online's import of goods and services.

Click the green Next button in the bottom right corner of the screen after choosing your file (not shown).

Step 3: Connect Your Columns to Fields in QuickBooks

You can select which of your columns to import into each field that QuickBooks Online collects using this page.

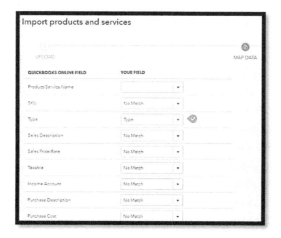

The left column lists the fields that can be loaded into QuickBooks. The right column in QuickBooks indicates which column in your spreadsheet has the data for that field. If any of the QuickBooks fields on the left is absent from your spreadsheet, you should indicate No Match, as was done with the Income Account in the example above.

Once all of your columns have been transformed into QuickBooks fields, select the green Next button in the bottom right corner of the page.

Step 4: Review and import the data

On the final screen, you can look at the data that is being imported into QuickBooks Online. On this screen, you can make any hurried edits. The number of goods and services you should import should equal the number of rows in the spreadsheet, minus one for the header row.

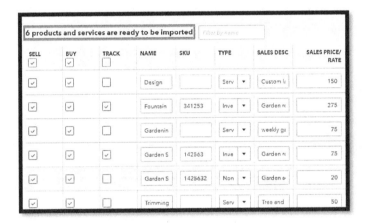

6 products and services are ready to be imported							Filter by name
SELL ☑	**BUY** ☑	**TRACK** ☐	**NAME**	**SKU**	**TYPE**	**SALES DESC**	**SALES PRICE/RATE**
☑	☑	☐	Design		Serv ▾	Custom l	150
☑	☑	☑	Fountain	341253	Inve ▾	Garden n	275
☑	☑	☐	Gardenin		Serv ▾	weekly g	75
☑	☑	☑	Garden S	142563	Inve ▾	Garden n	75
☑	☑	☐	Garden S	1425632	Non ▾	Garden o	20
☑	☑	☐	Trimming		Serv ▾	Tree and	50

Look over the goods and services listed in the items that will be loaded into QuickBooks Online.

After verifying your data, select the green Import button in the bottom-right corner of the screen to complete the import. After you receive notification that the import was successful, the new items ought to appear on the Products and Services panel.

How To Modify a Product or Service on the List

A product or service that you've already established can be changed. On the Product and Services screen, find the item or service you wish to update. Make any necessary modifications by selecting Edit from the menu on the item's information's far right.

136

How To Delete a Product or Service from the List

Once a product or service has been used in a transaction, such as when creating an invoice for a client, it cannot be deleted from QuickBooks. However, if an item is no longer required, you can deactivate it. Even while inactive items won't be shown on the list of goods and services, they will continue to show up in financial reports if they are used in a transaction.

Click on the drop-down arrow next to the Edit option and choose Make Inactive to deactivate an item. This item will no longer be listed in the category of goods and services.

CHAPTER SIX

INVOICING CUSTOMERS AND RECEIVING PAYMENTS

It always helps to repeat actions a few times to become accustomed to them when using new software. Recording any unpaid invoices for your clients in Quickbooks now, for instance, will help you remember what you read here. Additionally, you should keep track of all bank deposits you've made since the date you decided to use Quickbooks.

Getting started with Sales Transaction.

You can see the status of sales transactions, open invoices, and paid invoices very clearly on the Sales page. From within the page, you can also examine, make, and edit sales transactions.

Go to Bookkeeping, choose Transactions, and then pick All Sales to get to this page (Take me there).

View the status of transactions and invoices

The Money Bar, a crucial element of the Sales page, will be visible after you go there. It provides you with a fast view of open and recently paid invoices and quickly displays the status and dollar amounts of your sales transactions. Additionally, it displays any unbilled fees, charges, time activities, or estimates.

The list allows you to view information about certain transactions and can show:

- ❖ Invoices
- ❖ Sales receipts
- ❖ Estimates
- ❖ Payments
- ❖ Credit notes

❖ Delayed charges (QuickBooks Online Plus and Essentials only)
❖ Billable time activities (QuickBooks Online Plus only)

The list makes it simple to see any transaction's status and determine if it is Open, Closed, Paid, Partially Paid, or Overdue.

You can easily alter the list so that it displays the details you require:

❖ To see only the items you are interested in, filter the list.
❖ View only the info you require by altering the columns.
❖ In order to work with the data included in lists in different ways, export lists to Microsoft Excel.

Keep in mind that '365 days' is the default view for all transactions. If an invoice was not created during the previous 365 days, the Invoices page won't show up.

Simple to control Sales transactions

From the Sales page, it's simple to:

❖ From the New transaction dropdown menu, you create new invoices, payments, sales receipts, estimates, credit notes, delayed charges, and billable time activity.
❖ Do anything about a transaction. For instance, by choosing Receive payment in the Action column, you can pay an invoice right from the list.
❖ Print transactions or delivery notes for individual customers or a specified group (for invoicing and sales receipts).
❖ Delete, invalidate, or copy transactions.
❖ Send transactions, and when sending just one, personalize the message that goes with it.
❖ Update the estimations' status.
❖ For QuickBooks Online Plus and Essentials only, add more customer entries such as charges, time activities, and credits.

You can now use the Sales page to your advantage.

Create And Send Invoices

Send your customers an invoice if you expect to get paid for the goods and services you provide in the future. You can include the good or service you're selling in an invoice that you send to your client via email.

You'll learn how to make new invoices and how to examine overdue invoices. We'll also provide information on how to manage things if you utilize an external payment processing platform like QuickBooks Payments, where clients can pay their invoices online.

Step 1: Create And Send Invoices

If you are using Old experience

1. Choose + New.
2. Choose Invoice.
3. Select a customer from the Customer dropdown menu. Ensure that all of their information is accurate, particularly their email address.
4. Check the invoice's date. Change the due date in the Terms dropdown if necessary. The term "net" denotes how many days there are until a payment is expected. The due date can be altered if necessary; the default is 30 days.
5. Choose a product or service from the Product/Service column.
6. If necessary, enter a quantity, rate, and amount change.
7. If you must charge sales tax, tick the Tax box.
8. When finished, you have a number of options for saving or distributing the invoice:
a. When you're prepared to email your customer with the invoice, choose Save and send. If necessary, edit the email, then click Send and close.
b. Choose Save and close to send the invoice at a later time.
c. Choose Save to print a printed invoice. Choose Print or Preview next.
d. Choose Save and share link if you want to SMS your customer a link to their invoice.

If you are using the new experience

In QuickBooks, there are various ways to construct an invoice. You can turn your estimate into an invoice if you give it to the client and they accept it. A fresh invoice can also be made from scratch.

1. Choose + New.
2. Choose Invoice.
3. Pick a customer from the dropdown menu after selecting Add customer. Verify that every piece of information, including the email address, is accurate.
4. Review the Terms, Due Date, and Invoice Date. If necessary, provide new dates or conditions. Note: The term "Net" in the Terms section denotes the number of days until the payment is expected.
5. Pick a product or service from the dropdown menu by selecting Add product or service.
6. Choose between a flat rate, an hourly rate, or an itemized charge to determine how much to charge. If necessary, enter a quantity and a rate.
7. Choose Manage to edit the content or layout of your invoices. Next, pick a choice from the side panel. Your selections are saved by QuickBooks, which then applies them to all previous and upcoming invoices.
8. When finished, you have a number of options for saving or distributing the invoice:
9. When you're prepared to email your customer with the invoice, choose Review and send. If necessary, edit the email, then choose Send invoice.
   a. Choose Save and close to send the invoice at a later time.
   b. Choose Print and download to print a paper invoice.
   c. Select Receive Payment if the customer has already paid you.
   d. Choose Share link to send your customer a text message link to their invoice.

Steps 2: Reviewing the unpaid invoice

Unpaid invoices are added to your accounts receivable account by QuickBooks. This account will appear on your balance sheet as well as other financial reports.

Go to Get paid & pay or Sales & expenditures whenever you wish to see your invoices, then choose Invoices. To find out where invoices stand in the sales process, look at the Status column.

You may encounter the following statuses:

- ❖ [Days] from now: The invoice has not yet been sent via email.
- ❖ Upon [days] Sent: The customer received the invoice through email from you.
- ❖ Upon [days] Viewed: The invoice was opened by the client.
- ❖ Deposited: The invoice payment from your client.
- ❖ The invoice is past due and underpaid. Overdue [days].
- ❖ Expired [days] Viewed: Your consumer opened the overdue invoice but failed to make payment.
- ❖ Undeliverable invoice: This is a delivery issue. Re-send after checking the email address.
- ❖ Voided: QuickBooks voided the invoice.

You must inform clients of impending invoice due dates. You could ping them with a reminder.

Step 3: Collect invoice payments

Customers can pay their invoices directly by credit card or ACH transfer if you use QuickBooks Payments. Everything is processed and taken care of for you. QuickBooks records transactions in the appropriate accounts when you receive payments. You can monitor payments made through an external platform in QuickBooks if you do.

Accessing recent transactions

Every transaction screen in Quickbooks has a recent transaction button, which is a clock with an arrow around it that can be found in the top left-hand corner. To access any recent transactions you've created, click this icon. As an alternative, you can view a list of recent transactions from all of Quickbooks by selecting the search button on the dashboard page. On the corresponding page for a customer, vendor, etc., you can also see recent transactions.

Setting Up Automatic Totals

Any group of items on a form can have a subtotal manually added to it by using the add subtotal button on sales transaction forms. Alternately, you can enhance subtotals by allowing Quickbooks to automatically subtotal your items by customizing your forms.

You can customize your forms in a web browser and then use them in a mobile app, but some actions, like customizing forms, can't be done in the iOS and Android mobile apps. You might be able to perform these actions using your mobile device's web browser, depending on your device's screen resolution.

To invoices, estimates, and sales receipts, you can add subtotals. Here are some examples of how to add subtotals to an invoice;

1. Select settings, and then add custom form styles.
2. After choosing the form you want to change, click Edit in the action column.
3. Click the content
4. Select the table section.
5. Scroll down the screen and click the bottom-left button that says "Show more activity options."
6. Select an option from the drop-down list after checking the group activity box.
7. Choose Subtotal Groups.

8. To save the settings, click done in the bottom-right corner of the window.

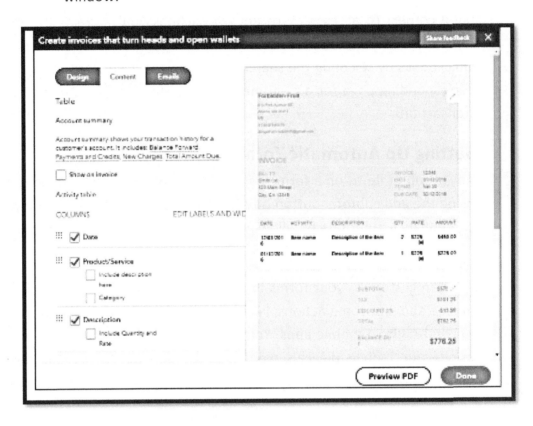

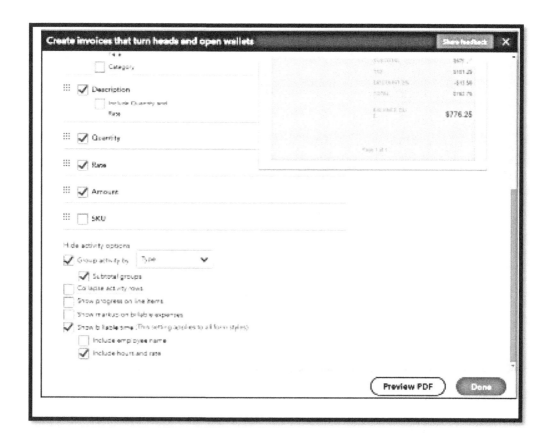

Note: If you want a similar look and feel across all the forms you use, repeat these steps to include subtotal for estimates and sales receipts.

Creating entries for billable time

In addition to tasks that are necessary for the operation of your business (such creating customer invoices or inputting accounting data), your staff may also handle tasks that are directly relevant to your customers. In the latter scenario, you might want to keep track of the time staff members spend working on projects for clients so you can charge your clients for that time. The time tracking capabilities that come with Quickbooks Online are the main topic of this section.

Make sure to enable time tracking settings in Quickbooks Online in order to track time utilizing its capabilities. Activate these two options by selecting setting > account and settings > time.

❖ Timesheets should have a service field.

❖ Make time available for billing

For more advanced time tracking requirements for your business, see Quickbooks time by clicking view plans (formerly known as Tsheets). One of many timekeeping applications that seamlessly link with Quickbooks Online to let your staff log time on mobile devices is this one. Any time entries they make automatically sync with your books and contain the necessary customer, job, and employee data.

Time-related activities entry

Let's say, for instance, that you wish to document the 4 hours that a worker put in on a consulting project. To open the Add time for window, adhere to following instructions;

1. Select Time entry from the Employees column by clicking the New button.

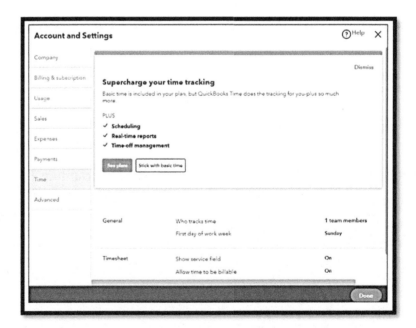

2. Select a worker from the Add time Panel.
3. Select the date when the work was completed.

4. Select Add Work Details.
5. Type a time value, such as 4 for four hours, in the duration field.
6. Specify the client for whom the work was done.
7. Select which service was rendered.
8. If necessary, switch on the chargeable (/hr) option.
9. Click on save.

How to add billable time to the an invoice

Create the invoice as usual, as I mentioned earlier, and then add billable time and cost. If you've been tracking costs for the customer and have entered time for the client, QuickBooks will ask you whether you want to bill for any of the time or costs after you've identified the customer. In the event that you select yes, QuickBooks shows the Choose Billable Time and Costs dialog box.

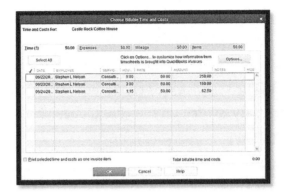

Select Billable Time and Costs dialog box

Each time you've entered a time for a customer is displayed on the Time tab of this dialog box. Click the Use column for the time to add these times to the invoice. The Use column is the first column from the left and is marked with a checkmark. Alternatively, you can pick every time by using the Select All option. then press OK. Each of these billable times is included as a separate line to the invoice by QuickBooks. The Create Invoices window's billable time information can be seen in this figure.

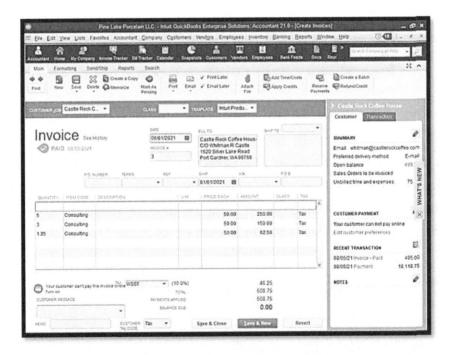

Create invoice window, billing for billable time.

QuickBooks places each time recording you log on a distinct line of the invoice if the check box labeled Print Selected Time and Costs As One Invoice Item is left deselected. However, if you click the box, QuickBooks will allow you to merge various time entries into a single invoice budget item. (If you're interested, you might want to play around with this feature a little.)

To view a list of the items, out-of-pocket expenses, or business miles logged on behalf of a client, click the Items, Expenses, or Mileage tab. Similar to adding time charges, you can add charges for these kinds of things to an invoice. Adding a markup to your out-of-pocket costs is also possible. By the way, click the Add Time/Costs button that displays at the top of the Create Invoices window if you want to go back to the Choose Billable Time and Costs dialog box while looking at it.

Printing A Batch Of Packing Slips Or Invoices

You might occasionally decide to publish a sales document later. In other instances, a client or customers may request a copy of each and every invoice or other document they have from a certain time period. Both of these scenarios are easily manageable by you;

1. From the left menu bar, select sale > all sales (Bookkeeping > Transactions > All sales).
2. Select one or more transaction types, customers, and other criteria as necessary by clicking the filter button.
3. In the transaction list, either choose all by clicking the checkbox at the top of the list, or click the checkbox next to each transaction you want to print or produce a packing slip for.
4. Select printing for sales transactions or packing slips by clicking the batch actions button.
5. The sale forms can be printed or downloaded from a print preview window that appears.

Recording customer payments

Sending an invoice is one thing, but recording a payment on the invoice is quite another. Or maybe you want to record a sales receipt rather than making an invoice. You'll observe that sales receipt transactions combine an invoice with a customer payment. Let me first discuss the payment to deposit account before we look at documenting payments.

Acknowledging deposits made to a deposit account

Undeposited funds accounts may still exist for older Quickbooks organizations, which may seem contradictory. Of course, you'll deposit the funds right away. This is now referred to as the payments to Deposit account in Quickbooks. Using the payments to deposit account simplifies bank account reconciliation for bank deposits made with two or more checks or for electronic payments that have been deducted.

The payments of deposit account's purpose is to make it possible for Quickbooks to replicate what posts to your bank statement. One lump payment is posted to your account by the bank if five cheques are deposited on a single deposit ticket. Instead of five separate deposits, you should ideally want your bank account in Quickbooks to represent that single payment. This is what the payments to Deposit account does. Consider this account as a storage space where you can compile customer payments and then aggregate them into sums that correspond to what the bank sends to your account. When you aren't trying to play Tetris by matching up which combination of individual payments is equal to the sum that the bank posted, your bank reconciliation procedure will move along much more quickly.

Recording payments for invoices

This portion of the book is for you if you choose to use Quickbooks' payments service, as Quickbooks will then automatically label your invoices as paid, mark the deposit as cleared, or match it with your bank deposit. Let's assume, though, that a client writes you a check or possibly uses Venmo or Paypal to send you money. There is a two-step process in these situations;

1. Record the customer payments.
2. Record the banking transaction.

Several methods exist for starting the payment of an invoice:

- ❖ On the customer page, click receive payment in the action column of the sales transaction list.
- ❖ On the sales transaction page, select new transaction > payment and select payment.
- ❖ Choose New > Receive Payment.
- ❖ Select the project on the projects page and click Add to project. The receive payment window is shown for the first method in the previous list, and it is already filled with data for the invoice you choose as well as a default payment amount. The receive payment window is blank in the second and third methods. Once you choose a customer, any unpaid invoices show up in the outstanding transactions section.

Payment history for a single invoice

1. Choose + New.
2. Click Accept payment.
3. Choose the customer's name from the Customer dropdown menu.
4. Choose the payment option from the Payment method dropdown.
5. Choose the account you want to deposit the money into from the Deposit to menu.
6. In the Outstanding Transactions section, tick the box next to the invoice for which the payment is being recorded.
7. If necessary, enter the Memo and Reference numbers.
8. Click Save, then click Exit.

Record partial payments made for an invoice.

1. Choose + New.
2. Click Accept payment.
3. Choose the customer's name from the Customer dropdown menu.
4. Choose the payment option from the Payment method dropdown.
5. Select the account to deposit the money into from the Deposit to menu.
6. Enter the sum your customer paid in the Amount received section.
7. In the Outstanding Transactions area, tick the box next to the invoice for which the payment is being recorded.
8. If necessary, input the Reference No. and Memo.
9. Choose Save and close.

Recording Bank Deposits

To prevent the money from being up in purgatory in your payments to deposit (undeposited funds) account, it's crucial to remember to record your bank deposits in Quickbooks. Once any recent bank deposits have been recorded, this account should always be at zero. Follow these steps to place a bank deposit:

1. List one or more client payments.
2. Pick the payments you want to deposit
3. Optionally, insert a bank service charge or payment processing cost.

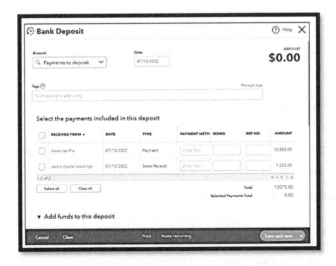

4. Verify that the net amount posted to your bank account matches the deposit total.
5. Select Save and New or Save and Close.

Keeping Tabs On Invoice Status And Receiving Payment

Any time you wish to receive a high-level overview of your sales activities, select sale, followed by invoices (sales and expenses > Invoices). You may quickly see via graphics how much money is owed on your unpaid and paid invoices. The total is divided into overdue and unpaid invoices by the unpaid invoices bar.

To check the underlying data for each transaction, including whether your customer has seen the invoice yet, click the status column for that transaction. You may view any payment dates and amounts in the status window as well. To hide the details, click the status window's close button or the status column for the transaction once more.

The meaning of "deposited" is exactly what you would expect. You deposited a payment that you had received. To help you keep track of how much is still owed, partially paid invoices display a balance column value that is different from the total, while past-due amounts are highlighted in orange. Sadly, the status column is unable to inform you of any outstanding invoices that have not yet been mailed or printed. Here are some alternatives.

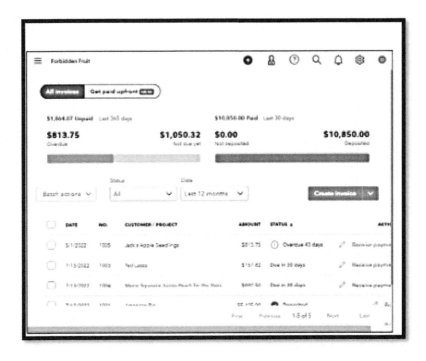

1. From the left menu bar, select sales (Bookkeeping > Transactions).
2. Switch on the Sales tab.
3. Select Send Later from the filter menu to check the delivery status.
4. Click the mark all checkbox at the top of the list or select the checkboxes next to any invoices you want to send.
5. Select Send Transactions after clicking Batch Action.

Note: By changing the delivery status to print later, you can utilize the same procedures to print invoices that you marked for printing later.

To keep track of outstanding invoices, you can also use the accounts receivable aging summary and accounts receivable detail reports. Follow these instructions to run either report;

1. From the left menu bar, select reports (Business overview > Reports).
2. Type accounts receivable in the section labeled "Find a report by name," then choose the relevant report from the list that appears.
3. A screen displays your report.

Returning funds to a consumer

There are times when you must refund money that a consumer gave you. It is unfortunate, but it does happen. You have two choices for giving clients their money back;

1. If you need to return money right away, provide a refund receipt.
2. Provide a credit memo that the client may use to offset a future invoice.

Eliminating Bad Debt

The terrible truth is that you might occasionally not be paid for goods supplied or services provided. Although it can be irritating, it is a necessary component of the hard-won expertise that one gains over time as a business owner or manager. Before you can write off bad debt, you must do some setup, which is as easy as creating a credit memo that you then use to make payments on the past-due invoices.

Establishing a bad debt item and account

Add a bad debt account to your chart of accounts as a first step. You can accomplish that by doing the following.

1. To display your chart of accounts, select setting > chart of accounts.
2. In the top right corner, select "new."
3. Depending on whether you're using business view or accountant view, the next few steps may alter since two separate screens will appear.

a. Business view

   i.   Type a name in the category Name field, such as Bad Debt.

   ii.   Select expenses from the select category menu, then click the next button.

   iii.   Click pick after selecting Uncategorized Expenses from

   iv.   If you'd like, fill out the description field.

   v.   To create a new account, click Save.

b. Accounting viewpoint

   i.   To filter the list of saving account numbers, enter uncat, and then select Uncategorize Expense.

   ii.   Select "Bad Debts" from the list in the Tax form section.

   iii.   In the account name area (iv), provide a name like Bad debt. You may also choose to fill out the description field.

   iv.   To create your new account, click Save.

Making a bad debt item is the next stage, so. Fortunately, both the business view and accountant view follow the same procedures here;

1. To display your item list, go to setting > Products and services.
2. Select non-inventory by clicking new in the top right corner.

156

3. Give it a label, like "bad debt."
4. You can choose to categorize the item of bad debt.
5. If you want, include a description.
6. Select "Bad Debt" from the list of income accounts.
7. Press "Save" and "Close"

Creating bad debt write-off transactions

You are now prepared to grit your teeth and begin writing off some uncollectible invoices after creating the Bad Debt account on your chart of accounts and a Bad Debt non inventory item.

1. Select "new" > "credit memo"
2. Pick and choose on your adversary
3. Select "Bad Debt" from the products/services section's first list of options.
4. Add the amount you are deducting to the amount column.
5. Optional: Type "write off bad debt" in the field labeled "message displayed on statement."
6. If you have additional non-paying clients to dispatch, click save and new or save and close.
7. Select new > accept payment.
8. Select your customer
9. From the section of outstanding transactions, pick one or more bills.
10. From the credits section, pick the credit memo you created.
11. Select Save and Exit.

CHAPTER SEVEN

WRITING CHECKS AND PAYING BILLS

The transactions you use in Quickbooks to fulfill your financial responsibilities are covered in this chapter. Accountants commonly refer to these transactions as accounts payable, or A/P, for short.

Looking At Expense And Bill Payment Methods

Since it isn't always clear from the user interface, let's first examine the many payment method choices you have for tracking expenses and bill payments.

1. **Electronic transactions:** such as Automated Clearing House (ACH) transfers, wire transfers, online bill payments, and debit card transactions, are direct debits from your bank account.
2. **Printed check**: Quickbooks gives you the option of batching checks for later printing or filling out a check form onscreen first.
3. **Credit card:** You can record credit card purchases and bill payments in the same way as you would a check. Simply select a credit card from the payment account options rather than a bank account.

Understanding The Transaction Types

The following is a list of the different sorts of accounts payable transactions you can enter:

❖ **Expense:** This category of transactions is ideal for capturing automatic withdrawals from your account for things like bank fees, energy bills, rent, and other payments in addition to costs you pay with a credit card.
❖ **Check:** Check transactions are almost identical to expense transactions, but you are presumed to be either documenting a handwritten check or intending to print or write a check when you record a check transaction.

❖ **Bill:** Using this type of transaction, you can enter the expense now and pay it later. On the A/P Aging summary and A/P Aging detail reports, you can keep track of unpaid bills.

❖ **Pay bills:** When it's time to pay one or more bills in full or in part, this type of transaction is involved. You have the option of printing a check or recording an online payment that your bank has planned for you. Once a bill is fully paid, it disappears from the A/P Aging Summary and A/P Aging detail reports.

❖ **Vendor credit:** A vendor credit might be compared to a reverse bill in which the vendor waives all or a portion of a bill or possibly makes a goodwill gesture in lieu of a future bill. In a manner similar to making a payment, vendor credits can be applied to outstanding invoices.

Entering An Expense

Transactions for expenses are used when money has already been spent, or when "the horse has already left the barn," as the saying goes. Instead of inputting a bill for expenses you want to pay later and a check for expenses you want to pay right away, you can enter expense transactions. Typically, costs are used to keep track of automatic bank account withdrawals, debit card purchases, handwritten checks, outgoing ACH transactions, and so forth. This is the procedure for entering an expense.

1. Select expense from the suppliers column by clicking the + New button at the top of the left-hand menu bar, or select expenses > Expenses (Sales and Expenses > Expenses), click New transaction, and then select expense.

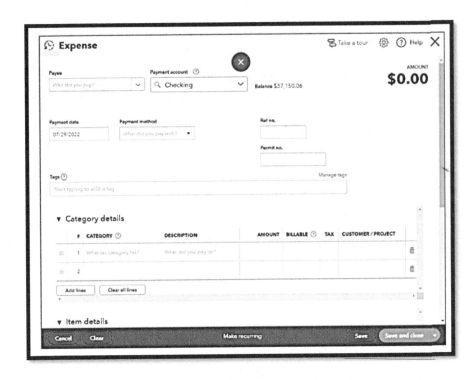

2. To add a new payee, click Add New from the drop-down list or choose the payee from which you incurred the charge.

3. Select an account for payments (this is typically a bank or credit card accounts)

4. Verify the date.

5. If applicable, fill out any custom fields that are supported by your subscription level as well as the fields for the payment method and ref number. If you are using that functionality, you can additionally add one or more tags.

6. You can enter payments you are making that are unrelated to inventory purchases in the category details area. Selecting a category—really an account from your chart of accounts—and entering an amount are the absolute minimal requirements. You can optionally enter a description and mark an item as billable. For billable charges, you must select a client or project. If your customer is required to pay sales tax on the reimbursement form, you may also choose to pick the Tax column.

7. If desired, describe any inventory purchases covered by this expense transaction in the item description section. You must select a good or service, give a quantity, and input a price or an amount, at the very least (Quickbooks calculates the rate if you enter an amount, or the amount if you enter a rate). The description is already filled in when you select the good or service. The inventory purchases can optionally be marked as chargeable. If you choose to do this, you must select a customer or project for billable costs. You may also choose to click the Tax column if the payment you receive from your client is taxed.

Writing A Check

When the window washer is tapping their toes by your desk, you can use check transactions to generate an actual check to cover the unpaid expense. Additionally, you have the choice to queue up one or more checks for bulk printing later by selecting print later. You have two options for writing a check:

❖ From the vendor column, select +New > Check.
❖ From the left menu bar, select Expenses > Expenses, click New transaction, and then select Check.

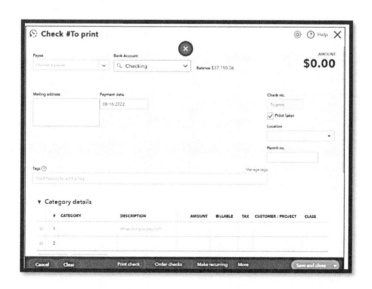

Note: The check window appears in both scenarios.

Hold onto your hat for the check-writing process because the screen is nearly identical to the expenditure page. Only the check number entry field and, as I previously indicated, the option to print the check later change. The rest all function in the same way. The bottom of the screen, however, offers a variety of command options.

- ❖ **Cancel**: If you click the button to exit without saving the transaction, the transaction is discarded and the check window is closed.
- ❖ **Print check**: stores the transaction and opens a window for printing a preview copy.
- ❖ **Order checks**: This leads to a Quickbooks page where you can order different paper checks. Be disappointed since they only sell blank checks; you won't find your name on the payee line.
- ❖ **Set up a recurring**: check on your own schedule, such as a monthly rent payment that you wish to print a check for in person each month.
- ❖ **More:** the void check command is hidden in this submenu, ostensibly so that you can only void checks that you have knowingly created.
- ❖ **Save the transaction:** close the check window, or save and new to make room for a new transaction.

Entering A Bill

If you haven't already realized, invoices and bills are two different things in Quickbooks. According to Quickbooks, a bill is a payment request from a vendor, but an invoice is a transaction you create to seek payment from a client.

You can any of the following to enter a bill:

- ❖ Click new transaction, then select bill under costs in the left menu bar.

❖ From the vendor column, select + New > bill.

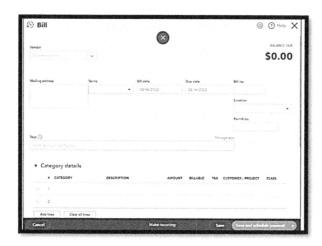

The bill window is visible in both scenarios.

The following fields are among those that you won't see in the other two windows:

Note: Include here the payment terms you intend to employ for this invoice, such as Due on Receipt, Net 15, Net 30, and so on. In order to create a new type of payment term, you can also select add new.

❖ **Bill date:** This is the corresponding field in the expense and check window for the payment date. Put the date your vendor sent you the bill here.

❖ **Due date:** You can change the default due date, which is calculated automatically depending on your selection in the Terms section.

❖ **Bill no. :** This is the equivalent of the reference number and check number fields in the expense and checks windows, respectively. This field is used to insert the invoice number from your vendor.

❖ **Cancel:** If you choose to leave without making a purchase, the transaction is discarded, and the bill window is closed.

❖ **Make recurring:** establishes a reoccurring check according to a schedule you choose, such as yearly property tax obligations.

- ❖ **Save:** keeps the transaction and bill window on the screen while saving the transaction.
- ❖ **Save and schedule payment:** This option saves the transaction and then sneakily displays Quickbooks Online Bill Pay, which lets you pay up to two invoices for free each month and an additional $1.50 per check after that. If you want to pay your bills with a credit card, there is a 2.9 percent fee. If you prefer to use other methods for paying your bills, you can also select save and new or save and shut.

Paying Bills

Since you are either recording an already-occurring financial event or paying for an immediate need by printing a check, you usually won't need to go back and review spending or checks that you enter. Contrarily, unless you schedule a payment online, bills always require follow-up.

Quickbooks provides two options for bill payment. The pay bills command is the first, and it's made to help you fast deplete your bank account by paying numerous invoices. Alternately, you can use the write checks command to pay each vendor separately as part of the slow bleed strategy.

Paying multiple invoices all at once

This brings you to the transaction screen for paying invoices, where you have a few display options:

- ❖ From the vendor column, select Add New > Pay bills.
- ❖ Select Expenses > Expenses from the left menu bar, then select Pay Bills by clicking the arrow next to Print Checks.

The button on the expenditures window to the left of the new transaction button keeps track of your most recent selection. You can print checks, order checks, and pay invoices using this option. Until you make another decision, the status of this button will default to your most recent selection.

Either action opens the pay bills window, which is intended to make paying multiple bills at once easier. Another option is to use a check to pay one bill at a time.

Recording vendor credits and refunds

A vendor credit could be viewed as a negative expense. Vendor credits can happen if you return items that you have already paid for or if a service didn't live up to your expectations and the vendor gives you a credit to use on future purchases. Or, you might be fortunate enough to have your vendor's refund check in hand. In any case, the procedure starts with the recording of a vendor credit transaction.

Entering a vendor credit

To record a vendor refund or credit check, complete these steps:

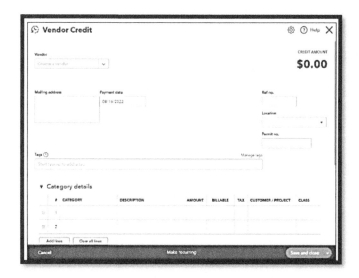

1. Select + New > Vendor credit.
2. Pick the merchant who provided the credit.
3. Type in the credit date.
4. Type a positive number for the credit or return amount.
5. If the credit refers to costs other than those associated with buying merchandise, you can choose the account used on the original bill in the category information section.

6. If applicable, optionally list the inventory items you returned in the item information section.
7. Add a digital copy of the credit as an optional attachment in the Attachments section.
8. Select either save and new or save and close.

You can use a credit memo provided by the vendor to pay an existing or upcoming charge.

Applying vendor credits against bills

Depending on your method of bill payment, you might not even need to consider asking for credit. Paying a bill is not the only way to do so, though. You can pay bills using the checks window, as you can see under the heading "Writing a check to pay a bill." In either case, applying a credit memo to an overdue payment is a straightforward procedure. There are a couple more steps to take, though, if you have a vendor refund check burning a hole in your pocket.

Recording vendor refund checks and payment

Follow these steps only if your vendor provided you with an actual check or electronic payment rather than a credit memo; otherwise, make sure that you entered a vendor credit note first;

1. Click the other column's + New > Bank Deposit option.
2. Select the bank account into which you will deposit the check, or, if you want to take the check to the bank alongside other checks, select Payments to Deposit (Undepoisted Funds).
3. In the Add Funds to the Deposit section, enter the vendor's name in the received form field.
4. From the Account column, select Account Payable (A/P).
5. Optional: provide your ref no., payment method, and description.
6. Fill out the amount column with the refund check amount.
7. Record any additional sums you choose to include on the same bank deposit, if applicable.

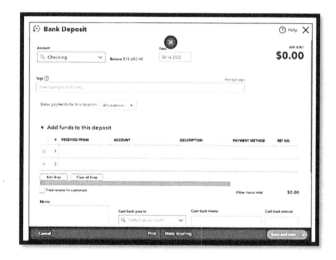

8. Select Save and Exit.
9. Select Add New > Pay Bills.
10. Pick the bank deposit transaction that you saved in step 8 from your saved list.
11. Select Save and Exit.

Managing Recurring Transactions

Your accounting transactions may become less repetitious to some extent with the aid of recurring transactions. That is, unless you have a subscription called "easy start," which doesn't.

Create a new recurring template

Here's how you can create a new template:

1. Access Settings.
2. Choose Recurring transactions.
3. Choose New.
4. After choosing the desired transaction type, click OK.
5. Give the template a name.
6. Choose a Type: Reminder, Scheduled, or Unscheduled.

Duplicate an existing template

Create templates more quickly by duplicating existing templates.

1. Access Settings.
2. Choose Recurring transactions.
3. Select the template and then Duplicate from the Action column dropdown menu. The duplicate copy will have every setting, excluding the title.
4. Increasing the number of recurring transactions

By following these steps, you may also immediately add new transactions to the list of recurring transactions;

1. To view the list of recurring transactions, select setting > Recurring Transactions.
2. Select a transaction type by clicking the new button to open the select transaction type dialog box, and then click "OK."
3. After completing the recurring transaction window in the manner outlined in the section above, click save.

Making changes in recurring transactions

Select settings > recurring transactions to view the list of current recurring transactions and manage them. A recurring transaction can be changed by clicking edit in the action column. Only future transactions are impacted by any modifications you make to recurring transaction templates. Any current transactions that have been posted to your books must be manually edited.

When you make changes to a customer or vendor record in Quickbooks, such as by recording an address change, the system automatically adjusts recurring transactions.

The following options are also included in the action column.

- ❖ Use: enables you to enter an unplanned transaction or reminder into your records.
- ❖ Duplicate: From already-existing recurring transaction templates, it generates new ones. The template could be used, for instance, to schedule monthly insurance payments. Additionally, you can utilize this choice to make backup copies of intricate transactions, such a thorough diary entry for a paycheck.
- ❖ Delete: gets rid of unnecessary recurring transaction templates.

In many situations, rendering a record inactive in Quickbooks corresponds to deleting the record. Recurring transactions can be deleted, and Quickbooks does not have an undo option, so be cautious before doing so. You can also print a report of all the recurring transaction templates you currently have. The recurring template list report will be seen when you select Report from the left menu bar, put recu in the search box, and click on the report's name.

Reviewing And Creating Transactions With Spreadsheet Sync.

With the spreadsheet sync capability, advanced users of Quickbooks Online can update or produce invoices and bills as well as purchase and sales records, effectively extending Quickbooks into Microsoft Excel spreadsheets. So, in this section, we'll concentrate on how to amend and/or create vendor-related transactions in Excel using spreadsheet sync.

1. Launch either a new or existing Excel workbook into which Quickbooks is to insert a new worksheet.
2. To view the spreadsheet sync task window, select home > spreadsheet sync in Excel.
3. Log in or click. click Get started if prompted
4. Select Manage Records
5. From the list of available templates, pick purchases and sales receipts or invoices and bills.
6. Optional: Select the Quickbooks option to import existing records. If requested, click ok or clear data based on the message that appears to notify you that any current information may not be imported.
7. The template worksheet's transactions or unposted changes will be discarded.
8. If you choose invoices and bills, you may also choose credit notes or supplier credit notes from the list of transaction types.
9. To import your past transactions from Quickbooks into Excel, click OK.
10. Optional: If you modify any of the transactions or add any new transactions, click Post Data to Quickbooks at the bottom of the spreadsheet sync task pane.

After closing the spreadsheet sync task pane, open it again whenever you need it by going to Home > Spreadsheet Synchronization in Excel.

When changing transactions, use caution because it is simple to remedy one issue while creating another, such as when there are inconsistencies between the payments made against invoices or bills. Examine the template thoroughly and go over all the notes and warnings.

CHAPTER EIGHT

PAYING EMPLOYEES AND CONTRACTORS

Paying your employees and any contractors who work for you is your duty as an employer. We will thus examine both duties in this chapter. Payroll administration involves more than just giving your employees paychecks. You must send amounts withheld for benefits and deductions to the relevant parties after creating paychecks. The tax returns are handled for you by Quickbooks payroll with the relevant taxing authorities.

Users of Quickbooks Online previously had two options for preparing payroll:

1. Making use of self-service payroll using Quickbooks
2. Employing full service payroll with Quickbooks.

Intuit has changed its products to make the distinction between these two approaches less clear. All Quickbooks payroll plans are now equipped with tax forms and automated tax deposits. Initially, you could not choose to forego the automatic filings and tax payments; however, you can now do so if you so want. Each of the three plans also includes Auto Payroll, which instructs Quickbooks to handle payroll automatically if it is turned on. Much of your payroll process may be set and forget thanks to Auto Payroll, automatic tax deposits, and automated payroll return findings.

How To Do Payroll In Quickbooks Online

Consider adding QuickBooks Payroll to your package if you already use QuickBooks Online and need to pay staff. Your payroll expenses can be seamlessly transferred to the relevant general ledger accounts by using the same system that you use to handle your company's books. Discover how to complete the first pay run after you set up payroll in QuickBooks Online in a few easy steps. If you are subscribe to a QuickBooks Payroll plan, you can even perform payroll as frequently as you need at no additional cost.

Additionally, by adding QuickBooks Payroll to the current QuickBooks Online subscription, your company will gain access to additional HR and pay processing capabilities, including same- and next-day direct payments, employee benefits, and automatic tax preparation and filing. For the first three months, payroll is discounted by 50% for new users. Register right away for QuickBooks Payroll.

Checklist for Payroll Setup: Information to Have on Hand

You must have the employer and employee information on hand before setting up and processing payroll in QuickBooks. You can use the following checklist to make sure you have the necessary employer and employee data.

Employer Details

- ❖ Types of employee compensation You will enter data that you typically give your employees, like overtime, paid time off (PTO), bonuses, and commissions.
- ❖ Options for employee benefits: You must list all of the benefits you provide. Keep in mind that all plans with QuickBooks Payroll provide access to health benefits. It also provides alternatives for 401(k), retirement, flexible spending accounts (FSA), and workers' compensation on a pay-as-you-go basis.
- ❖ Information about the business bank account: In addition to the account number, you need the complete routing number of the checking account you will use to deposit payroll taxes and issue payroll checks.

Note: You ought to keep your payroll account separate from the checking account you use for regular business operations.

Employer data and documentation

- ❖ Basic information on your employees, such as their legal names, dates of birth, and dates of employment, is required.

- ❖ Direct deposit authorization form: Employees must complete a direct deposit authorization form if you choose to pay them using direct deposit rather than paper checks.
- ❖ PTO policy and balance: If you provide vacation and sick leave, you must be aware of how many PTO hours you have allotted to each employee for the entire calendar year.
- ❖ Pay rate and schedule: If necessary, you can create several pay schedules in QuickBooks.
- ❖ Payroll deductions: You should keep track of the health insurance, retirement, and garnishment contributions made by your staff.
- ❖ Form W-4: When you hire a new employee, you must have them fill out and sign a W-4 form so that you may enter their withholding information and other necessary facts to accurately compute payroll tax deductions.
- ❖ Payroll history: To ensure proper tax calculations, you should have your previous payroll data on available if you paid employees throughout the current calendar year.

The total number of sick and vacation days an employee accrued under your old payroll system should be included if you are switching to QuickBooks Payroll in the middle of a fiscal year.

Steps In Doing Payroll In Quickbooks

Step 1: Navigate Payroll.

You should head to the "Payroll" tab after signing in to your QuickBooks account to get going. There is a "Get Started" button if your QuickBooks Online subscription was just purchased. To move on to the following screen, click on it. The system will ask you a few questions when you first sign up for QuickBooks Payroll, such as if you need HR support and whether you need to keep track of employees' working hours.

You can manually choose one of the plan's three payroll alternatives, but these questions will assist match you with the appropriate one. You can sign up for a 30-day free trial of QuickBooks, and it will suggest the best payroll plan for you.

Step 2: Provide a General Description of How to Pay Your Employees

The system will ask you whether you have already paid staff for the current calendar year in the following stage. You must select "Yes" if you're transferring from a manual system or another payroll program to QuickBooks Payroll.

Keep in mind that later on in the setup process, the system will want you to provide year-to-date (YTD) payroll information as well as tax payments made for each employee. To guarantee that your W-2 forms are accurate at year's end, you must provide information about earlier paychecks that were sent to employees before the start of your QuickBooks Payroll subscription. You can get detailed pay records from your former payroll provider in addition to getting YTD data from the most recent payroll you submitted for each employee.

The system will ask you to specify the date that you intend to conduct your first payroll in QuickBooks, in addition to payments to employees in the current calendar year. The physical address of the workplace where the majority of your employees are located will also have to be entered.

Step 3: Add Employees

When you enter your workplace, a new window that allows you to enter basic personnel data and payroll information into the system will open. To begin entering the necessary information for each person on your payroll, even those who are no longer employed by your business but were paid during the current fiscal year, click the "Add an employee" button.

Step 4: Complete the employee information

You have the option to enter your employees' email addresses as you enter basic staff information into QuickBooks. This enables the system to send them a link so they may access QuickBooks Workforce, the provider's self-service web portal, to check their pay stubs and W-2s. Even better, the solution has the ability to allow workers to use QuickBooks Time to monitor and record their working hours.

You must complete the employee information fields shown below in order to set up QuickBooks Online Payroll.

❖ Pay schedule: In the "How often do you pay (employee)" box, select "create pay schedule" to specify a pay schedule for your staff members. Choose the appropriate timetable from the dropdown menu, which includes options like weekly, twice in a month, and monthly. Additionally, you will have the choice of having the plan you just made serve as the standard schedule for subsequent employees who are added to the system.

❖ Employee pay: In the "How much you pay (employee)" area, enter the employee's salary. Additionally, you need to provide the staff's default workdays and hours per day.

- ❖ Employee contributions/deductions: Check the relevant contribution and as well as the deduction items in the "Does (employee) have any deductions" section.

- ❖ Employee withholding information: You will utilize the details from Form W-4s in the "What are (employee's) withholdings" section. Choose whether you need the tax form for the current year or one from a previous year when you click "Enter W-4 form." And QuickBooks keeps both the new and old forms. This makes it possible for you to print one straight from the system to distribute to employees and record the appropriate data.

- ❖ Information about the YTD payroll: If you paid the employee this year, utilize the data from the most recent payroll check to enter the YTD payroll information into the system. The sums paid during the current quarter but before you started using QuickBooks Payroll will also be requested by QuickBooks, so take note of this.

- ❖ Payment method: To pay the employee, choose either direct deposit or (manually) check from the dropdown menu in the "How do you want to pay (employee)" area. Use the data from the direct deposit authorization form and the that of the voided check that you requested from the employee if you decide to use direct deposit.

- ❖ It is crucial that you make sure the YTD totals are correct. This information is essential to ensuring the accuracy and dependability of your reporting. It will also affect restrictions on donations to 401(k) and retirement accounts, as well as state and federal taxes that have an annual ceiling. You can now execute your first pay run after setting up payroll in QuickBooks is complete.

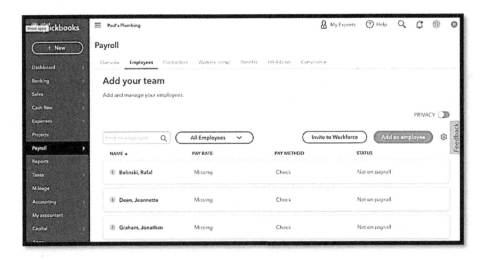

Step 5: Click "Run Payroll"

Click the "Run payroll" button in the top right corner of the screen while you are on your "Payroll" dashboard.

Step 6: Type in the current hour.

It should be noted that employees on salary, the system will automatically fill in the total hours depending on the employee's initial setup's preset amount of work hours. You must manually enter the actual working hours for hourly employees in the "Regular Pay Hrs" column or transfer the time data from the time tracking software to the system.

Your staff's work hours will immediately appear in QuickBooks Payroll for those subscriber to the Elite or Premium plans and utilize QuickBooks Time (included in both tiers) to record and manage employee attendance. These hours are then available for you to evaluate and approve. Feel free to update the system if the staff's working hours change.

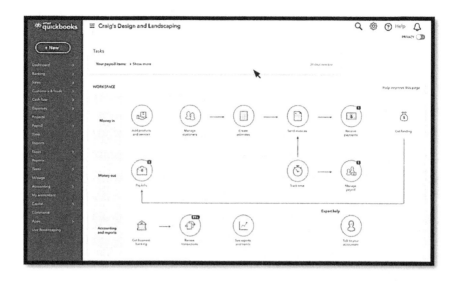

Step 7: Review and Submit Payroll

Your final opportunity to evaluate and make changes to the payroll data is at this stage. Check out the payment method to make sure that employees who ought to be paid by direct deposits and paychecks show up correctly, in addition to the number of hours worked and other pay information. Review the employee and employer tax contributions as well.

Click the "Preview payroll" option at the bottom right of the screen once you have done checking the time data and pay information for your employees.

If everything appears to be in order, press the "Submit Payroll" button in the bottom right corner of the screen. After that, you can print the employees' payroll cheques and/or direct deposit remittances advise. If you are using QuickBooks Online as your accounting program, a bill will be generated immediately for each payroll handled, making it simple to reconcile your payroll account.

Managing Payroll Tax

Payroll tax management is simple with QuickBooks Online. Payroll preparation and production don't mark the end of the process. You must submit payroll taxes and the file payroll tax returns on a schedule set by the IRS.

Payroll taxes payment

Depending on how much you are owing, you can pay payroll taxes weekly, monthly, or quarterly by adhering to IRS requirements (called your payroll tax liability). Federal tax deposits must be made using an electronic money transfer. The Electronic Federal Tax Payment System (EFTPS), a free service offered by the United States Department of Treasury, is used by the majority of people to deposit Federal taxes, and QBOP makes use of the EFTPS.

To view the Payroll Tax Center and pay your payroll taxes, select Taxes Payroll Tax. After you've paid your employees, the Payroll Tax Center shows any outstanding taxes, along with their due dates and deadlines for electronic payments. Click on the View Your Tax Liability Report link on the Payroll Tax Center page to print the Payroll Tax Liability report and get an idea of how much you owe. The Pay Taxes page, which shows the payroll tax amounts you owe to various taxation authorities and the deadlines for making payments, appears when you click on the Pay Taxes button in QBO.

Your obligations for payroll taxes, broken down by payroll tax authority.

The sums you see are estimations of your liabilities if you "look ahead," or choose to view payroll tax bills before their due date.

QBO displays the total amount you owe, broken down by tax item, when you click on the Create Payment link next to a line. You have the option to use EFTPS to pay the responsibility electronically or manually at the top of the screen. Choose to make the payment yourself if you're inputting historical payrolls to provide accurate payroll information for the current year (as you've likely already made the payment and just want to record it in QBOP).

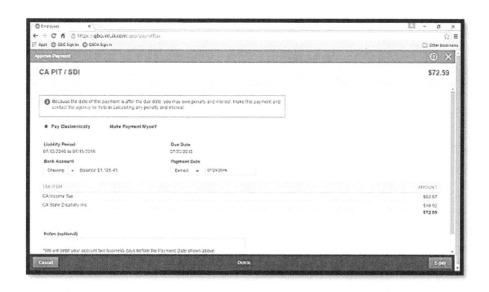

A payment of payroll taxes.

This illustration uses a hypothetical corporation and a prospective payment that was made a few days after the due date. As a result, QBO shows a notification at the top of the screen warning that late payments may incur interest and penalties and outlining the next steps you should take.

Once you've finished reviewing the payment information, which includes the payment method (manual or electronic), the bank account from which you'll make the payment, and the payment date, click the E-pay button or the Record Payment button in the lower right corner of the screen (depending on whether you're making the payment manually or electronically). The payment confirmation window in QBO contains a list of the payment method, type, obligation, due date, payment date, and payment amount.

Note: For each liability for payroll taxes, repeat this procedure.

Preparing payroll tax forms

Every three months, a federal Form 941, which specifies the total pay you paid, when you paid them, and the total taxes you withheld and paid to the appropriate taxing authorities during the quarter, must be completed and submitted. The IRS will accept paper submissions of the form as well.

If you live in a state that charges a personal income tax, check your state's website for the payroll tax reporting requirements since you typically need to complete a similar form for your state as well. You might also need to fill out and submit a state unemployment form in your state. On the Payroll Tax Center page, under Quarterly Forms, QBOP displays the reports you must complete and send.

The Quarterly Tax Forms page lists the payroll tax returns that you must complete and submit.

The QBOP presents a page where you may opt to submit the form electronically and see a preview of it once you click the link next to each form. An example of the form with data filled in is displayed when you select the View button. Using the tools provided in the form preview, you may review, save, and print the form. Additionally, by navigating to the form's bottom, you can view the filing instructions.

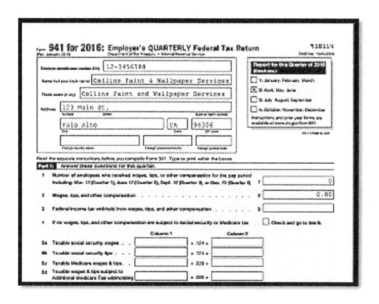

An example of a Form 941 used by the federal government to report payroll tax information

Paying Contractors

You can set up your contractors as vendors in QuickBooks. When you need to file their 1099s, you already have all of their information because QuickBooks keeps track of all of their relevant payments. For each product, follow these steps to set up contractors.

Understand who needs a 1099.

Any non-employee you may pay $600 or more in a calendar year (although electronic payments, like those made with a credit card, are not considered). Check the IRS regulations before you begin to determine who you must file 1099s for.

Please take note that the 1099 E-File Service only works with contractors that have US addresses.

Ask your contractors to complete a W-9 form.

We advise having your contractors complete a W-9 before you begin. This provides the information you need to speed up setup. W-9 forms are available for direct download from the IRS.

Setting up 1099 eligible contractors

To set up your 1099 contractors, select your payroll provider.

Step 1: Add a vendor for a contractor.

In QuickBooks, add the contractor as a vendor if you haven't already:

1. Click Payroll and then choose Contractors.
2. Choosing Add a contractor
3. Enter the information for your contractor or choose the Email this contractor button to have them complete it.
4. When done, choose Add contractor.

Step 2: Track contractor payments for 1099s

You must begin keeping track of the contractor's payments now that you have added them as a vendor.

1. Go to Sales or Get paid & pay, then Vendors.
2. Open the profile of the seller you want to keep an eye on.
3. Choose Edit.
4. Track Payments for 1099 checkbox must be chosen and checked.

Behind the scenes, QuickBooks will start keeping track of all of their payments. The tracked payments can be added to the form easily when you're prepared to file your 1099s.

Paying contractors

Contractors are paid in the same manner as other vendors. You can enter and pay a bill that a contractor sends you when necessary.

Reporting 1099 vendor payments

Now comes the challenging part. Both the 1099 contractor summary and detail reports are available in Quickbooks, but neither report includes information on payments you have already paid; instead, it only lists outstanding bills. These reports might be considered accounts payable reports for contractors.

You need to take the following actions in order to view payments you've made to 1099 qualified contractors:

- ❖ Make sure your business is set up to prepare 1099s.
- ❖ The 1099 transaction detail report should be prepared. This lists the contractors you've paid more than the $600 threshold outlined by the IRS.

Since you are not required to provide a 1099 NEC for credit card payments made to contractors, those payments are not included in the report. Instead, the contractor will receive a form 1099-K from the contractor's payment processor.

In your place, Quickbooks electronically files 1099s with the IRS, electronically delivers 1099s to your contractors, prints and mails hard copies of 1099s to your contractors; however, you are still responsible for the cost of these services. Here are the costs.

- ❖ First three forms, $3.99 for each subsequent form up to 20, and no fee Filing 1099 forms by January 15: the first three forms are $12.99, the next 20 forms are $2.99 apiece, and the additional 20 1099s are free. Your expense would be $63.82 ($12.99 + $2.99 x 17 + $0 x 5) if you had to file 25 forms.

❖ For 1099s submitted on or after January 16: there will be a $14.99 fee for your for 1099s over 20. Your expense would be $82.82 ($14.99 + $3.99 x 17+ $0 x 5) if you had to file 25 forms.

A 1099 kit that enables you to print your 1099s on paper is also available for purchase.

Due to the new e-filling automation in Quickbooks, you must wait for specific times of the year to complete the following procedures in order to access the 1099 process:

1. Select Workers > Contractors from the Payroll > Contractors menu.
2. Press the Prepare 1099s button in the page's centre.
3. Select Let's begin: Let's Get Started will be replaced by a button that says, "Continue your 1099s," if you have only partially finished the 1099 procedure.
4. Press Next. You are asked to classify the contractor payments you made.
5. Press Next: You can see details about the contractors you've hired on the following page.
6. Click next after you have finished examining the contractor information. You can view the total payment you have made to each contract.
7. Select "Save and finish later" if you are not yet ready to create 1099 forms: The 1099 transaction detail report is available for printing at any time of the year. Credit card payments are reported to IRS by the credit card company, so if you made payments to any of your 1099-eligible merchants using a credit card, those payments won't show up in the 1099 transaction detail report.

CHAPTER NINE

WORKING IN REGISTERS

There are other ways to work with transactions in Quickbooks Online besides the windows and list. Registers can also be used. Some people believe that entering transactions, especially checks, into a register is more efficient. The majority of people need to find it simple to use a register to swiftly discover the transactions that have an impact on a certain account and locate specific transactions.

Understanding Registers

You may view all transactions affecting a certain account in registers. Much of the information found in traditional paper registers, such those provided by banks to record handwritten checks, is also found in quickbooks online registers. Choose Gear > Accounting > Chart of Accounts in your company column to see the register for a specific account. It's important to have in mind that the first time you examine the chart of accounts, you might need to click the button that says "see your chart of accounts" for it to show. The register for a certain account can then be viewed by clicking the view register link in the action column.

Quickbooks Online by default presents the most recent transaction first, but you can alter how Quickbooks Online presents register information. Registers have one important restriction that you should be aware of: not all accounts can use them. All balance sheet accounts, with the exception of retained earnings, can be found to have registers. These balance sheet account types can be found in Quickbooks Online:

- ❖ Bank
- ❖ Accounts payable
- ❖ Accounts receivable
- ❖ Credit card

- ❖ Other current liabilities
- ❖ Long term liabilities
- ❖ Equity
- ❖ Other current assets
- ❖ Fixed assets
- ❖ Other assets

When you add new account to the chart of accounts or when you browse the chart of accounts page in Quickbooks Online, these account category kinds are displayed.

If you utilize account numbers, all asset accounts—such as 1000 and 10,000—begin with 1, all liability accounts with 2, and all equity accounts with 3. Although most accountants advise that you go by these criteria when you give the accounts in your chart of accounts numbers, this numbering strategy is not infallible.

Each transaction's information in the register's columns is identified by column headings, and the right edge of each register page displays the account's running balance. According to accounting regulations, every transaction in a bank account register has an impact on both the bank account and the other account. Every transaction has an impact on at least two accounts (due to double entry bookkeeping, a foundational tenet of accounting). As long as the register is sorted by date, the amount displayed in the balance column reflects the account's running balance.

We learn how to sort a register so that it displays in a different order than the usual transaction date order in the section "additional things you may do in a register." Have in mind that the balance column won't show any information if any other column is sorted before the Date column because the information wouldn't make any sense.

The most recent transactions are displayed at the top of the register by default, but you can change the register's appearance to utilize the Paper Ledger node if you'd prefer. Quickbooks Online displays transactions in paper ledger mode in chronological order. to how transactions would appear in a paper bank account ledger. In a paper register, transactions are entered as they happen, with the earliest transactions showing up at the top and the most recent transactions showing up at the bottom.

Entering And Editing Transactions

You could feel more at ease entering a check, a sales receipt, or a bill payment on a bank account register than on a transaction screen. But even if you aren't, you'll probably find it quite simple and useful to view a transaction in a register.

Not all of Quickbooks Online's registers allow you to enter transactions; specifically, you cannot enter transactions in the accounts receivable or payable registers because these registers require that transactions be tied to a specific customer or vendor, which calls for a transaction form like an invoice or a bill.

Entering a transaction

We will concentrate the discussion in this section on bank account registers since the most frequent transactions put directly into a register, such as handwritten checks, generally affect the checking account. You can add a transaction to the register after clicking the bank account's link to access the register.

You must make the attachment column in the register visible if you want to attach files to transactions. Select Table Gear Setting > Attachments to achieve this. You have the choice to add an attachment as you enter a transaction by selecting the option to display the attachments column automatically, or you can amend the transaction afterwards to add an attachment.

Quickbooks Online automatically guides you toward entering the most logical transaction for a particular register. Depending on the register you open, there may be a check, a deposit, a journal entry, etc. In the case of a bank account register, quickbooks online displays the add check link. Click the Add link under the Date column to enter the type of transaction that Quickbooks Online suggests. Imagine, however, that you want to record a different kind of transaction in a bank register. Open the relevant register and take the following actions to begin a new transaction and enter it:

1. To open the Add list box, press Ctrl+Alt+N, or click the down arrow next to the add check button.
2. Choose the type of transaction you wish to input from the list that appears; in our example, we chose sales receipt.
3. Modify the transaction date as appropriate.
4. Press tab and, if necessary, modify the transaction's reference number.
5. Select Tab and enter a name.
6. Press tab, then enter any note information you wish to record for the transaction in the memo column.
7. Press tab and enter the transaction's amount in the relevant field.
8. Press tab to move the mouse pointer to the Reconcile and Banking Status column in Quickbooks Online. The status of the transaction is indicated by a character in this column, either C for Cleared or R for Reconciled. The transaction is neither cleared nor reconciled if the column is empty. Normally, when you download or reconcile transactions, this column is updated. This column also indicates if a transaction was added or matched when transactions were downloaded via the account's bank feed if the account is also electronically linked to your financial institution.
9. Press tab: The location of the insertion pointer in Quickbook online depends on the type of transaction you are entering. However, quickbooks online sets the entry point in the account column if you are entering a check, a deposit, an expense, etc. Use the table's Gear settings button to add the attachment fields in order to attach an attachment to the transaction. then select the add attachment button located in the transaction window's lower left corner.
10. Press the transaction's save button to finish the process.

When entering a transaction straight into the checking register, you cannot alter the sales account for a sales receipt. To modify the account if necessary, you can, however, edit transactions through the relevant transaction form.

Editing a transaction

You can amend a transaction in the register by clicking it, making the necessary adjustments, or by clicking the transaction and then the edit button if you want to utilize the transaction window for the particular sorts of transactions you chose. Quickbooks Online shows the transaction in the check window if you want to enter a check transaction.

Additional Actions You Can Take In A Register

If you could only add and amend transactions, registers wouldn't be very useful. You must be able to locate transactions with ease. Additionally, the ability to print a register is always useful.

Sorting Transactions

Especially in a bank account register, the volume of transactions over time might cause the register page to grow exceedingly long. Skimming through the register or eyeballing it can be ineffective methods for looking for a transaction. Instead, you might be able to locate a specific transaction by sorting the register.

The transactions are sorted by date, in decreasing order from latest to earliest; observe the downward pointing arrow in the date column heading. You can sort by any column in the register by just clicking that column heading.

Printing a Register

Many people find it most convenient to print the data that shows in the register when conducting research. Click the print button next to the register's table gear settings button (located at the right edge of the register, above the balance column), and Quickbooks Online will display your register formatted for printing along with printing options in a new browser tab called the print tab. Choose the printer you want to use and any additional options, such as the pages to print, the quantity of copies, and the layout orientation, on the left side of the tab. Click print when you have finished setting the preferences. You can exit the print tab to re-display your registration in your Quickbooks company once the report has finished printing.

There is no requirement that you print to paper. To print the report to a PDF file, for instance, click the change button next to the destination printer and choose one of the PDF options, like Save as PDF or Microsoft Print to PDF. If you sign into Google Cloud Print, you can even decide to save to Google Docs. Alternately, you may export the register to an excel spreadsheet and filter and analyze it as much as you like by clicking the export to excel button next to the table gear button.

CHAPTER TEN

ADMINISTERING BANK AND CREDIT CARD ACCOUNTS

You can save time by using bank feeds or online banking, which eliminates the need for human data entry. The download and categorization of transactions begins as soon as you link your accounts. All you need to do is provide your approval.

QuickBooks Online Credit Card Account Setup Instructions

For businesses that have primary and secondary cards on one statement, setting up credit card accounts in QuickBooks Online is frequently the most challenging task. Whether you have one credit card or several credit cards, I will demonstrate how to set up your credit card accounts in QuickBooks Online so you can watch your expenses in real-time.

With regard to the quantity of cards you have and whether or not you also have staff cards, there are two approaches to set up credit cards in QuickBooks Online. You'll need a copy of your credit card statement to start the process outlined below. Register with QuickBooks Online.

Method One - Single Card, No Employees

- ❖ Click the Accounting Tab, then select Chart of Accounts.
- ❖ Click the new green button to create the credit card accounts.
- ❖ In the Account window, add:
- ❖ Account Type = Credit Card
- ❖ Detail Type = Credit Card
- ❖ Name = credit card name plus the last four digits of the card number
- ❖ Number = enter your chart of accounts number

- ❖ Description = leave this blank
- ❖ Is sub-account = leave unchecked
- ❖ Balance = leave this blank
- ❖ Click save and close

Method Two- Master Credit Card with Multiple Secondary Cards for Employees

- ❖ In the chart of accounts screen, click the New green button to create a generic parent credit card account.
- ❖ In the Account window, add:
- ❖ Account Type = Credit Card
- ❖ Detail Type = Credit Card
- ❖ Name = Credit Card plus "Corp or Parent"
- ❖ Number = enter your chart of accounts number if applicable
- ❖ Description = enter "this account to reconcile all sub-credit card accounts"
- ❖ Is sub-account = leave blank
- ❖ Balance = leave this blank
- ❖ Click save and new to add the real credit cards as sub-accounts
- ❖ In the Account window, add:
- ❖ Account Type = Credit Card
- ❖ Detail Type = Credit Card
- ❖ Name = add "credit card name+Employee's first and last name initial+card last 4 digits"
- ❖ Number = enter your chart of accounts number
- ❖ Description = leave blank
- ❖ Is sub-account = select the parent credit card account you created above
- ❖ Balance = leave this blank
- ❖ Click save and new to repeat the process to add the remaining sub-accounts.

Setting Up A Bank Or Credit Card Account

Step 1: Connect a bank or credit card account

You are free to link as many personal and professional accounts as you like.

Note: There are several stages involved in opening an American Express Business account.

1. Select Bank transactions under Bookkeeping, then Transactions, or choose Banking.
2. Choose Connect account if this is your first time setting up a bank account. Or, if you've already created an account, choose Link account.

    Note: For security purposes, if you are switching from QuickBooks Desktop, you must connect your bank and credit card accounts once again.

3. Enter the name of your bank, credit card, or credit union in the search area. Note: You can upload your bank transactions manually if you can't find your bank but still want to add your transactions.
4. Choose Continue. then use your user ID and password to log in to your bank.
5. Take the steps shown on the screen. This could involve the security checks that your bank demands. The connection can take a while.
6. Choose the accounts you want to link, then pick an account type from the selection. Select the account type in QuickBooks that corresponds to your chart of accounts.

If the appropriate account type isn't displayed in the dropdown,

To add a new bank or credit card account to your chart of accounts, select + Add new.

  a. For Newly opened bank accounts:
     ❖ Select Bank under Account Type.

- ❖ Choose either Savings or Checking under Detail Type.
- ❖ Select Save and then close after giving the account a name.
b. Regarding fresh credit card accounts:
  - ❖ Select Credit Card under Account Type.
  - ❖ Select Save and close after giving the account a name.
7. Choose how many transactions you wish to download in the past. You can obtain the 90 days' worth of transactions from some banks. Others are able to go back up to 24 months.
8. Choose Connect.

Connect your bank account from your chart of accounts (optional)

1. Chart of accounts can be found by selecting Bookkeeping (Take me there).
2. To connect to an account, locate it.
3. Choose the View register option from the Action column menu. Next, choose Connect bank.
4. For guidance on connecting your bank to QuickBooks, go to the on-screen prompts (these steps are the same as listed above, starting with step 5).

Step 2: Download recent transactions

Transactions are downloaded by QuickBooks so you don't have to manually enter them. To download the most recent transactions, refresh the bank feed.

1. To choose bank transactions, go to Bookkeeping, then Transactions (take me there), or go to Banking
2. Choose Update.

Step 3: Sort downloaded transactions into categories

You must verify and categorize your transactions after QuickBooks downloads them to ensure that they are properly categorized.

Record And Make Bank Deposit

Multiple payments from different sources are frequently deposited at once when making a deposit at the bank. Typically, the bank keeps a single record with a single total for all transactions. They won't match the way your bank recorded the deposit if you enter the same payments as separate records in QuickBooks.

To ensure that your records correspond to your actual bank deposit in these circumstances, you can combine transactions using a special feature in QuickBooks. How to record bank deposits in QuickBooks Online is shown below.

1. Transfer the transactions you need to group into your Undeposited Funds account.
2. Then combine them by using the bank deposit feature.

Step 1: Add transactions to the account for undeposited funds.

Payments for invoices and sales receipts that you want to combine should go into the Undeposited Funds account if you haven't already. Before you record a deposit, everything is held in this account.

Step 2: bank deposit and QuickBooks transactions together

A distinct record is created in QuickBooks for each bank deposit. For each of your deposit slips, make a single deposit.

1. Click + New
2. Select Bank Deposit.
3. Select the account you wish to deposit the money into from the Account menu.
4. For every transaction you want to combine, click the appropriate box.
5. Verify that the sum of the chosen transactions matches the amount on your deposit slip. As a guide, use your deposit slip.
6. Choose Save and close or Save and new.

Important: The bank deposit window displays all transactions made in your Undeposited Funds account. Place it in the Undeposited Funds account if you don't see one that has to be added.

Include bank or processing fees

Some banks add up processing and service fees. In QuickBooks, don't make changes to the initial transactions. As an alternative, include the fee while using the bank deposit window.

1. Scroll down to the box labeled Add money to this deposit.
2. Add the cost as a line item.
3. Determine who the cost was from
4. From the Account dropdown, choose Bank Charges.
5. Enter a negative value for the fee amount. Enter -50, for instance, if the cost was $50.
6. Examine the deposit sum and bank fee.
7. Choose Save and new or Save and close.

Note: Here's how to open a bank charges account if you don't already have one: The Account dropdown menu has a + Add New option. Choose Expenses as the account type and Bank Charges as the detail type in the account creation panel. Simply rename the account "Bank fees" or something like.

Manage bank deposit

Review previous bank deposits

1. Click the Reports menu option under the Business overview.
2. Scroll down to the section under "Sales and customers."

Step 3: Choose the Deposit Detail report

All of your completed bank deposits are listed in the report. To view additional information, choose certain deposits.

Remove a payment form a bank deposit

Made a payment addition by error? No issue. If you want to withdraw a certain deposit payment:

1. Select All Sales under Transactions under Bookkeeping.
2. Locate the payment you wish to delete and open it. The appropriate status is "Closed."
3. Remove the check from the box next to the payment you want to delete.
4. Choose Save and close or Save and new.

The money will be returned to the account for undeposited funds. It can be included in a different deposit.

Delete a bank Deposit

If a bank deposit needs to be deleted in order to start over:

1. Click "Bookkeeping," then "Chart of accounts."
2. Locate the bank account where you made the deposit, then click Account history.
3. Find the bank deposit and click on it to view more information.
4. Click Delete.

Every payment made on the deposit is returned to the account for undeposited funds. You can create a fresh deposit to start anew.

Why It's Important to Record Deposits in QuickBooks Online

Maintaining accurate and current records of your bank transactions is one of the principles of excellent bookkeeping. You must enter a deposit into QuickBooks Online in order to keep track of any transactions made through your bank account. This holds true even for deposits from the business owner's investments or other sources of non-income.

How to Use QuickBooks In Processing Credit Card Payments

This will demonstrate how to use QuickBooks Payments to process credit card payments in QuickBooks Online. To record credit card payments using a sales receipt and a customer invoice, we'll first go over how you can set up QuickBooks Payments as you'll need an account to receive payments.

How to Setup QuickBooks Online Payments

Step 1: go to the payment settings.

Select Account and settings from Your Company, the first column, by clicking the gear symbol in the upper right corner of your QuickBooks Online screen, as shown below.

Select Payments from the Account and Settings screen's left menu.

Step 2: Open a QuickBooks Payments Account application

Step 3 should be taken if you have a QuickBooks Payments account. You must register for one if you don't already have one by selecting the green Learn more button in the Payments settings window.

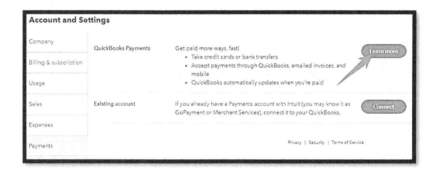

You'll be directed to the QuickBooks Payments account application window, which has three components, after clicking Learn more, as seen below.

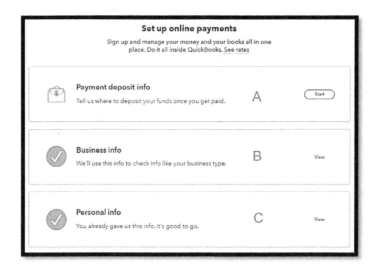

1. Payment deposit information: QuickBooks will inquire as to which of your bank accounts should be used to deposit payments made by credit card and to charge credit card fees. Choose a different bank account, then click the Add button if you haven't already added it to your chart of accounts. Click the green Save button after choosing the account.
2. Business information: Information about your company, including its name, industry, and address, will be requested.
3. Personal information: When prompted by QuickBooks, you can enter your entire name, address, and phone number.

Each component of QuickBooks Payments should include a start button if this is your first time configuring it. If not, a View button should appear, as shown in the above screenshot (items B and C).

Click the green "Get set up" button at the bottom of the screen once all three sections have been finished (not shown in our image).

Step 3: Review payment settings

Similarly to Step 1, navigate to the payment preferences section. You should see the following on your Payment settings screen now that you have registered for QuickBooks Payments:

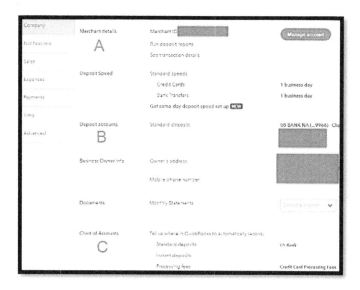

1. Merchant information: In order to access the QuickBooks Payments account, click the green Manage account icon.

2. Deposit accounts: You'll deposit credit card proceeds into this section's mentioned bank account, and you'll withdraw processing fees from it. The QuickBooks account where the transactions are recorded will not be impacted by changing the bank account in this case.

3. Accounts Chart: This field specifies the QuickBooks expense account to classify the processing fees as well as the QuickBooks bank account to record deposits.

Click anywhere in the Chart of Accounts area to choose which account should be used to record processing fees.

Next, select an expense account to charge your credit card processing costs to by clicking on drop-down menu next to Processing fees (under Charts of Accounts). When choosing an account from drop-down list that appears, click + Add New to create a new account if the account is not yet in QuickBooks. Choosing an expenditure account is followed by clicking the green Save button.

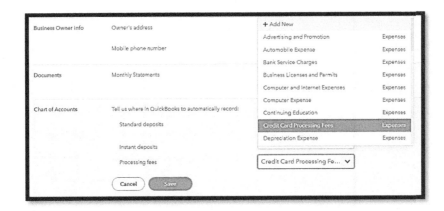

How to Use a Sales Receipt to Record a Credit Card Payment

In a previous section, you learned how to make and transmit sales receipts. You may now generate sales receipts to track customer payments made with credit cards, debit cards, and bank transfers after you have a QuickBooks Payments account.

Step 1: make a sales receipt.

Select Sales receipt in the first column under Customers by clicking + New at the top of the left menu bar.

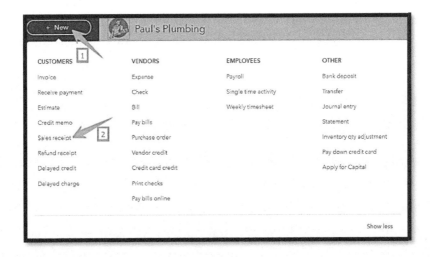

Step 2: Enter Your Credit Card Details

Select the appropriate payment option from the drop-down menu under Payment method to accept payments made by bank transfer, credit card, or debit card.

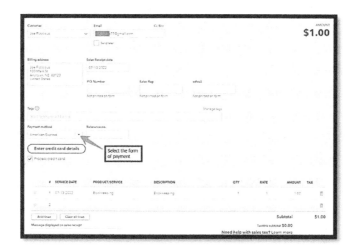

Click on Enter credit card data to enter the customer's credit card account information after choosing the payment option.

Click the green "Use this information" button after entering all the credit card details. You will be informed that the credit card transaction hasn't yet been completed and that you have 10 minutes to complete it before the credit card details are erased from the sales receipt. You'll be taken to the sales receipt screen after being informed that you have 10 minutes left.

Step 3: Saving Sales Receipt & Processing Credit Card Payment

The final four digits of the credit card number that will be charged are now displayed on the Sales Receipt screen. Click the green "Save and send" button to complete the transaction.

Step 4: Verify the Credit Card Transaction Processed (Optional)

Reopen the sales receipt by selecting All Sales from the left menu bar, then looking for the just created sales receipt transaction. Open the sales receipt and check that the Payment method section says "Transaction executed."

To view the transaction's details, click on Transaction executed.

By selecting the Print or Refund buttons, you can print the transaction details or give the consumer a refund.

How to Input Credit Card Payment Information on an Invoice

If your customer chooses to pay an invoice online by clicking Pay Invoice in the email you sent them, you won't need to go through this process. By selecting Company settings in the first column, clicking Sales, and then clicking the gear icon in the top-right corner of the screen, you can enable online payments.

Step 1: Access the screen that reads "Receive Payment."

Select Receive payment in the first column by clicking + New above the left menu bar.

Step 2: Fill out the Receive Payment Screen's Credit Card Information

The Receive Payment screen should be filled out just as it is in our instructions on how to accept payments, with the exception of changing the payment type to a credit card. Select the credit card processor from the drop-down option under Payment method.

To get a window where the customer can enter their credit card account information, click Enter credit card details:

Click the green Use this info button to proceed after entering the credit card details. You have 10 minutes to complete the transaction before the credit card information is deleted even though the charge hasn't yet been made to the card.

Step 3: Save the payment to complete the credit card transaction.

The final four digits of the credit card that will be debited are now displayed on the Receive Payment screen.

Resulting Events

It will take some time for the money to be moved from QuickBooks Payments before the credit card payments you received are shown in your bank account register. QuickBooks will record the deposits and associated processing fees to the account registers you chose in the QuickBooks Payments settings outlined above after the money has arrived in your bank.

What Advantages Come With Making Payments Using a QuickBooks Account?

❖ By selecting the Pay Now button on their emailed bills, your clients can submit payments online.

❖ Through the mobile app for QuickBooks Online, you may collect payments from customers using a mobile device.

- ❖ In general, payments are made to your bank account two to three business days after the transaction date.
- ❖ For QuickBooks Payments to function with QuickBooks Online, there is no software to install.
- ❖ Considering that QuickBooks Payments is connected with QuickBooks, your accounts and financial statements are constantly current.

Credit Card Account Reconciliation Instructions

You will learn how to reconcile credit card accounts in QBO in this section. This process is essential for ensuring that the credit card activity in QuickBooks corresponds to your credit card bills. You can easily reconcile credit cards in QuickBooks with the help of this course.

Step 1: Go to the Credit Card Reconciliation Screen

Select Reconcile by placing your cursor over Accounting in the left menu bar.

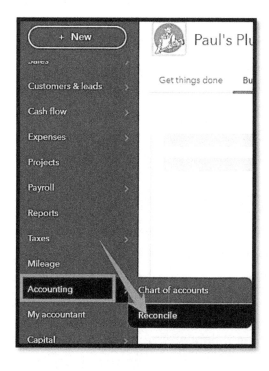

Step 2: Choose the Account and enter the information for your statement.

Below, we'll walk you through how to fill out the fields on the credit card reconciliation screen.

1. **Account:** Make your selection for the credit card account you want to reconcile.
2. **Last statement ending date:** According to QuickBooks, this credit card account's most recent statement reconciliation was on this day. If this is the first credit card reconciliation, there won't be a date.

   Never skip a month.

   You cannot skip months since a reconciliation always begins with the reconciled balance from the previous month. You must start with the most recent reconciled statement and move ahead one month at a time if it has been a while since a reconciliation.

3. **Beginning balance:** According to QuickBooks, the reconciled ending balance of the previous statement serves as the current statement's

212

beginning balance. If you are reconciling a credit card for the first time, this amount will be zero.

Check the starting balance.

The beginning balance determined by QuickBooks must coincide with the ending balance on the most recent statement reconciled for your reconciliation to be successful. The beginning balance may be incorrect if there have been any modifications to previously reconciled transactions; in this case, QuickBooks gives a link to help you locate the altered transaction.

4. **Ending balance**: Enter your credit card statement's ending balance.
5. **Finance charge**: Enter the finance charge (if applicable) from your credit card statement if you haven't already done so in a separate transaction. Include the expenditure account or category to capture the expense as well as the date the charge was assessed. When the reconciliation is finished, QuickBooks will automatically record this charge.

Click the green Start reconciling button after entering all of your statement data.

Step 3: Match Credit Card transactions

QuickBooks will show a screen with a summary of the reconciliation in the top half and detailed transactions in the bottom half after the previous step is finished.

1. **Statement ending balance:** The statement balance that was entered on the previous screen is carried over and should be the same as the final number that appears on your credit card statement.

2. **Cleared balance:** QuickBooks determines the cleared balance by adding charges you mark as cleared and subtracting payments you indicate as cleared to the beginning balance from the previous page.

3. **Difference:** Before you can complete a reconciliation, the difference between the cleared balance and the statement's closing balance must be zero. If the difference isn't zero, you'll notice an exclamation mark, which means you need to reconcile those records.

4. **Radial buttons for cleared transactions:** If a transaction displays on your credit card statement, click the radial button in the right-most column for that transaction. The transaction will be added to the cleared balance once you press the radial button (item B).

How to Proceed if the credit card transactions don't match the entries in QuickBooks

Investigating unmarked transactions on your bill after tracking transactions from the platform to it is how transactions between QuickBooks and your credit card statement are matched.

Track Transactions to Your Statement

Start by finding each transaction indicated on your credit card statement that is listed in the QuickBooks screen above. If you locate it, mark the transaction's spot on your statement with a checkmark by clicking the radial button for it (item D).

Any transaction in QuickBooks that isn't on your bank statement needs to be looked into. Don't erase the transaction because it might have an impact on other accounts or periods, even though your QuickBooks accounting blunder is the most likely culprit.

The following are some of the most typical mistakes that might result in inaccurate QuickBooks credit card transactions:

1. **Transactions that are same:** If you accidentally produced a transaction that is identical, the original transaction will be displayed on the statement, but the duplicate won't. For instance, you might have entered a new transaction rather than matching the credit card activity to an existing transaction if it was imported from the bank. If so, you ought to remove the redundant transaction.

2. **Incorrect account:** It's possible that the questionable transaction was inadvertently reported on this account as a charge made with a separate credit card. If so, update the transaction and give it the proper account designation.

3. **Wrong date:** During the reconciliation process, you can encounter various problems if you submit the incorrect statement date. For instance, if the statement date is too early, certain essential transactions might be missing; conversely, if the statement date is too late, some additional transactions might be included. Make sure your QuickBooks statement date matches the date on your bank statement at all times.

Review Unmarked Transactions on Your Statement and Look into Them

You marked each transaction on your statement that was seen in QuickBooks when you traced from QuickBooks to your statement. Now scan your statement for any transactions that lack a mark. Unmarked transactions must be added to QuickBooks if they are valid. Once it has been added, select the radial button in the right-most column to designate the transaction as cleared.

Add another QuickBooks tab.

When performing reconciliation, you should use two or more open tabs rather than just one. This will allow you to work on the reconciliation screen in one tab while making the necessary modifications to transactions in another, which will speed up the process. To accomplish this, in your web browser, right-click on the reconciliation screen tab and choose "duplicate" to open a new tab. You must refresh the original tab after the modifications are saved in order to see the new interface.

Step 4: Verify There Is No Difference

The discrepancy between your statement's ending balance and cleared balance should be zero if all the selected transactions in QuickBooks match the transactions on your credit card account. In the event that it isn't, look over our troubleshooting advice to identify inconsistencies on your statements or in Intuit.

The transactions in this sample reconciliation have all been linked to a credit card statement.

Click the green Finish now button in the top-right corner of the screen after your reconciliation is finished.

Step 5: Make a payment on the credit card balance (Optional).

If you choose to make a payment against this credit card amount, QuickBooks will ask you in a message that appears when it has confirmed the reconciliation is finished.

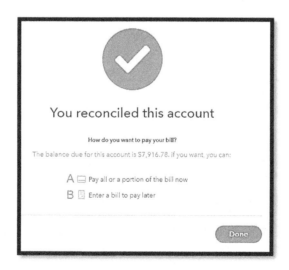

You can write a check or create a bill later by navigating directly to the Write Check or Create Bill pages, so you don't need to make a decision right away. However, if you wish to pay right away, choose one of the following:

- ❖ To access the Write Check page and draft a check for the credit card balance you desire to pay, click Pay all or a portion of the bill now. You shouldn't alter the category's default setting, which should be the credit card account you recently reconciled.
- ❖ To access the Create Bill screen, click on Enter a bill to pay later. From there, you can enter a bill for the balance you are to pay by the due date indicated on the credit card statement. Verify that the category corresponds to the credit card you recently reconciled, that the bill date matches the statement date, and that the due date matches the due date on the credit card statement.

Because doing so transfers some of your credit card debt to a current accounts payable (A/P), you should enter a bill. The benefit is that your credit card payment and due date are now visible with your other accounts payable, serving as a reminder for you to pay the bill before it is past due.

Press the green Done button once you've finished configuring your payment or have made the decision to postpone it.

Credit Card Reconciliation Advantages

Identifies missing transactions: For the account to reconcile, you must add any transactions that appear on your statement but have not yet been entered in QuickBooks.

Identifies incorrect amounts: The account won't reconcile if the same transaction has different amounts in QuickBooks and the bank statement.

Searches for duplicate transactions: You can find transactions that shouldn't be in QuickBooks by looking at those that didn't show up on your bank account for the month.

- ❖ Displays false or fraudulent charges: You should check any charges that appear on your bank statement but aren't included in QuickBooks to see if they're valid. Put them on the platform once they have been given permission

218

CHAPTER ELEVEN

WORKING WITH PURCHASE ORDER, ESTIMATE, PROJECT AND TAGS

Working With Purchase Order Feature

You provide yourself (and others in your firm) a useful tool you may use to expedite your internal ordering, inventory management, and bookkeeping operations when you generate a purchase order in QuickBooks Online. Many organizations skip the task of inputting purchase orders into their accounting software since they are non-posting entries, which have no influence on your financial results. You could lose time and money if you make this error.

This section will show you how to make a purchase order in QuickBooks Online, which is simple to do.

What is a purchase order?

Purchase order is a letter that a customer sends to a vendor in order to place an order for goods or to make a commitment to pay for services in the future. Purchase orders are used for two things.

Purchase orders are used to formally order goods or services from vendors and specify the terms of the order (the quantity of each product you intend to purchase or what sort of service you intend to use, the price you expect to pay for the products or services, how and when the vendor should deliver the products or services, etc.).

=Purchase orders also act as internal controls that stop your staff from accepting and paying for goods or services that you did not order or from overpaying for goods that you planned to buy at a price that is different from what your vendor charges you.

Your technique for reconciling your bills depends heavily on purchase orders. Using purchase orders provides your staff with a document they can use to confirm the validity of any orders your company gets. If the order is for a product, your team can add it to your inventory after accepting it and begin immediately turning it into revenue for your company.

Purchase orders are used by your accounting department to ensure that you aren't being charged for goods or services you never planned to buy. When they get the invoice for these things, they use purchase orders to make sure you pay the right amount. This is crucial since adjustments to the prices of your vendors will directly affect your gross margin and overall profitability.

How to create purchase orders

It's simple to create a purchase order with QuickBooks Online. If you have a QuickBooks Online Plus subscription (buy orders are not accessible in QuickBooks Online Self Employed, Simple Start, or Essentials), you can set it up instantly even if you've never used this function.

A step-by-step guide for establishing your first purchase order in QuickBooks Online can be found below. Remember that Intuit is constantly enhancing the QuickBooks Online user experience, so your screen may not exactly like the examples below.

1. From the QuickBooks Online dashboard, pick Purchase Order from the Vendors list by clicking the New button in the upper left-hand corner of the screen.

2. A window with the purchase order form will open. The form created in the QuickBooks Online "test drive" file can be used exactly as is, or you can alter or add new fields by selecting the gear icon in the top right corner of your screen.

   You might want to add the following fields:

   ❖ Cancel On Date (useful if you don't want backorders)
   ❖ Ship Date
   ❖ Delivery Date

There will be an automatic numbering pattern for your purchase order. If you are on the dashboard or another non-form screen and would like to change the numbers, click the gear icon and choose Account and Settings.

Select Expenses on the following screen, then modify your purchase order parameters by clicking the pencil icon to the right of the Purchase Orders line. If you need to enable Purchase Orders in QuickBooks Online, you can do it here as well.

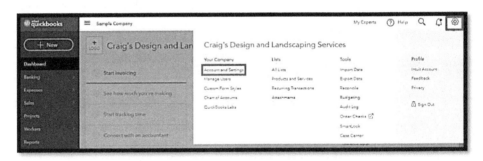

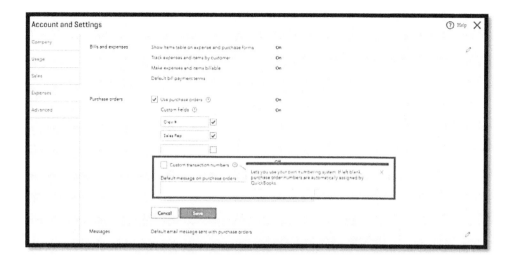

3. Complete the information on the purchase order as shown in the screenshot below:

i.   From the drop-down menu, select the Vendor. The "Add New" option is located at the top of the drop-down menu, and you can enter vendor information instantly by clicking there.

ii. If you want to send the purchase order, provide your email address. If you want to copy other people (such your accountant or bookkeeper) on the purchase order, you may either use the Cc/Bcc link or separate numerous email addresses with commas.

iii. If the vendor's mailing address doesn't appear automatically, you can enter it here.

iv. From the Ship To drop-down option, select the customer's name if you want to drop-ship this order to them.

v.   Include the purchase order's date.

Verify that the shipping address is accurate. If it needs to altered, you can do so here.

vi. The following fields are optional: "Ship via" designates the method of delivery for the order. Both "Sales Rep" and "Crew #" are custom fields. Fill in any of these fields as required.

223

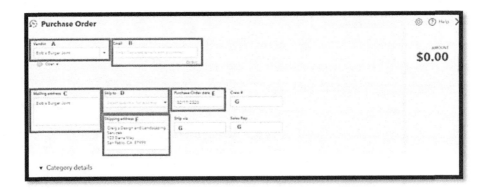

4. Complete the purchase order's "order" section (outlined in the below screenshot).

i. You can fill out the "Category information" box in QuickBooks Online even if you don't use Products or Services (A). Similar to an expense entry, you will select the chart of accounts category in this section using the drop-down box (B). Then, if desired, provide a description (C), and last, enter the line's value (D). If you want to bill the purchase to a customer, you can select a customer (E) from the drop-down menu; this will be useful when you convert the purchase order to a bill.

can enter category and client names instantly from the order screen, just like with expenses and sales entries. Simply select "Add New" from the drop-down menu at the top of any of these fields.

You can add lines if you require more than the two that are already there (F). You can also delete every line on this section of the purchase order (G), however before clicking this button, make sure you want to delete every line on this section because there is no "undo" function available.

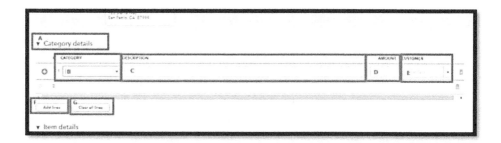

ii.   Your purchase order entry is made considerably simpler if you employ the products or services. Fill out the purchase order's "Item details" section (H), selecting a good or service from the drop-down menu (I). By selecting "Add New" at the very top of the drop-down menu, you can add a good or service instantly. If you have already supplied this information for the good or service, the description (J) and rate (K) will automatically populate. If necessary, you can also change these fields. the quantity of the product or service you are ordering after that (L). The amount field (M) will calculate automatically unless you manually modify it.

You have the ability to add a customer's name to each line of the purchase order, just like in the "Category information" section, and you can add more lines if necessary or remove all of them.

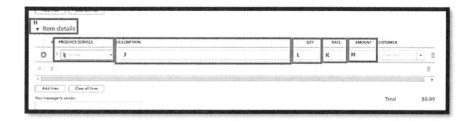

5. If you'd like, you can add a memo (O) or a message to your vendor (N) to the purchase order. These extra entries can clarify the purchase order for your team or your vendor.

You may also click within the box and choose files from your computer or drag and drop files into it to add attachments (P) to the purchase order. Click the "Attach to email" button if you want to send the attachments with the purchase order through email (Q).

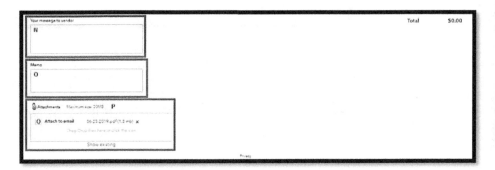

6. Review, save, and transmit your QuickBooks Online purchase order at this point. To avoid unintentionally ordering 10,000 units of something instead of 10, make sure the order total (R) is what you anticipate, and then save the purchase order. You'll see that there are a few choices available to you when it comes to saving.

i. The purchase order is saved when you press the "Save" button (S), allowing you to return to it or continue working on it later. In order to prevent QuickBooks Online from logging you out and erasing your progress while you are working on a large order, click this button every few minutes.

ii. There is a green button with a drop-down menu to the right of the "Save" button (T). You can choose to "Save and send," "Save and new," or "Save and close" by clicking the arrow to the right of this button.

By clicking "Save and Send," you can email your vendor with the purchase order. When you select "Save and close," the purchase order is saved and the window is closed. If you're inputting multiple buy orders at once, "Save and new" will save the purchase order you're working on and open a new purchase order page for you to complete.

226

iii. At the bottom center of the screen, there is an option to print your purchase order (U). Additionally, you'll have a choice to make the purchase order a recurring entry (V), which is useful if you consistently place the same order.

iv. The "Cancel" and "Clear" buttons (W) are carefully tucked away on the bottom left corner of the screen, far from the Save buttons, so you can't accidentally click on them and lose your progress. This is useful if you want to scrap completely the purchase order before you save it.

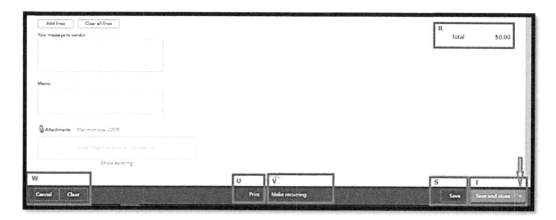

Why you should create purchase order

Some companies prefer to create their purchase orders outside of their accounting software, utilizing an inventory management system, a POS system, or perhaps even a paper form. Many opt to merely maintain the buy orders outside of their accounting system rather than going through the extra effort to produce the purchase order in QuickBooks Online or to set up an automatic sync between two different computerized systems.

This appears like a logical justification at first. Purchase orders have no effect on the financial data of the company because they are non-posting transactions. Considering that they are merely informational documents, spending the effort to enter them into QuickBooks Online feels like extra, pointless work.

However, as was already indicated, your accounting division will use purchase orders to guide them in deciding whether or not to approve processing payment for a supplier's invoice. Additionally, they can assist you in managing your inventory and cash flow by using the Open Purchase Order report, but they can only do this if you make the purchase orders readily available to them.

Let's imagine, for instance, that sales haven't been as strong as you had hoped. This not only means you don't need to buy more inventory because you already have enough for any prospective sales, but it also probably means you don't have the money on hand to cover any fresh incoming orders. Your accounting staff can run a quick report after you've submitted your purchase orders in QuickBooks Online to see if any new inventory is expected to arrive soon, how much you ordered, and whether you should think about canceling or delaying the order.

Delete a Purchase Order

QuickBooks Online or SOS Inventory can be used to start the elimination of a purchase order. Our cloud-based app will be synchronized with QBO to make sure the data is accurate on both platforms.

You can start deleting a purchase order in QBO by:

i.   Click on the "Advanced Search" menu icon in the search menu.
ii. Next, select the option for "Purchase Orders," click "Search," and then pick the particular purchase order you wish to cancel.
iii. Select "More" and then "Delete" from the menu that appears at the bottom of the page.

Whether you are switching from QuickBooks Desktop to QuickBooks Online and want to improve your inventory functionality or discover that your current inventory system is lacking the potent features SOS Inventory adds to QuickBooks Online, making the switch to the top-rated inventory app for QuickBooks Online sets your business up for efficiency, easier transactions, and greater control over every aspect of the business.

Working With Estimates

Do you prepare estimates, bids, quotations, or proposals for prospective customers before beginning work on a project? You may make estimates in QuickBooks, email them to customers, and then turn them into invoices once the task is completed. Creating and tracking estimates is a key aspect of growing your company's earnings. So, let's go over the fundamentals of creating an estimate in QuickBooks Online (QBO).

What is an estimate and what is its purpose?

An estimate is a document that provides prospective consumers a list of items and services as well as the prices for each. It is critical to understand that an estimate is not a sales order. Potential clients have not yet made a purchase decision. Estimates in QBO provide a breakdown of prices so your consumer understands exactly how they spend their money.

The importance Estimations

❖ Estimates in QuickBooks Online are an important aspect of running a growing business. It is critical to keep things structured and precise not only for your consumers, but also for your employees.

❖ Estimates are a method of converting potential consumer interest into a sales transaction in QBO.

❖ In addition, connecting QuickBooks Online with Method allows your sales team to make QuickBooks estimates from anywhere and at any time.

❖ Let's take a look at how to make an estimate in QuickBooks Online.

How to Make an Estimate

Estimates are quick and simple to construct in QBO. We've broken down the steps so you can easily navigate the QuickBooks Online estimate process.

Locate the estimation screen

Step 1: Locate the estimation screen.

Find the Add New button in the upper-left menu bar of your QuickBooks Online dashboard, and then click Estimate in the drop-down menu options under Customers.

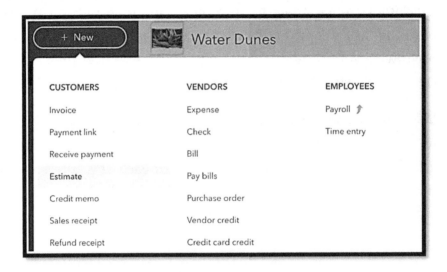

Enter customer details

Step 2: Enter customer details

There are a few vacant boxes to fill up on the estimates page. The first is the customer information. You can choose an existing customer from the drop-down list or create a new one by clicking the Add new button.

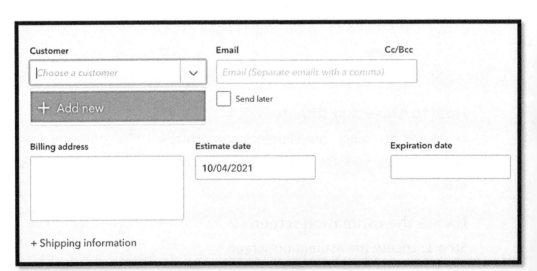

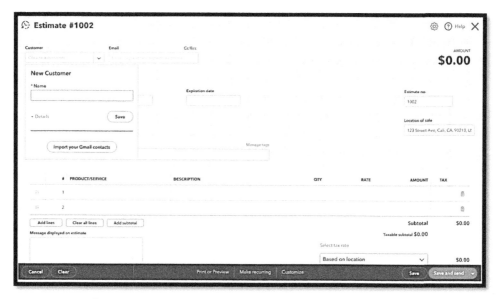

Customer information includes the billing address, mailing address, email address, phone number, and other information. You can also attach documents and make notes to the customer profile as needed.

You can also add more client information by clicking the More Details button.

Enter estimation details

Step 3: Enter estimation details

After finishing the profile, go to the search bar in the Product/Service column and select the products or services (items) you intend to provide to your potential customer.

To add a new item, use the same search bar and press the Add new button. When filling out the item information and descriptions, be sure to include the item's quantity and price.

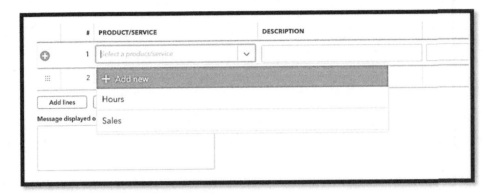

You can also include files and a customer note with the estimate.

QuickBooks Online estimates allow you to create invoice notes ahead of time for when the estimate converts into a sales transaction. This is a useful feature, and if you want to improve the efficiency of this flow, stay reading to find out how Method might assist.

Save and send your Estimate

Step 4: Save and send your Estimate.

One of the most crucial procedures is to save the QuickBooks Online estimate by clicking the save icon in the lower-right corner of your screen.

If you're wondering how to send an estimate in QuickBooks Online, simply click the bottom-right green Save and send button.

Changing an estimate into invoice

Step 5: Changing an estimate into invoice

When your customer accepts the estimate, it's time to convert it into an invoice.

Go to your dashboard and look for the Sales tab in the left menu bar. Select All Sales from the drop-down menu selections.

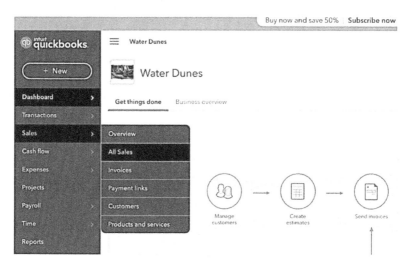

On this screen, click the blue Estimate tab to see your list of estimates. Find the one you wish to convert into a sale and click it.

Make any final modifications negotiated with your customer and double-check the entire estimate.

Then, in the top-right corner of the screen, click the Create invoice button to convert the estimate into an invoice.

Note: You cannot change the status of an estimate once it has been converted into an invoice.

The secret to smoother running of Estimates

Now that you know how to produce an estimate in QuickBooks Online, you can concentrate on improving your QBO estimates by syncing with Method.

Grasp the value Method delivers to your organization begins with an understanding of some of the limitations of QuickBooks Online estimates.

Limitation in Quickbooks online Estimates

Did you realize QuickBooks Online lacks an automated estimate approval process?

That is correct.

As a result, mistakes occur, especially when a team of sales representatives, administrative personnel, and an accounting team are all attempting to develop estimates and manage bills.

With the limits of QuickBooks Online estimates, it can be difficult to grow your business, and many QBO users work around this by requesting consumers to accept estimates by email. This does not always work out as anticipated.

- ❖ Customers frequently fail to respond to estimate emails.
- ❖ The following are the main drawbacks of QuickBooks Online's current estimate approval system:
- ❖ There is a greater possibility that you will misplace the approval email in your inbox.

Customers' lack of commitment as a result of QBO's informal approval procedure.

By automating the estimate-to-invoice process, syncing QuickBooks Online with Method can help you overcome these constraints and close sales faster.

Managing Project

The Projects tool helps you keep track of and arrange all moving pieces. You may also manage project-specific reports, add project income and expenses, and add historical transactions for new projects from a single dashboard. This makes it easier to manage your work and track your progress. So, let's go ahead and talk about how to set up and create Projects in QuickBooks Online.

Steps for configuring and creating projects in QuickBooks Online

Turning on Projects
Step 1: Turning on Projects

First, if you haven't already, enable the Projects function. Follow the procedures below to activate the projects:

- ❖ Open QuickBooks Online and select Settings, followed by Account and Settings.
- ❖ Locate the Advanced tab now.
- ❖ Next, locate the Projects section and click Edit to enlarge it.

- ❖ Select the Organize all job-related activity in one location checkbox.
- ❖ Now, click Save to exit your settings.

The project menu appears immediately in the main navigation bar.

Create your first Project

Step 2: Create your first Project

Follow the steps below to create your first project in QuickBooks Online.

- ❖ To begin, navigate to the Projects menu and then select New Project.
- ❖ Give your project a meaningful name that you will remember easily.
- ❖ Next, using the drop-down option, select the customer for whom you are working.
- ❖ Add your project's records or details now.
- ❖ Select Save.

Your project list will grow as your company receives more work.

Add project income and expenses

Step 3: Add project income and expenses

Now that you've started your first project, it's time to start adding income and expenses. Follow the steps below to enter project income and expenses. Adding transactions to projects has no effect on how they are classified or affect your accounts. You are simply labeling them so that you can track specific project income and expenses.

- ❖ First, proceed to your project.
- ❖ Click the Add to project button to create a new transaction.
- ❖ Select Invoice, Receive Payment, Expense, Estimate, Purchase Order, Bill, or Time later.

When you select Add to Project, new items are instantly tagged. The time option allows you to record work done by one of your employees on the same day. If you need to add a weekly timesheet to your project, you must first complete some additional procedures before adding your timesheet. Check out the additional procedures to determine your hourly time charges if you are not utilizing QuickBooks Online Payroll.

- ❖ Navigate to the Projects menu.
- ❖ Select the Hourly cost rate. The hourly cost rate windowpane is displayed here.
- ❖ Click Add next to an employee's name.
- ❖ Now, click the calculator icon to get the hourly cost calculator.
- ❖ Enter your hourly employee pay and business taxes on an hourly basis.
- ❖ You must also account for their additional employer taxes, employee compensation, and overhead.
- ❖ When you've completed the preceding steps, click Add and then Save to add their hourly cost rate.
- ❖ You must repeat these processes for each employee.
- ❖ Now, click on Done.

If you use QuickBooks Online Payroll (Enhanced and Full-Service), follow the instructions below to add a weekly timesheet to your project.

- ❖ Go to Add New and select Weekly Timesheet.
- ❖ Later, select your employee and the week for which you are entering time from the drop-down menus.
- ❖ To select a customer or project, select the project from the drop-down menu. This step associates the timesheet with the project.
- ❖ Fill out the timesheet completely. You can also change an employee's salary rate from normal to other rates as needed before the deadline.
- ❖ If you intend to bill your client for a certain project hour, tick the billable (/ hour) box and modify the billable rate (the price you are charging your customers)

Add existing expenses and timesheets

Step 4: Add existing expenses and timesheets

You can also import costs and timesheets (billable or non-billable) from outside the Projects menu. To add existing expenses and timesheets, follow the instructions below.

- ❖ To begin, go to the Expenses menu.
- ❖ Next, look for the transactions and open them.
- ❖ From the Customer/Project drop-down menu, select the project. Do this for each item you want to tag. It is not the same as the expense payer.
- ❖ Click the Save and Close button.

Add existing timesheets (billable or non billable)

- ❖ To order the list, open the sales menu and click on the Type column.
- ❖ Now, locate the timesheet and open it.
- ❖ Select the project from the drop-down menu under Customer/Project. You must do this for each employee whose time you need to tag.
- ❖ Select the Save and Close option.

Add existing invoices and estimates
Step 5: Add existing invoices and estimates

You may simply produce new invoices for a project, but you should exercise caution while adding current bills.

You may easily generate new invoices for a project, but you must exercise caution while updating current bills.

The best time to add existing invoices to projects is before they are paid. When you add a paid invoice to a project, it is segregated from the related payment. It will also have an impact on the state of the invoice, which may be unpaid. You must re-add payment to avoid mistakenly charging clients twice.

Adding invoices that are associated with more than one transaction, billable expense, or timesheet is not recommended. When you add a linked invoice to a project, only the invoice is added. You must add project-related transactions and link them to the invoice.

Existing forecasts can be added to projects until they are converted into invoices.

Track profitability

Step 6: Monitor profitability

Every project page includes the relevant cost and profitability information ("job costing"). As a result, you can easily track yourself.

Turn off Projects

To disable the Projects function, you must log in with the master admin credentials.

- ❖ First, navigate to Settings and seek for Account and Settings.
- ❖ Next, select the Advanced tab.
- ❖ Locate the Projects section and select Edit to enlarge it.
- ❖ Uncheck the box Organize all job-related activity in one location.
- ❖ Select Done after clicking Save.

Tagging Transactions

Tags are customized labels that allow you to track transactions in whatever way you want. Invoices, costs, and bills can all be labeled. To examine how specific sections of your business are performing, group tags together and run reports. They have no effect on your books. Instead, they allow your team to keep track of the information that is most important to you.

Create Tag group

Step 1: Create Tag group

    1. Begin by organizing tags into groups:

2. Navigate to Settings and then Tags.
3. Select the New dropdown, followed by the Tag group.
4. Give the organization a name.
5. Choose a color from the dropdown menu.
6. When you're finished, click Save.

Assume you own an event planning company. You might want to look at how much money you made and spent on events this year. Make a new group called "events." Then, for specific events, create tags and add them to your events group.

Create new tags and tag transactions

Step 2: Make new tags and tag transactions

While working on a form, such as an invoice or expense, you can add tags:

1. Enter the name of the tag you want to create in the Tags field. Then click + Add.
2. Choose one of the groups and apply the tag to it.

This both creates and tags the tag. Simply put the name of an existing tag in the Tag field and choose it to add it to a form. You can add as many tags as you want, but only one tag per tag group can be selected.

Get insights from tags

Step 3: Get insights from tags

Run tag group reports to see how tagged transactions are performing:

1. Navigate to Bookkeeping or Banking, then Tags.
2. Look through the list for a group.
3. Select Run report from the Action column.

You'll observe how everything in the group affects your bottom line because groups include both money in and money out transactions.

Edit tags and tag groups

1. Navigate to Settings and then Tags.
2. Locate the tag or tag group you want to modify.
3. Click the Run report dropdown in the Action column. Then, choose Edit tag or Edit group.

CHAPTER TWELVE

SYNCHRONIZING WITH FINANCIAL INSTITUTIONS

As you are aware, QuickBook's incredible capabilities and connectors offer a variety of practical solutions for every business accounting software. To handle all of your business payment difficulties, QuickBooks provides a secure payment method. Here, you may instantly link your bank accounts to QuickBooks Online. You can easily keep track of your business payments throughout this, including data and time.

How QuickBooks Online Connects to Your Financial Institution

Using your account information from your financial institution's website, QuickBooks Online establishes a connection with your financial institution. If you'd rather update your accounts and transaction information manually,

Connect Your Online Banking Account

1. Launch a web browser and go to quickbooks.intuit.com to sign into QuickBooks Online.

2. Click Connect an account in the Bank accounts area of the Home screen.

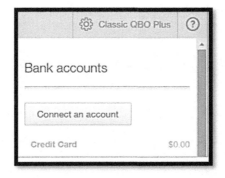

3. Type the name of your bank or the website address for online banking in the Search area. Then click Search or hit Return. The tiny magnifying glass icon to the right of the entry area is for search.

4. The search results will now be listed in QuickBooks Online. This is the filtered list that appeared when we typed "First Bank" in the example.

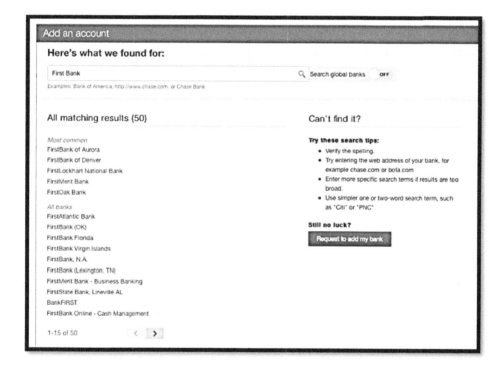

5. In the list of results, click your financial institution. The login screen for your financial institution will appear.

6. After entering your login information to access your bank's online banking, click Log In. QuickBooks will connect securely to your banking institution and display information about your accounts there.

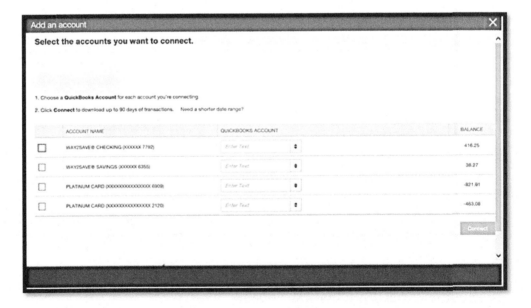

7. Choose the accounts you wish to download, then give each one a specific account type.

8. Click Connect to finish the account setup after selecting your accounts and giving them a type.

Connect bank and credit card accounts to QuickBooks Online

You can save time by using bank feeds or online banking, which eliminates the need for human data entry. The download and categorization of transactions begins as soon as you link your accounts. Simply give them your approval.

Step 1: Connect a bank or credit card account

You can link as many personal and professional accounts as you'd like.

1. Select Bank transactions under Bookkeeping, under Transactions, or under Banking. Choose Connect account
2. If this is your first time setting up a bank account. Or, if you've already created an account, choose Link account.

   Note: For security purposes, if you are switching from QuickBooks Desktop, you must connect your bank and credit card accounts once again.

3. Type the name of your bank, credit card, or credit union in the search field. Note: You can manually upload your bank transactions if you can't find your bank but still want to add your transactions.
4. Choose Continue. then input your user ID and password to log into your bank.
5. Comply with the instructions displayed on the screen. This could involve the security checks that your bank demands. The connection can take a while.
6. Choose the account types from drop-down menu after choosing the accounts you wish to connect. Select the account type in QuickBooks that corresponds to your chart of accounts.

If the appropriate account type isn't displayed in the dropdown,

To add a new bank or credit card account to your chart of accounts, select + Add new.

To create a new bank account,

❖ Choose Bank under Account Type.
❖ Select Savings or Checking under Detail Type.
❖ Type a name for the account, then click Save and close.

To create a new credit card account,

❖ Choose Credit Card under Account Type.
❖ Type a name for the account,
❖ Then click Save and close.

7. Decide how many transactions you wish to download in the past. You can obtain the 90 days' worth of transactions from some banks. Others are able to go back up to 24 months.
8. Choose Connect.

Connect your bank account from your chart of accounts (optional)

1. Click "Bookkeeping," then "Chart of accounts."

2. Locate the account you wish to connect to.
3. Choose View register from the dropdown menu in the Action column. Next, choose Connect bank.
4. Comply with the guidelines displayed on the screen to link your bank to QuickBooks (these steps are same as listed above, starting with step 5).

Step 2: Downloading recent transactions

Transactions are downloaded by QuickBooks so you don't have to manually enter them. To download the most recent transactions, refresh the bank feed.

1. Select Bank transactions under Bookkeeping, Transactions, or Banking.
2. Choose Update.

Categorizing And Matching Online Bank Transactions In QuickBooks Online

The most recent transactions are downloaded by QuickBooks immediately after connecting your bank and credit card accounts. It searches for them and makes an effort to match them up with transactions that you've already put into QuickBooks. If it is unsuccessful in doing so, it makes a new transaction record for you. The match or newly formed transaction only has to be approved.

Note: To save you time and effort, QuickBooks can automatically match transactions performed with QuickBooks Payments.

Step 1: Download latest bank and credit card transactions

Every night at roughly 10 PM PT, QuickBooks downloads the most recent transactions for the majority of banks. Some could require a bit more time. Whenever you want to get the most recent transactions available, you can update your accounts manually:

1. Select Bank transactions under Bookkeeping, under Transactions, or under Banking.
2. Choose Update.

All of your bank and credit card accounts are updated as a result.

Tip: To continue with the update if you receive a warning requesting more authentications, just follow the instructions displayed on the screen. While some banks don't demand it, others do for extra security.

If you are having problem downloading your transactions, follow these steps.

Step 2: **Review and categorize the downloaded transactions**

1. Select Bank transactions under Transactions under Bookkeeping or Banking.
2. Pick the account tile you want to review.
3. To begin your review, click the For review tab.

The For review tab is where QuickBooks sends downloaded transactions. Go over each one in detail.

You can choose to add, match, or view multiple matches for each. Follow the instructions for each option in the section:

Matching with an existing transaction

Match indicates that QuickBooks compared the downloaded transaction to a previously entered one. They are connected by this, preventing duplication.

All you need to do is confirm the match is accurate.

1. Use the Match option in the Action column to locate a downloaded transaction.
2. Make a note of the date, the description, the payee, and the sum paid or received.

3. To widen the display, choose the downloaded transaction.
4. Examine the QuickBooks records that match. This could be the transaction that matches the one you just submitted in QuickBooks.
5. To find out additional information, click the link next to each match.
6. Verify that this is the right match. Check in particular the fields on forms for the existing transaction in QuickBooks that say Deposit to, Payment Method, and Bank account.
7. Close the open transaction if this is the proper match.
8. Choose Match.

Since you already entered the transaction, QuickBooks now recognizes the downloaded transaction as such. It links the two together to prevent duplication. Your job is finished.

Knowing why there are transactions that don't have a match

There are instances where some transactions can't match their records from the past. Here are some potential explanations.

1. The transaction is more than six months old
2. The payees and amounts do not match;
3. The dates do not match or are near.

   Note: Even if you choose the Find match option, you can still equally find a match.

4. There is a multicurrency problem with the exchange rates, or the transaction doesn't pass through the home currency at some specific point.
5. The bank account on the payment is different from the bank where the match is been located.
6. The payment has been reconciled.
7. The transaction has already been matched to another thing.

Confirm paired bank transfers

QuickBooks will trace outgoing and incoming bank transfers among both two of your linked bank accounts by looking for matching transfer amounts and dates.

When you import a transfer into QuickBooks Online, you will be presented with a suggested transaction pairing, which you can accept or reject. If the pairing is approved, it will mark the transaction as evaluated for both streams.

1. Click Transactions under Bookkeeping, then choose Bank transactions. Verify your paired bank transfers as prompted:
   ❖ Choose Record transfer from the Action column to authenticate the pairing.
   ❖ To end the pairing, choose Unpair after selecting the transactions to reveal the information. Next, decide between Categorize and Find match.

To view the settled transactions

1. Click Transactions under Bookkeeping, then choose Bank transactions.
2. Click Categorized, then search the list for the transaction.
3. To examine the transaction information, click Transfer to [...] in the Added or Matched column.

Editing a settled transaction

1. Click Transactions under Bookkeeping, then choose Bank transactions.
2. Click Categorized, then search the list for the transaction.
3. Click Undo in Action column.
4. After returning to the For review tab, the transaction can be examined as usual.

Adding a new transaction

Add signifies the absence of a matching transaction in QuickBooks. Instead, it used the information from your bank or credit card to begin a completely new transaction for you.

All you need to do is confirm there isn't a match and give the task your approval.

1. Use the Add option in Action column to locate a downloaded transaction.
2. To enlarge the screen, choose the transaction.
3. Examine the suggested Category. QuickBooks wants to classify the transaction under this account. For instance, QuickBooks would advise classifying a petrol expense under travel expenses. The category and the account can both be changed at any time.
4. If necessary, switch the supplier or client.

   Tip: Choose the Find match option if you believe that you have previously input this transaction into QuickBooks. Look over the list of potential matches, and if you discover one, choose it.

5. Examine and include any additional information that might be required or omitted.
6. When everything is in order, choose Add.

In order to create and add a new transaction to your accounts, QuickBooks utilizes this information.

It should be noted that QuickBooks occasionally classifies transactions into the Unrelated Income and Unrelated Expense accounts. These accounts are transient. Always classify transactions into revenue or spending accounts directly, if at all possible.

View and review multiple matches

View denotes that QuickBooks discovered multiple candidate matches. Simply choose the appropriate one, and you're done.

1. Use the View option in the Action column to locate a downloaded transaction.
2. Choose View.
3. Examine the QuickBooks records that match. The potential matching transactions that you've already inputted in QuickBooks are listed here.
4. To find out additional information, click the link next to each of the match.
5. Verify that one of these matches. Check in particular the fields on forms for the existing transactions in QuickBooks, such as Deposit to, Payment method, or Bank account.

   Note: Depending on the transaction you are actually matching, the fields you see may change.

6. Evaluate the possible matches.
7. Once the right match is made, finish the open transactions.
8. Choose the right match, then click "Match."

Viewing images for check transactions

For every check transactions that are awaiting approval, QuickBooks has worked with a number of institutions to automatically provide front and back check photos. This may facilitate the examination and comparison of transactions.

The check images load immediately if QuickBooks is already linked to a participating bank; further action is not necessary.

To view the check images

1. Choose a downloaded transaction with a particular number in the Attachment field from the For Review tab.

2. To view a picture, choose one of the check image attachments in the transaction information.
3. You can inspect the front and back of the check in the picture panel that opens and extend it to fill the entire screen.
4. Examine the exchange as usual. Images can be found later in your Attachments list under Settings if you match or add the transaction.

Notes:

❖ Your bank is not supported if associated bank transactions don't have check images attached automatically. However, as it is seek to collaborate with some other financial institutions, it might be supported in the future.
❖ Verify if images are incompatible with multi-currency enabled.

Step 3: Reviewing matched or added transactions

The downloaded transactions are entered into QuickBooks after you have match or add them. In the Categorized or Reviewed tab, you can check your work to make sure everything is in order.

After your review, it's a good to briefly check this.

1. Select Bank transactions under Transactions under Bookkeeping or Banking.
2. Pick the account tile you are to review.
3. Select the Reviewed or Categorized tab.
4. To review the transaction, click the link right in the Added or Matched column.

Follow these instructions to undo or unmatch a transaction if you need to alter it or move it to another account. Prior to your monthly reconciliations, make all necessary revisions.

Splitting transactions between multiple accounts

For easier tracking, you might divide transactions between different accounts, such as a big business travel bill.

1. Navigate to the For review tab.
2. To widen the view, choose the downloaded transaction.
3. If the Action column's Match option is selected, change the Find match option to Categorize.
4. Close to the Add button, choose Split.

This will opens the Split transaction window

1. Choose the categories (the accounts) you want to divide the transaction into from the Category selection.
2. Fill out a sum for each split.
3. Pick a client for every split.
4. When finished, choose Apply and accept.

Excluding personal or duplicate transactions

To maintain the accuracy of your accounts, exclude personal or duplicate transactions:

1. Navigate to the For review tab.
2. Check the box next to each transaction you want to Exclude.
3. Choose Exclude.

The Excluded tab is where excluded transactions are moved. They won't be re-downloaded or added to QuickBooks.

Opening Text files In Microsoft Excel Or Google Sheet

Open text file in Excel

1. Click File > Open > Browse on the Ribbon, then choose the text or CSV file you want to open.

   The first of three steps in the Text Import Wizard is displayed.

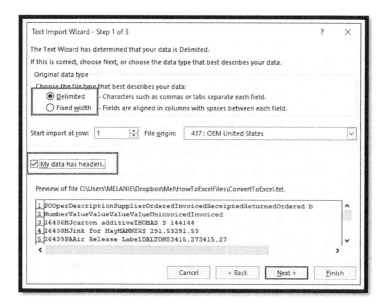

2. You have the option of selecting Delimited or Fixed Width as the file type, relying on the data that the selected file contains. Select Delimited if the data is delimited by a character such as a comma, semicolon, space, or tab. Check the box labeled My data has headers if the first row of the data contains column headings.

3. Press Next.

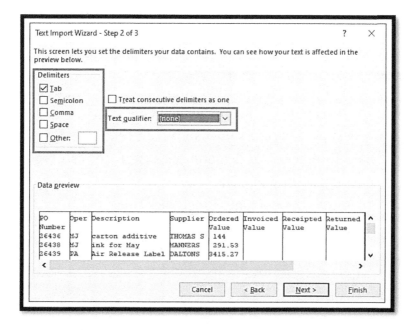

4. In Step 2, choose the text file's tab delimiter as the type of delimiters to use. choose the text qualifier next. Although the text qualifier for this example is (none), in some circumstances the data may be encased in quotations.

5. Press Next.

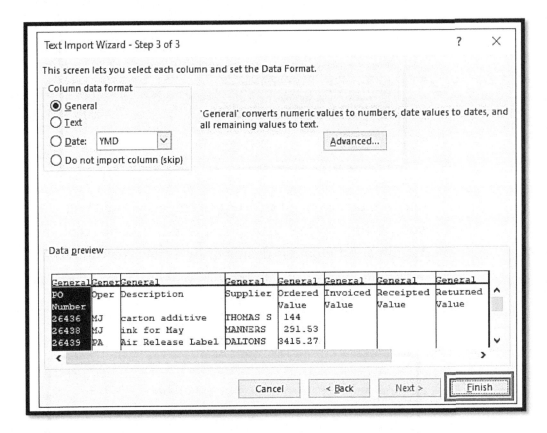

6. You can actually specify the data type present in each column in the text import wizard's final step. You can leave the selected Column data format set to General because Excel can typically detect the data type automatically.

7. To import the data into Excel, click Finish.

	A	B	C	D	E	F	G	H	I	J
1	PO	Oper	Descriptic	Supplier	Ordered	Invoiced	Receiptec	Returned	Ordered l	Rcpted less
2	Number				Value	Value	Value	Value	Uninvoice	Invoiced
3	26436	MJ	carton ad	THOMAS S	144				144	
4	26438	MJ	ink for Ma	MANNERS	291.53				291.53	
5	26439	PA	Air Releas	DALTONS	3415.27				3415.27	
6	26440	MJ	Engineeri	ATTWOOD	2525.89	1936.77	1956.96		589.12	20.19
7	26442	MJ	F1 belting	GGC LTD	609.94				609.94	
8	26444	PA	Eatlight p	STEVENS	196.87	234.1	196.87			-37.23
9	26445	MJ	Methylate	sOCI(NZ)	457.38	457.38	457.38			
10	26450	MJ	"3/4"" BS	SGB LTD	300.15	300.15	300.15			
11	26451	MJ	Waste and	WATER IS	6537	6537	6537			
12	26453	DJ	Freight	FREIGHT 4	21.9	21.9	21.9			
13	26454	DP	plant hire	HIRE PLAN	60.94	60.94	60.94			
14	26455	DP	frame by	FRAMERS	1217.25	1217.25	1217.25			
15	26456	MJ	Aluminum	BENNETS	91.91	91.91	91.91			
16	26457	DP	photocopi	COPYCENT	292.5	292.5	292.5			
17	26460	SB	May clean	S ALLY	4837.5	4837.5	4837.5			
18	26462	DP	phone acc	TELECOM	40.77	40.77	40.77			
19	26463	DP	phone acc	TELECOM	201.46	201.47	201.46			-0.01
20	26466	DP	Pager	TELECOM	19.12	19.13	19.12			-0.01
21	26467	DP	Mobile	TELECOM	78.78		78.78		78.78	78.78

Import text file using Get data

Utilizing the Get and Transform Data tool is an alternative method of importing data into Excel from a text file.

1. Click Data > Get and Transform Data > From Text/CSV in the Ribbon.

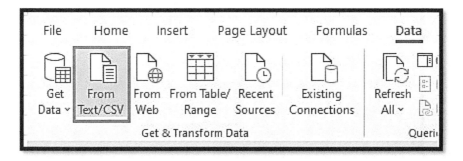

2. Click Import after choosing the file to import.
3. The file is displayed in a dialog box with the delimiter already chosen and the text broken into sections by Excel based on the information contained in the text file. To import the data into Excel, click Load.

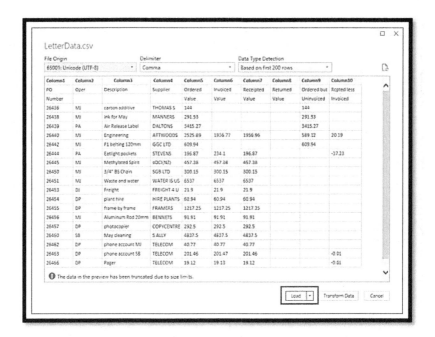

The data is now visible in a new Excel sheet. Table Design and Query, two new tabs on the Ribbon, as well as a Queries & Connections pane showing on the right side of the screen, are now available. As a result, if any information in the TXT file were to change (externally to Excel), the data presented in Excel would also change.

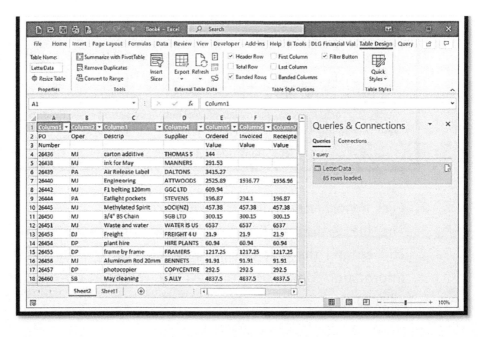

4. In the Ribbon, choose Table Design > External Table Data > Unlink to remove the link between the imported data and the external TXT file.

5. A table of the data is imported into Excel. Select Table Design > Tools > Convert to Range from the Ribbon to change it into a typical Excel range.

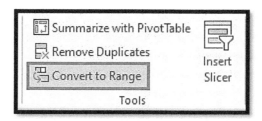

The Ribbon's Table Design and Query tabs vanish together.

Open text file in Google sheets

1. Click Import in Google Sheets' File menu.

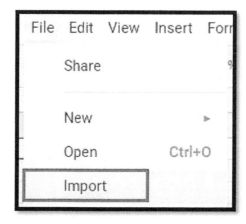

2. Select the necessary file by clicking Upload, followed by the blue Select a file from your device button.

The default parameters for importing are automatically selected when the name of the file to be imported is displayed under File.

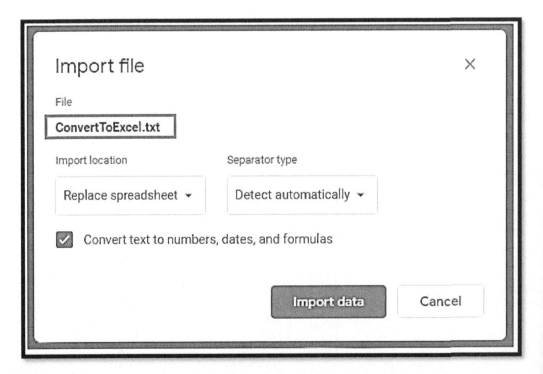

3. Select the appropriate choice from the drop-down list under Import Location to alter the import location.

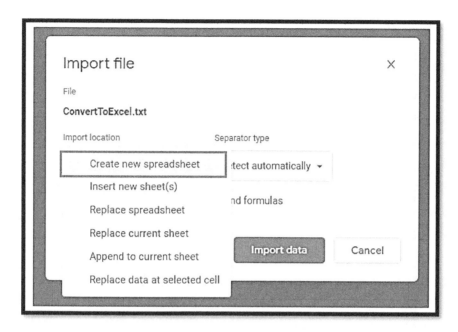

Select a character to distinguish by from the drop-down list on the right to modify the separator type.

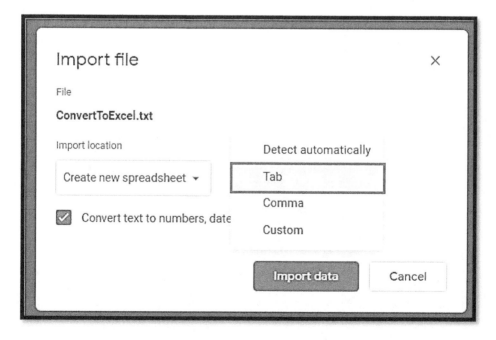

4. Keep To import the file into a new Google sheet, choose the checkboxes next to Convert text to numbers, dates, and formulas, and then click Import Data.

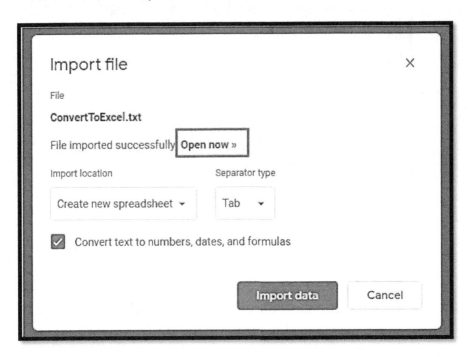

5. Select "Open now."

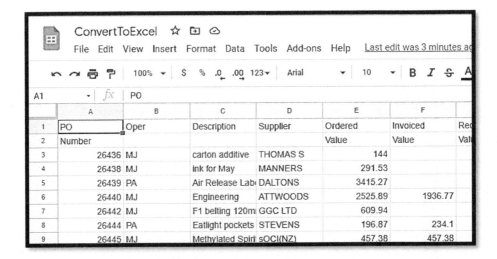

PART 2: BUDGETING, REPORTING AND ANALYSIS

CHAPTER THIRTEEN

CREATING BUDGETS IN QUICKBOOKS

A budget is a spending and revenue plan. It might offer you a sense of how your financial condition will evolve over time. It can also assist you in setting objectives and determining why you reached, exceeded, or failed to meet them.

Budgets are used by many firms to make reasonable guesses about how their finances will look in the following months or years. This is accomplished by reviewing the business's income and expenses for the previous month, quarter, or year in order to develop a budget for the coming year.

This section will guide you how to establish a budget for your company using QuickBooks data. Will also guide you on how to analyze and amend your budget, as well as generate reports that compare your actual income and expenses to your budget.

Creating A Budget

To begin, you must have the appropriate subscription level, either Advanced or Plus. You can upgrade if you don't already have this subscription level. To upgrade, go to Account and Settings under the Your Company heading after clicking the gear-shaped Settings symbol in the Header. Locate the Usage tab and scroll to the bottom to find an Upgrade Now button.

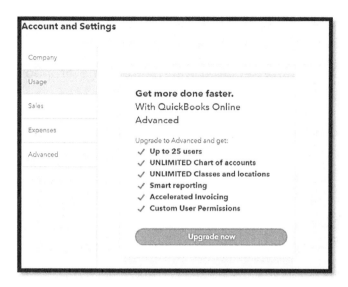

You are to log in as an administrator in addition to having the relevant subscription level. To check your user status, go to the gear-shaped Settings icon and select Manage Users. There, you may observe administrators and, if necessary, add a new user.

A budget can be created at any moment, but the optimal time is at the start of your fiscal year. You may view your first month of the year by navigating to Account and Settings under the Your Company heading after selecting on the gear-shaped Settings icon in the Header.

Navigate to the Accounting area at the top of the Advanced tab. Check the month you have set aside for the first month of the fiscal year. You may alter the date by clicking the pencil-shaped Edit icon.

Step 1: Examine your company's fiscal year.

Check that the start of your fiscal year is right in QuickBooks. A budget can be created at any time, although it is best to begin at the start of the fiscal year.

1. Navigate to Settings and then Account and settings.
2. Go to the Advanced tab.

3. Examine the First month of fiscal year field in the Accounting section. If it is inaccurate, click Edit.
4. Choose the required month from the dropdown menu and click Save.

Step 2: Get your budget data

You can skip this step if you already have the data you wish to use for your budget. If not, you can actually base your budget on data from either the current or previous fiscal year. If you intend to use past data, run a Profit and Loss Detailed report to ensure that all transactions and accounts appear to be correct.

The report can be run as follows:

1. Locate and open the Profit and Loss Detail report.
2. Select a timeframe from the Report Period selection. Select Last Year, for example, if you wish to use data from the prior year. Select This Year-to-date if you wish to use data from your current fiscal year.
3. Check that the beginning and finish of the year correspond to your fiscal year.
4. Choose Run report.
5. If you don't want to revisit the report, click the print or export icon to print or download a copy.

Create your budget using this information as a guide.

Step 3: Create your budget

You can construct a budget from scratch or duplicate an previous one's. If this is your first budget, you can start here, then when you've added your first budget, you will see how to clone a budget.

If you have QuickBooks Online Advanced membership, you may also import a.csv file to generate a budget.

Please keep in mind that QuickBooks Online generates the budget accounts list directly from your chart of accounts. If your budget requires extra accounts, add them to the chart of accounts before creating the budget.

1. Navigate to Settings and then Budgeting.
2. Choose Add budget.
3. Give the budget a name in the Name column.
4. Select the fiscal year for which you are constructing the budget from the Fiscal Year menu.
5. Choose whether you want the budget to display monthly, quarterly, or annually from the Interval dropdown.
6. If you want QuickBooks to prefill your budget with actual data from the chart of accounts, select the actual date year from the Pre-fill data? dropdown.

   Please keep in mind that if you utilize the pre-fill data and then change your mind, you will have to start anew to delete the data. Select the X to close the budget and begin over.

7. Make use of the Subdivide by dropdown to further subdivide the budget.
8. When you're finished, click Next or Create Budget.
9. Enter your monthly budget for each account. If necessary, go to the report you saved in Step 2.
10. When you're through with your budget, choose Save or Save and close.

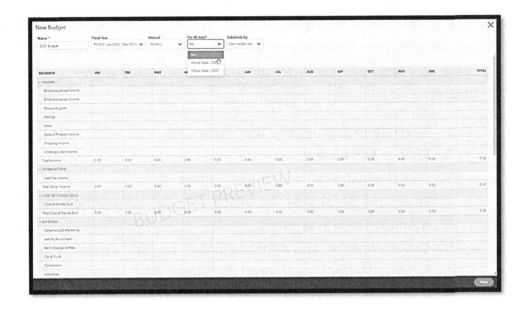

Copy and existing budget

You can make a duplicate of an existing budget instead of beginning from scratch. This kickstarts your new budget by utilising data from the previous year. Here's how to duplicate a budget:

1. Go to Settings and then Budgeting.
2. Locate the budget you want to replicate.
3. In the Action column, select the option, then Copy.
4. Enter the new budget name and fiscal year on the Copy Budget screen.
5. Click Create Budget.
6. Adjust the budget amounts as needed.
7. Choose Save or Save and close.

This copies the budget and saves it as a new budget.

Upload a budget in the form of a.csv file (Advanced only)

You can import your budget from a.csv file into QuickBooks Online Advanced. If you've never created a budget before, you must first create one (which can be blank) before you can see the.csv import option. Here's how to make a budget from a.csv file:

Step 1: Create a new budget.

You can skip this part if you've previously generated a budget.

1. Navigate to Settings and then Budgeting.
2. Choose Add budget.
3. Give the budget a name in the Name column. (This budget can be deleted later.)
4. Click Next.
5. Choose Save or Save and close.

Step 2: Download a budget template.

Download a budget.csv template now that you've make your first budget. QuickBooks formats the template based on the chart of accounts and fiscal year months. The template can then be used to generate your budget, ensuring that your data is compatible and imports without issues.

1. Go to Settings and pick Budgeting if you aren't already there.
2. Select Budget Import.
3. Click the Sample.csv link to get the template.
4. Save the file somewhere you can readily find it, such as your computer's downloads folder.

Step 3: Create your budget using the template

1. Launch Excel or Google Sheets and open the.csv budget template.
2. Enter your budget for each account for the entire month.

   Important: Do not add any additional columns or rows. If you require additional accounts, add them to your chart of accounts before downloading the template.

3. When you're done, save your modifications.

Step 4: Upload your template.

When you're done, re-import your budget into QuickBooks:

1. Navigate to Settings and then Budgeting.
2. Select Budget Import.
3. Click Browse, then locate and open the template.
4. Click Next.
5. Your budget is now in QuickBooks. Perform a short review.
6. Give your budget a name in the Name area.
7. Examine the cells. Check that the proper amounts are in each account. If you need to make adjustments, choose a field and make your modifications.
8. When you're done, choose Save or Save and close to save your budget.

Edit A Budget

If you need to make modifications to a budget, do so in QuickBooks:

1. Navigate to Settings and then Budgeting.
2. Locate your budget on the list.
3. Select Edit from the Action column.
4. Make changes to each account one month at a time.
5. Select the Gear at the top of the budget to change the time period from monthly to quarterly or yearly. Then choose Quarter or Year.
6. Choose Save or Save and close.

Delete A Budget

Be cautious if you decide to eliminate a budget. Budgets that have been deleted cannot be recovered.

1. Navigate to Settings and then Budgeting.
2. Locate your budget on the list.
3. In Action column, choose the Edit dropdown and then click Delete.

Create Budget Reports

You can run special budget reports to keep track of your budget objectives.

1. Navigate to Settings and then Budgeting.
2. Locate your budget on the list.
3. In Action column, choose Edit, then Run Budget Overview report or Run Budgets vs. Actuals report.

CHAPTER FOURTEEN

ULTILIZING QUICKBOOKS REPORT

When running a business, you'll want a simple way to keep track of how things are progressing. This can be accomplished by running reports. You can run reports on any data that QuickBooks Online stores for you.

QuickBooks Online makes it simple to build management reports in addition to quick reports. This is a collection of additional reports for particular managerial analysis, and they are put together in a professional manner suitable for passing on to other parties.

The Reports Page

Click on the Reports menu option in the left-side Navigation Pane to begin using reports. You'll see that the Reports page is divided into three tabs: Standard, Custom, and Management Reports.

All of the usual reports are split into distinct parts on the Standard tab. The Favorites section is located at the top of the Standard page. Any report that you start by clicking the start button will display here.

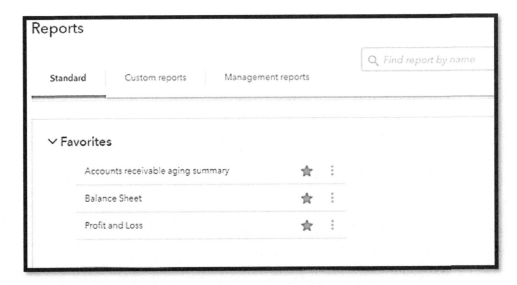

Following the Favorites section, you will see a list of all the reports made available to you based on your subscription level and whether you have extra services, such as Payroll, enrolled in. To discover more about any report, hover your cursor over the question mark icon that shows when you roll your mouse over its name.

Finding The Report You Want

Business Overview

Directly below the Favorites section, you will see the Business Overview section. This contains reports such as:

- ❖ Audit Log
- ❖ Balance Sheet Comparison
- ❖ Balance Sheet Detail
- ❖ Business Snapshot
- ❖ Profit and Loss Detail
- ❖ Profit and Loss Year-to-Date Comparison
- ❖ Profit and Loss by Customer
- ❖ Profit and Loss by Month
- ❖ Profit and Loss
- ❖ Quarterly Profit and Loss Summary
- ❖ Statement of Cash Flows

If you have created a budget and have the correct subscription level, you will also have Budget Overview and Budget vs. Actuals here.

Who Owes You

After the Business Overview section is the Who Owes You section. Here you will see charts such as:

- ❖ Accounts Receivable Aging Summary
- ❖ Collections Report

- ❖ Customer Balance Detail
- ❖ Customer Balance Summary
- ❖ Invoice List
- ❖ Invoices and Received Payments
- ❖ Open Invoices
- ❖ Statement List
- ❖ Terms List
- ❖ Unbilled Charges
- ❖ Unbilled Time

Sales and Customers

After the Who Owes You section follows the Sales and Customers section. You will actually find reports for:

- ❖ Customer Contact List
- ❖ Deposit Detail
- ❖ Estimates & Progress Invoicing Summary by Customer
- ❖ Estimates by Customer
- ❖ Income by Customer Summary
- ❖ Inventory Valuation Detail
- ❖ Inventory Valuation Summary
- ❖ Payment Method List
- ❖ Physical Inventory Worksheet
- ❖ Product/Service List
- ❖ Sales by Customer Detail
- ❖ Sales by Customer Summary
- ❖ Sales by Customer Type Detail
- ❖ Sales by Product/Service Detail
- ❖ Sales by Product/Service Summary
- ❖ Time Activities by Customer Detail
- ❖ Transaction List by Customer
- ❖ Transaction List by Tag Group

What You Owe

The next section is called What You Owe. The reports here include:

- ❖ 1099 Contractor Balance Detail
- ❖ 1099 Contractor Balance Summary
- ❖ Accounts Payable Aging Detail
- ❖ Accounts Payable Aging Summary
- ❖ Bill Payment List
- ❖ Bills and Applied Payments
- ❖ Unpaid Bills
- ❖ Vendor Balance Detail
- ❖ Vendor Balance Summary

Expenses and Vendors

The following section is for Expenses and Vendors. The reports here include:

- ❖ 1099 Transaction Detail Report
- ❖ Check Detail
- ❖ Expenses by Vendor Summary
- ❖ Open Purchase Order List
- ❖ Open Purchase Order Detail
- ❖ Purchases by Product/Service Detail
- ❖ Purchases by Vendor Detail
- ❖ Transaction List by Vendor
- ❖ Vendor Contact List

Sales Tax

The Sales Tax section has reports that include:

- ❖ Sales Tax Liability Report
- ❖ Taxable Sales Detail
- ❖ Taxable Sales Summary

Employees

The Employees section has reports for:

- ❖ Employee Contact List
- ❖ Recent/Edited Time Activities
- ❖ Time Activities by Employee Detail

For My Accountant

The next section is For My Accountant. You can find reports like:

- ❖ Account List
- ❖ Balance Sheet Comparison
- ❖ Balance Sheet
- ❖ General Ledger
- ❖ Journal
- ❖ Profit and Loss Comparison
- ❖ Profit and Loss by Tag Group
- ❖ Profit and Loss
- ❖ Recent Automatic Transactions
- ❖ Recent Transactions
- ❖ Reconciliation Reports
- ❖ Recurring Template List
- ❖ Statement of Cash Flows
- ❖ Transaction Detail by Account
- ❖ Transaction List by Date
- ❖ Transaction List with Splits
- ❖ Trial Balance

Payroll

The final category is Payroll. You can find reports such as:

- ❖ Employee Contact List
- ❖ Recent/Edited Time Activities
- ❖ Time Activities by Employee Detail

Examining standard reports

You can now begin studying QuickBooks' reports now that you've seen them. Click on the title of any report to begin viewing it. You may also look for a specific report by typing a portion of its name into the search bar. When it appears in the search results, click on it to access the report.

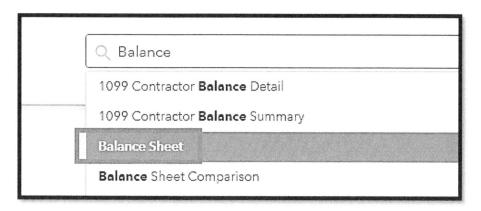

When you click on the report, it will open in a new window. The top section of the window allows you to personalize the report, while the bottom section displays the actual report.

Customizing a Report

The default versions of each report you examine may not contain the exact information you want. Alternatively, they may be too complex for the audience to which you must present the report.

To overcome this, you can tailor a report to your preferences. You can first set the Report Period at the top of the report's screen. You can select from predefined time periods or enter the dates yourself.

This Year-to-Date is the default time period. Other predefined report periods are: All Dates, Today, This Week, This Week-to-Date, This Month, This Month-to-Date, This Quarter, This Quarter-to-Date, This Year, This Year-to-Date, This Year-to-Last-Month, Yesterday, Recent, Last Week, Last Week-to-Date, Last Month, Last Month-to-Date, Last Quarter, Last Quarter-to-Date, Last Year, Last Year-to-Date, Since 30 Days Ago, Since

The dropdown arrow behind the Save Customization button allows you to expand or collapse the top customization menu. More options are visible when the window is extended.

The extra options available here will vary based on the type of report you run. You can often modify how columns are displayed by, whether columns or rows are displayed without values, whether to compare to another time period, and whether to employ a cash or accrual accounting technique. After making your changes, click the Run Report button to view the revised report. You can also modify the resulting report. A menu bar directly above the report changes depending on the type of report generated.

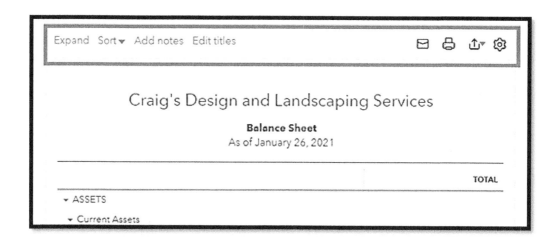

The first option is to expand or collapse the report. If your report is overly long, this will delete certain layers of detail. You can test this to determine if it removes too much important information.

You can also customize how the report's information is organized. The methods for sorting data vary depending on the type of report. You can also choose whether to sort in ascending or descending order.

When you click the Write Notes text, a text box at the bottom of the form will appear where you can add unique notes regarding the report.

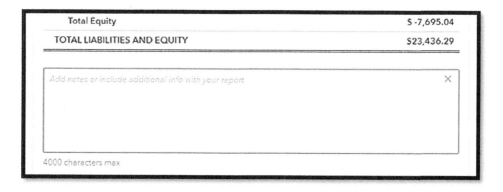

You can also edit the titles in the report. By clicking the Alter Titles link, you will be sent to a window where you can edit each title in the report.

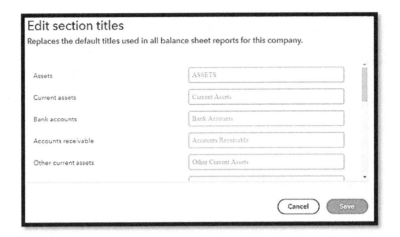

The business name and report title can also be edited by clicking on the pencil icon that appears when you hover over them on the report.

You can also email, print, save, or change settings using the four icons in the upper right. It will use the report as you see it when you email, print, or save it. As a result, if you expanded or collapsed a section by clicking on one of the section's dropdown arrows, it will use that view when completing the operation.

The options icon allows you to customize various display settings dependent on the sort of report you've created. You can modify the visible columns and the display density to conserve space, for example.

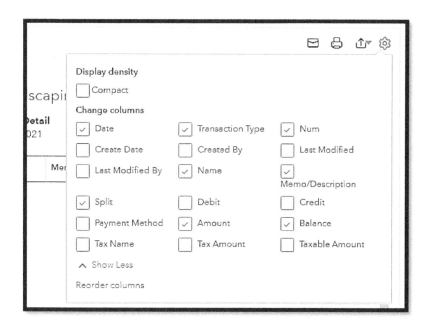

On some reports, you can as well reorder columns. When you click this link, a side panel will appear where you may drag and drop to reorder the columns.

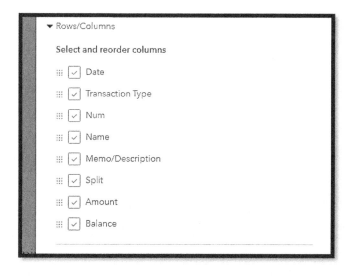

In addition to all of the options we've seen to customize, you can customize even more by selecting the Customize link at the top. This will bring up a screen with further customization options. There are four types of options: General, Rows/Columns, Filter, and Header/Footer.

Many of the same options exist in the General category in terms of time periods and accounting technique. You can also select number formats such as dividing by 1000, not including cents, and how to display negative numbers. Negative numbers can be shown with the negative sign before or after the number, or in parentheses.

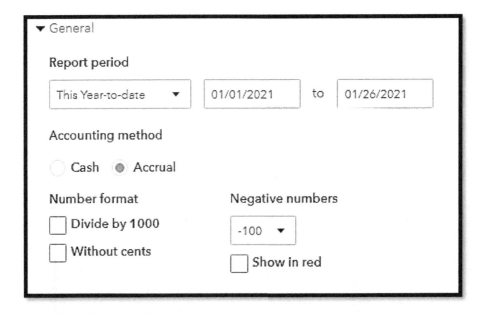

In the Rows/Columns section, you can specify which rows and columns are visible and in what order. This is the same option that showed previously when you clicked on the gear-shaped settings symbol above the report and then on Reorder Columns.

You can choose which data to filter out in the Filter category based on the type of data in your report. Check the boxes next to the fields you want to appear in your final report.

You can edit the header and footer information in the final category. It comprises both the data and the text alignment.

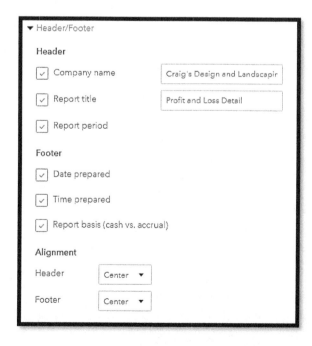

When you're done tweaking, select the Run Report button at the bottom to rerun the report.

Saving a customized report

After you've completed all of your tweaks, you may save them so you don't have to recreate them to get your settings back. Click the Save Customization button next to the Customize button to do so. A popup will appear with several saving options.

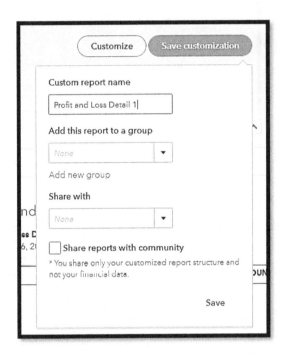

In this window, you can give the report a name and organize it into a group. To create new groups, click the Add New Group button. You can also make your settings available to others. To save the customized report, click the Save button.

Viewing a Customized Report

Return to the Reports page and select the Custom Reports tab to view the newly created customized report. The table will be empty if you haven't yet built a customized report. If you have previously saved a customized report, it will be visible in the table.

The table has fields for the report name, creator, date range, when it is emailed, and an action column for completing operations. The Action column has an edit function as well as a dropdown menu that allows you to export the custom report as a PDF, Excel, or delete it.

By clicking on the name of the customized report, you can view it.

Editing and Scheduling a Customized Email Report

By selecting the Edit link in the Action column, you can alter the name of the report, add it to a group, share it with others, or create an email schedule.

Toggling the Set Email Schedule switch opens a form where you may schedule when the report will be emailed. The recurrence can be adjusted to daily, weekly, monthly, or twice a month. You can also specify when and how often the emails should be sent.

You can specify the recipients and write a customized title and message text in the Email Information section. Check the box at the bottom to attach the report as an Excel file as well.

When you're finished, go to the bottom and click the Save and Close button. When you get back to the Custom Report page, you will notice a timetable in the Email column.

Reviewing management reports

Management Reports is the third tab on the Reports page. The set includes three predefined reports: Company Overview, Sales Performance, and Expenses Performance. Each of these reports is a collection of other reports that are presented professionally with a cover page and table of contents.

The Profit and Loss report and the Balance Sheet report are included in the Company Overview management report.

The Profit and Loss report, Accounts Receivable Aging Detail Report, and Sales by Customer Summary report are all part of the Sales Performance management report.

The Profit and Loss report, the A/P Aging Detail report, and the Expenses by Vendor Summary report comprise the Expenses Performance management report.

When you click the View link in the Action column, you'll be sent to a Print Preview screen where you can see how the report will look. Other options in the Action column dropdown include editing, sending, exporting as PDF, exporting as DOCX, and copying.

Customizing Management Reports

To edit a management report, select Edit from the Action column dropdown. This will launch a new form in which you can modify various components of the report. Customization options include the cover page, table of contents, preliminary pages, reports, and end notes.

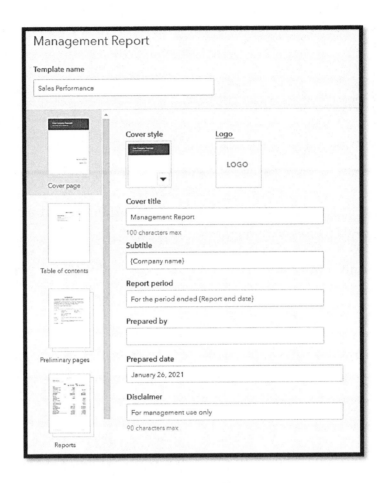

You can choose from four different cover page styles and insert your company's logo. The cover title, subtitle, report period, who prepared it, when it was prepared, and a disclaimer are all changeable. Variables supplied by QuickBooks Online, such as Company name, are denoted by curly brackets.

You may enable or disable the table of contents by using the checkbox at the top. You can also choose to change the name of your table of contents.

You can add some extra pages to your report in the preliminary pages. A text editor displays here, allowing you to format the pages you want to include.

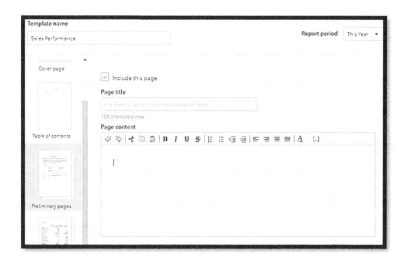

You can make some changes to the data shown in each report in the reports section. Change the title, period, and whether to compare with the preceding period or year by clicking on the pencil-shaped edit icon, depending on the type of report. By clicking the trash can-shaped icon, you can also remove the selected report from the management report.

By selecting the Add New Report option at the bottom of the screen, you can add new reports to this management report. This will add a new row with a dropdown menu where you can select your report.

The final category is for adding closing remarks. You can choose whether or not to include this page here. You can also provide breakdowns of line item sub-accounts. In the text editor window, you can also create a page title and fill in the page content.

After you've completed creating your management report, you may do a few things with it using the buttons at the bottom of the page. The Print or Preview button at the bottom allows you to preview and print. If everything is right, the report will load as a PDF for printing.

There is an Advanced button at the bottom where you can configure a few more options. Clicking this will open a window with fields that you can place into your header or footer. Fields are variables that are surrounded by curly braces. By default, the fields available are Company name and Report end date.

Finally, click the Save and Close button to create your management report. Your new management report will be shown in the table's Management Reports tab.

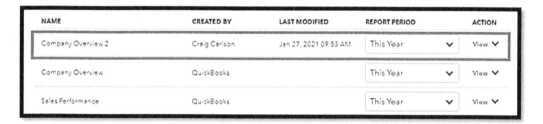

Printing A Report

QuickBooks' most lauded feature is reporting. In QB, users can produce various financial statements and reports. Users can generate profit and loss statements, cash flow statements, and much more with a single click. Let's get started with "Printing Reports in QuickBooks PRO and Enterprise."

To print reports in QuickBooks, follow the steps outlined below.

1. From Reports, navigate to the Reports Center window.
2. Choose the correct report.

3. You can effortlessly tag and search certain reports using the program's new Smart Search feature.
4. Select the print option when you click on the report.
5. Select Printer under Print to.
6. Choose the name of your printer from the drop-down menu.
7. Users can also store reports as pdf files for a backup copy.
8. Select "ASCII text file" from the File menu.
9. Choose the orientation in which the report should be printed.
10. It is advisable to produce a landscape printout of graphs and tables when producing presentations.
11. To acquire a complete hardcopy of your reports, select All.
12. Make sure your printer has extra paper.
13. Choose "Smart Page Breaks."
14. Choose Fit report and enter the number of pages you want the report to print on.
15. Select "Print in Color (Color Printers Only)" if you want a color printing.
16. Select Preview. Make changes in accordance with your needs.
17. Select print.

Users who want to save the report as a pdf can use QuickBooks' built-in pdf generator. During the presentation, reports in pdf format might be used. This is also an excellent format for providing reports via email.

Reports that QuickBooks users can generate

- ❖ Trial Balance
- ❖ Profit and Loss Statement
- ❖ Invoice List
- ❖ Account Payable Detail/ Summary
- ❖ Vendor Balance Summary
- ❖ Balance Sheet detailed/summary
- ❖ Profit and loss details
- ❖ Audit Log

❖ Customer Balance Summary
❖ Accounts Receivable Detail/ Summary

The amount of reports that QuickBooks users can generate is not limited to this list. Users can also construct a custom filter to generate a completely customized report template. This template can then be applied to reports as they run. One of the most essential features of QuickBooks reporting is the ability to generate multiple printouts with a single click.

Customizing Report

QuickBooks' financial reports provide you with a wealth of useful information about your company. Your reports can be customized in a variety of ways. You can filter them to display only certain accounts or clients, or you can format the layout so that the appropriate data appears where it should. Here's how to tailor reports so that they highlight the information that's most important to you.

Run a report

Step 1: Run a report.

1. Click Reports under Business overview, or simply click Reports.
2. Locate and launch a report. Advice: "Detail" versions of standard reports can be run if you have QuickBooks Online Essentials, Plus, or Advanced.
3. To change details like the report dates, use the report's basic filters.
4. Click on Customize.

The customization window is then displayed.

Customize a report

Step 2: Customize a report

Multiple filters can be used to customize your report. The same set of filters are used in most reports. Only certain reports can use certain filters.

Here is a list of the options you have:

- ❖ **General section:** Modify the number format, reporting period, and accounting method in the general section.
- ❖ **Rows/Columns section:** Select which rows and columns will show on the report in the Rows/Columns section.
- ❖ **Filter section:** Choose which clients, distribution accounts, suppliers, clients, accounts, and products should be included in the report.
- ❖ **Header/Footer section:** Select the information that go there.

Save custom reports

When you've found the ideal combination of filters, save them so you can run the same report later.

1. Choose Save customization after customizing a report.
2. Give your document a title.
3. Choose Save.

Example of custom reports

1. Choose the Filter icon located in the Customization window.
2. Pick a distribution account from the dropdown menu.
3. To include certain accounts in the report, check the appropriate boxes.

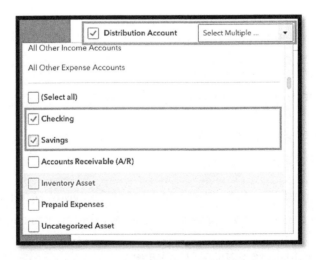

4. Select Run report when you are prepared.

View all accounts by type

Instead of individual accounts, you might group them by type, such as assets or accounts payable.

1. Click the Filter icon in the Customization box.
2. Select one of the All selections from the Distribution Account dropdown, such as All Asset Accounts.

3. When you're ready, click Run report.

Display certain clients, providers, products, or services.

1. Click the Filter icon in the Customization box.
2. Choose the consumers, vendors, and products and services to include in your report.

3. When you're done, click Run report.

Filter everything by class or location

You can filter report columns by class or location if classes and locations are enabled.

1. Click the Rows/Columns icon in the Customization box.
2. Choose either Classes or Locations from the Columns dropdown.

3. When you're ready, click Run report.

Manage and automate custom report

Step 3: Manage and automate custom report

1. Click Reports under Business overview, or simply click Reports.
2. Choose the tab for custom reports.
3. Locate a report and open it.

Automate custom reports

Schedule them to run automatically if you want custom reports on a regular basis:

1. Click Reports under Business overview, or simply click Reports. After that, choose the Custom reports tab.
2. Select your unique report from the list.
3. From the Action column, choose Edit.
4. To enable it, click Set email schedule.
5. Include the emails of the recipients to whom you want to send the report.
6. Complete the form and make the appointment.
7. Choose Save and then close.

Display customized reports for a specific groups

Additionally, you can add reports to a group to restrict access to them.

1. Choose Save customization after creating a custom report.
2. Pick a group from the Add this report to a group dropdown menu.
3. To include the report in the group, choose Save.
4. Select the Reports option. After that, choose the Custom reports tab.
5. Locate the team on the list.
6. From Action column, choose Edit.
7. To activate it, choose the Set email schedule option.

8. Include the email addresses of the recipients to whom you want to send the report.
9. Complete the form and make the appointment.
10. Choose Save and then close.

Delete custom report from a group's.

Additionally, reports from a group may be deleted.

1. Click Reports under Business overview, or just click Reports. After that, choose the Custom reports tab.
2. On the list, locate the group.
3. For the report you want to delete, choose Edit from the Action column.
4. Choose Yes and Delete.

Note: QuickBooks Online Simple Start does not offer this feature.

Export a custom report in Excel or PDF format.

A customized report can be exported in Excel or PDF format.

1. Select Reports from the Business Overview menu, or simply go to Reports. After that, choose the Custom reports tab.
2. On the list, locate the customized report.
3. To edit the report you want to export, choose Edit in the Action column.
4. Choose Export As Excel or Export As PDF.

The report can be downloaded as a pdf or excel file.

Share custom reports

Step 4: Share custom reports

Reports in PDF format can be quickly shared via email. The simplest way to inform your team is as follows:

1. Click the email icon on a report that is open.

2. Choose Email.
3. Complete the form.
4. Edit the body message to make it clear what to expect to the audience.
5. When you are prepared, choose Send.

Sharing report in excel format

Share edit access with team members

Giving other file users complete access to edit customized reports is possible if you:

1. On a report that is open, click Save customization.
2. From the Share with dropdown option, choose a user.
3. When you are prepared, choose Save.

Share reports only once, please. Duplicate reports could be produced if the same report is shared with users who already have access multiple times.

Exporting Reports From Quickbooks

Exporting to Excel

QuickBooks is a powerful accounting program. Despite all of its advantages, we occasionally find ourselves wishing we had MS Excel to run a few calculations or build a custom report.

The amazing thing is that you don't have to choose between the two. The program makes exporting reports from QuickBooks to Excel a simple. You may enjoy all of the benefits of QuickBooks while still being able to handle some of the work in Excel.

In four steps, learn how to export a QuickBooks Online report to Excel.

If you utilize the online version of QuickBooks, exporting QuickBooks reports to Excel is a simple. What you should do is as follows:

1. Navigate to Business Overview > Reports (or just find the Reports menu if you are in the Accountant view).
2. Choose the report you want to export.
3. Select Export and then click on Export to Excel at the top of the report.
4. Save the Excel document.

Many QuickBooks Online reports can be automated. Coupler.io allows you to export selected reports from QBO to an Excel workbook and refresh it on a regular basis. The section How to export from QB to Excel automatically will go over automated exports. Manual exports are covered in depth further down.

QuickBooks Online manual report export

Step 1: Navigate to Business overview > Reports in the Business view. Simply select Reports from the menu in the Accounting view.

Assuming you're already logged in, your first step should be to navigate to the Business overview area and select Reports from the submenu.

Step 2: Find the required report.

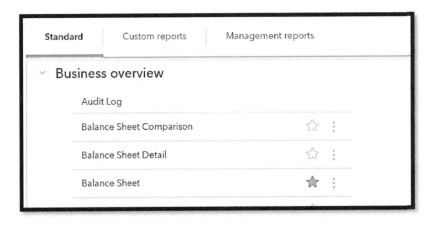

The next step is to locate the report that you wish to export. You have the choice of scrolling through the suggested selections, referring to the reports you've starred, or searching the report list. When you've located the appropriate report, click on it to access it.

Step 3: Select the export option.

Once the report has been accessed, look for the exporting button in the top right corner. When you click it, a choice appears that allows you to export the document in Excel or PDF format. Choose where to save the file by selecting the Excel export option.

Step 4: Save and double-check the file.

The final step is to save the file and, if necessary, examine it. That's all. Your QuickBooks to Excel export is now finished!

However, depending on your goal, you may need to take additional actions. Let's take a look at the most prevalent ones.

How to Automatically Export a QuickBooks Online Report

Manually exporting each report you require is a waste of time. This task can be automated by using an external tool. Coupler.io can automate practically any QuickBooks to Excel export – there are over 25 reports available.

However, it is only applicable to QuickBooks Online. QuickBooks desktop version is not supported, and there is no need because the desktop version enables for report scheduling. Coupler.io is a useful tool to utilize in conjunction with QBO because QBO does not offer automatic exporting on its own.

Once you've configured the export, it will run on a regular basis and retrieve reports without your intervention. You'll be able to spend less time manually exporting and more time analyzing data from your daily reports.

How to Export QuickBooks Reports to Excel Including All Users

QuickBooks Online allows you to export your whole customer list. It's in the Reports area, under the aptly called Customer Contact List report. You can export this QuickBooks report to Excel to further study it.

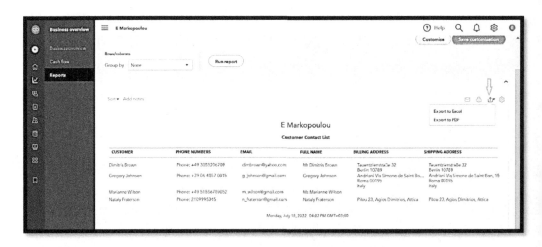

QuickBooks Desktop provides a more detailed view that includes all user activities. Go to Settings > Audit log to access it. The report displays all of the users' activities, however it cannot be exported. There are only two options: print it or save it as a PDF.

Accessing the Audit Trail report is another option. Go to Reports > Accounts & Taxes > Audit trail to find it. This report displays user actions in your QuickBooks instance and may be filtered by user or action type.

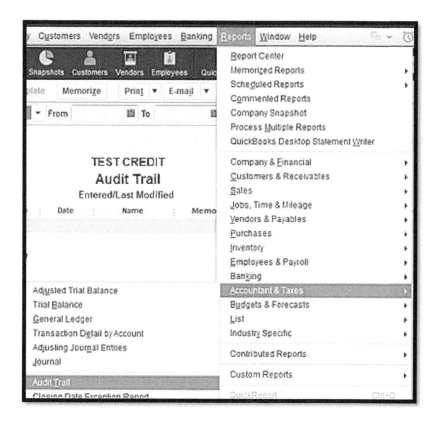

However, not all elements of user accounts can be exported in a report. User permissions cannot be included into a report; instead, they can be viewed by navigating to the Company tab and viewing a list of users. This tab displays the rights granted to particular users.

How to Save a QuickBooks Report to an Excel Spreadsheet

QuickBooks Online currently does not support updating existing Excel files during export. If you don't have the desktop version, your only option is to manually add the exported file as a new worksheet to your existing spreadsheet.

If you have the desktop version of QuickBooks, you can export the QuickBooks report to Excel and amend it while the report is being exported.

Troubleshooting Report Export to Excel in QuickBooks

Despite the fact that the process of exporting reports to Excel is fairly simple, technical challenges do arise from time to time. Here's how to solve the most common issues.

QuickBooks export to Excel is not working.

If you are using the desktop version of QuickBooks, you may notice that the export button is greyed out and that you are unable to conduct an export. If you do not have a desktop version of Microsoft 365 installed, it may not work. If you use Microsoft Excel from a web app, your desktop QuickBooks program may refuse to export.

Aside from that, here are a some things you could try to resolve this issue.

- ❖ Make changes to both Excel and QuickBooks.
- ❖ Repair the Microsoft Office suite.
- ❖ Reinstall Excel as well as QuickBooks.

If the report contains zeroes instead of your data and the advice above does not help, go to your Excel instance and update the Protected View settings.

Exporting To PDF

QuickBooks includes a PDF printer that allows you to save your statements, reports, and forms as PDF files. To create PDF files, you can alternatively utilize a third-party PDF printer, such as Adobe PDF. Third-party PDF printers, like any other printer, allow you to pick the printer in the Print settings box. PDF files are minimal in size and may be viewed on any computer or device that supports the PDF format. PDF files can also be used to archive reports, examine customer papers before sending them, and share information in corporate meetings.

Reports or Forms PDF

1. In QuickBooks, select the report or form you wish to print.
2. Select "Print" from the "File" menu to utilize a third-party PDF printer. Then, from the list of options, choose your PDF printer. Alternatively, choose "File" and then "Save as PDF" to use the QuickBooks PDF printer.
3. Select either "Print" or "Save." Then, choose where you want to save the PDF file on your hard drive.

Statements in PDF

1. Select "Customers" and then "Create Statements."
2. Select a customer from the drop-down menu.
3. Click on "View Selected Customers" and then "E-mail."
4. Select "Send Now" or "Send Later" to email a PDF statement to your customer.

Exporting To Google Sheets

QuickBooks Online Advanced now allows you to export QuickBooks reports to Google Sheets. Please keep in mind that payroll reports can't be exported to Google Sheets.

Before you start...

If this is your first time exporting data:

- ❖ Make sure you have a Google account
- ❖ Change your web browser settings to allow pop-up windows from QuickBooks Online

Exporting data to Google Sheets

1. Access your QuickBooks Online account.
2. Select Reports from the Business overview menu on the left.
3. Navigate to the report you wish to export to Google Sheets.
4. From the Export drop-down menu, choose Export to Google Sheets.

A verification code is provided to you to confirm your access and identity.

5. Enter the verification code that was emailed to you.
6. Go over the permissions information provided.
7. To accept permissions, click Allow.

   Your Google account is now open.

8. If prompted, sign in to Google.

Google Sheets connects to your QuickBooks Online account and facilitates data export.

Managing Google Sheets data that has been exported

Once the Google Sheet is created, any exported data will be preserved there and accessible via the same Google account. Intuit no longer has control over the exported data, and the Google Sheet cannot be loaded back into QuickBooks Online.

Please have in mind that any data saved to a Google Sheet will not reflect any subsequent changes made in QuickBooks Online unless another export is performed.

Custom Reporting With Spreadsheet Sync

Spreadsheet Sync's report templates can be used to analyze and show QuickBooks Online Advanced data. There are two types:

1. **Advanced reports:** Formatted pivot tables that can be automatically filled with QuickBooks Online Advanced data and then used to make charts and graphs are included in advanced reports.

   There are two such package templates: the Sample Management report and the Smart Profit & Loss report.

2. **Quickbooks Online reports:** Spreadsheet Sync allows you to create and edit QuickBooks Online reports. They are missing pivot tables.

a. You can also save QuickBooks Online Advanced transaction or account data to a data table.

b. These reports and tables are categorized. See the list below.

To update a report with the most recent QuickBooks Online Advanced data, click Refresh in the toolbar. (You can also fill out templates manually.)

Note: Spreadsheet Sync can only be opened and managed by QuickBooks Online Advanced account administrators.

Using the Smart Profit & Loss and Sample Management reports

The Sample Management and Smart P&L reports allow you to swiftly assess a company's or firms' financial health. They contain formatted pivot tables that can be segmented using slicers.

1. **Sample management report:** Three prepared spreadsheets are included in the Sample Management Report.
❖ Trial Balance
❖ Profit & Loss (standard)
❖ Balance Sheet
2. **Smart profit and loss:** this include one formatted spreadsheet for showing Profit and Loss data in detail

Types of Quickbooks online reports and data tables available in spreadsheet sync

To evaluate or show data from a company, use a QuickBooks Online report or data table template.

1. Begin by clicking the Build Reports button in the toolbar.
2. In the Report Builder box, select either Reports or Data Tables as the data source. Then, next to the type of template you want to use, select the carat >.

Types of Report

- ❖ New Reports includes an exchange rate report that has been updated.
- ❖ Reports include trial balance, profit and loss, and balance sheet spreadsheets for several periods.
- ❖ Accountant Reports summarize the general ledger, account list, and transaction list.
- ❖ A business overview contains a cash flow statement, a balance sheet, an inventory valuation summary, a profit and loss statement, and trial balance reports.
- ❖ Accounts Payable Management includes vendor balances and A/P summaries.
- ❖ Accounts Receivable Management includes customer balances and A/R summaries.
- ❖ Examine Expenses and Purchases, which includes vendor expenses.
- ❖ Standard QuickBooks Reports - Review Sales comprises product or service sales, department or class sales, revenue by customer, and sales by customer.

Types of data tables

- ❖ Transactions - Core are for downloading business data such as bills, invoices, and purchases.
- ❖ Transactions - Journals is a list of journal entries.
- ❖ Transactions - Bank are bank transactions such as deposits and payments.
- ❖ Contacts includes lists of customers and vendors.
- ❖ System Configuration is for downloading all other QuickBooks Online Advanced data including accounts, budgets, locations, and employees. such as accounts, budgets, locations, and staff, are downloaded.

Running Quickbooks Online reports or data table in Spreadsheet Sync

Follow these procedures to build and amend a QuickBooks Online report or data table:

1. From the toolbar, click Build Reports.
2. In the Report Builder task panel, pick the corporate data you want to use under Company or Group.
a. In the toolbar, select Firm Settings to add data from a company assigned to you by a QuickBooks Online Advanced account administrator.
3. Select the report or data table template you want to use by clicking Select data source.
4. Click Select data to get the report's filter data. (The filters will differ depending on the type of report.)
5. In the parameters window,
a. Put a name in the Presets area to save your filters as a preset, or select a previously saved preset.
b. Select Accounting Method or Basis, Class, Location, Customer/Vendor, or Item in the Filters section.
c. Under Date Macro, specify whether you want to receive data on a weekly, monthly, quarterly, or yearly basis, as well as the start and end dates of your data period. (For multiple period reports, select total time period and comparative time period filters.)
6. In the Filter data window for tables,
a. Add a name in the Presets area to save your filters as a preset, or select a previously saved preset.
b. Select the Date range and time period for your data under Conditions.
c. Select all conditions under Filters to categorize data by several fields, or single condition to filter for data that meets any of the conditions.

i. Create your filters by selecting Field and Operation from the dropdown menus and entering a Value.

ii. Click the plus (+) button to add more filters.

7. Select whether to download as an Excel Table or as Raw Data, and whether to add data to a New Sheet or the Current Sheet under Options.
8. A Successfully synced window will show once the report or table has been prepared.

Formatting your report

To format the report, you can also add or remove columns and rows. Your formatting preferences will be saved by Spreadsheet Sync. (Please keep in mind that deleted rows cannot be restored.)

Select Refresh in the toolbar, then All Sheets, and then Append in the Refresh window to add new data to the bottom of a report.

CHAPTER FIFTEEN

ANALYZING QUICKBOOKS DATA IN EXCEL

Filtering Data

Learn how to use custom fields in QuickBooks Online Advanced to organize and track data. Custom fields gives you access to track specific information across sales forms, purchase orders, and client profiles. Custom fields can be created to track everything from sales agents to particular customer details.

Custom fields can also be used to arrange lists, narrow search results, and filter financial reports. This gives you access to keep track of certain facts relevant to your organization.

Note: Do you wish to utilize this feature? You have the option to upgrade to QuickBooks Online Advanced.

Sort your lists by custom field

Make your invoice, customer, and spending lists easier to read. You can, for example, categorize your invoices by sales representative to discover which transactions they worked on.

1. Go to Navigation Bar, then select the Sales or Expenses menu.
2. Select Invoices, Expenses, or Customers.
3. Choose the Gear symbol from the list (not the Gear menu in the Icon Bar).

4. So to add a custom field as a column, check the box next to it.
5. Click the Gear symbol once more to close the window.
6. To sort the list alphabetically, click the Custom Field column header.

Search for transactions with a specific custom field

Each transaction is displayed using a unique custom field. For instance, if you developed a customer loyalty program custom field, you may use it to search for all transactions.

1. Click on the Search (magnifying glass) button.
2. Enter the name of the custom field. Select the Gear icon on any page then Custom fields to get a list of active custom fields.
3. In the search results, choose a transaction.
4. Select Advanced Search to see the whole list of transactions. From the dropdown menu next to the Contains or Equals field, select the custom field. Then click Search.

Incorporate custom fields into your reports.

When running reports, use custom fields to gain deeper insights into your organization. You can, for example, filter a report to display only the data that interests you.

Creating Custom Reporting With Pivot Tables

By selecting different columns with the custom reports builder, all users of QuickBooks Online Advanced may now simply construct pivot tables right in the reports area. Any dimension can be used to build summary tables.

Understanding Pivot Table

A tool to study and summarize vast volumes of data, examine related totals, and present summary reports, an Excel pivot table can be used to:

- ❖ Present a lot of information in an approachable way.
- ❖ The spreadsheet's total and aggregate numerical values.
- ❖ To see the specifics underlying any total, dive down and expand or collapse the data levels.
- ❖ Present your Excel data or printed reports in a clear and appealing manner online
- ❖ By using categories and subcategories, summarize the data.
- ❖ To focus on the most pertinent information, group, sort, and conditionally format various subsets of data.
- ❖ Pivot to examine various summaries of the original data by rotating rows to columns or columns to rows.

Making a pivot table in Excel

Making an Excel pivot table is perceived by many as being time- and labor-intensive. However, this is untrue! The technology has been improved by Microsoft over many years, and the summary reports in the most recent Excel versions are both incredibly quick and user-friendly. In reality, creating the summary table only takes a few minutes. And this is how:

1. Prepare your source material.

Organize the data into rows and columns before generating a summary report, and then export your data range as an Excel Table. To do this, pick all of the data, then click Table on the Insert tab.

One very pleasant advantage of using an Excel Table as the source data is that your data range becomes "dynamic." If your pivot table has a dynamic range, it will automatically grow and shrink as you remove or add entries, so you won't have to worry about the most recent data being missing.

Helpful hints:

❖ Give your columns interesting, distinctive titles; they will later serve as the field names.
❖ Make sure your source table has no subtotals, blank rows or columns, or any empty spaces.
❖ You can give your source table a name to make it simpler to maintain by selecting the Design tab and entering the name in the Table Name box in the worksheet's top right corner.

2. Create a pivot table

Go to the Insert tab > Tables group > PivotTable after selecting any cell in the source data table.

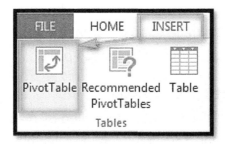

The Create PivotTable window will open as a result. Check to see that the appropriate table or cell range is highlighted in the Table/Range field. Next, decide where you want your Excel pivot table to be located:

❖ A table will be started in a new worksheet at cell A1 if you choose New Worksheet.

❖ When you choose an existing worksheet, your table will be inserted at the chosen spot in the worksheet. To position your table in the first cell, select it by clicking the Collapse Dialog button in the Location box.

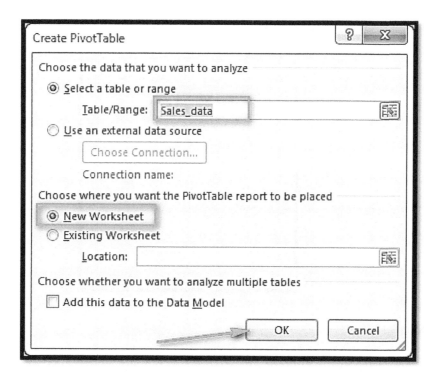

After selecting OK, a blank pivot table similar to this one will be created at the desired location:

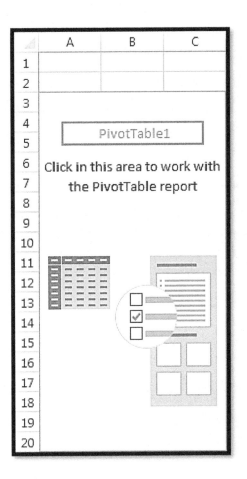

Helpful hints:

❖ A pivot table should often be placed in a separate worksheet; beginners are especially advised to do this.

❖ If you are building a pivot table from data in another workbook or worksheet, use the notation [workbook name] to include the names of the workbook and worksheet. For instance, [Book1] sheet name!range .xlsx]. Sheet1!$A$1:$E$20. As an alternative, you can use the mouse to pick a table or segment of cells in different worksheet by clicking the Collapse Dialog button.

❖ A pivot table and pivot chart could be made at the same time. To achieve this, open Excel 2016 or Excel 2013 and navigate to the Insert tab > Charts group. From there, choose PivotChart &

PivotTable. Click the arrow next to PivotTable in Excel 2007 and 2010 before selecting PivotChart.

3. Arrange the layout of your pivot table report

PivotTable Field List refers to the place where you deal with the fields in your summary report. It is divided into the header and body sections and is situated in the worksheet's right-hand corner:

* **The Field Section:** The names of fields that you can include in your table are listed in the Field Section. The names of fields match the names of the columns in your source table.
* **The Layout Section:** The Report Filter area, Column Labels area, Row Labels area, and Values area are all located in the Layout Section. The fields of your table can be rearranged and arranged here.

When you make changes to the PivotTable Field List, your table is updated right away.

Adding field to Excel pivot table

Select the checkbox close to the field name in the Field section to add the field to the Layout section.

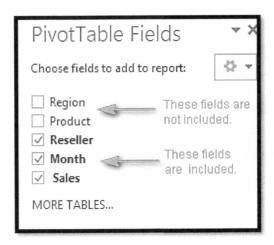

Microsoft Excel, By default includes the following fields to the Layout section:

- ❖ There are now non-numerical fields in the Row Labels section;
- ❖ The Values area now includes additional numerical fields;
- ❖ Date and time hierarchies from Online Analytical Processing (OLAP) are added to the Column Labels area.

Removing a field from a pivot table

You have two options for deleting a specific field:

- ❖ In the PivotTable pane's Field section, uncheck the box next to the field's name.
- ❖ Choose "Remove Field Name" from the context menu when you right-click on a field in your pivot table.

Setting up the fields in a pivot table

There are three ways in which you can arrange the fields in your Layout section:

i. Using the mouse, move fields among the four sections of the Layout section. The field can also be moved by clicking and holding the field name in the Field section and dragging it to a different location in the Layout section. This will shift the field from its present location in the Layout section to the new location.

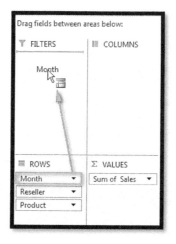

ii.   From the Field section, right-click the field name, then choose the location where you want to add it:

iii.   To pick a field, click on it in the Layout section. Additionally, this will show the choices that are accessible for that specific field.

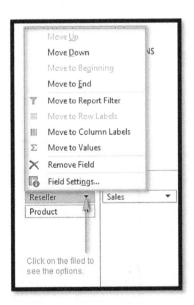

4. Selecting the Values field's function (optional)

If you put a numeric value field in the Values section of the Field List, Microsoft Excel will automatically apply the Sum function. The Count function is used when you enter text, date, Boolean, or other non-numeric data or empty values in the Values field.

However, if you like, you can select an alternative summary function. Right-click the value field you want to alter in Excel 2013 or Excel 2016, select Summarize Values By, then select the desired summary function.

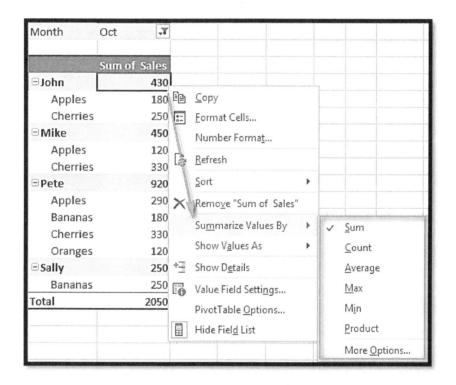

5. Display various calculations in value fields (optional)

One further helpful feature that Excel pivot tables offer is the ability to present values in various ways, such as showing totals as percentages or ranking values from smallest to largest and vice versa. Here you can find the complete set of calculating alternatives.

In Excel 2013 and 2016, the field in the table can be right-clicked to access the Show Values As option. This feature is also available in Excel 2010 and before in the Calculations group on the Options tab.

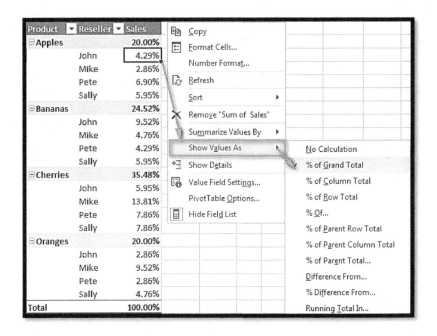

Working on PivotTable Field List

The primary tool you need to set up the summary table the same way you want it to be is the pivot table pane, which is also known as the PivotTable Field List. You might wish to adjust the pane to the preferences to make working with the fields more comfortable.

How to change the Field List view

Select the Tools button and select your preferred layout to alter how the sections are shown in the Field List.

By dragging the bar (splitter) that divides the pane from the worksheet, you can also resize it horizontally.

Opening and Closing the PivotTable pane

Simply click the Close button (X) in the top right corner of the pane to close the Pivot Table Field List. Making a second appearance is not always easy:)

Right-click anywhere in the table, then choose Show Field List from the context menu to bring up the Field List once more.

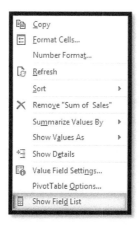

Additionally, you can use the Field List button on the Ribbon, which is found in the Show group of the Analyze / Options tab.

How to move a pivot table to a new location

Click the Relocate PivotTable button in Actions group on the Analyze tab in Excel 2013 and Excel 2016 (or the Options tab in Excel 2010 and previous) if you wish to move your pivot table to a different workbook, worksheet, or portion of the current sheet. Click OK after choosing a different location.

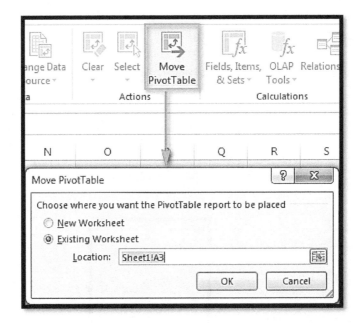

How to delete a pivot table in Excel

There are several ways to delete a summary report that you no longer require.

- ❖ Delete that sheet if your table is on a different worksheet.
- ❖ Select the whole pivot table using the mouse and then press the Delete key if your table is on a sheet along with other data.

❖ In Excel 2013 and Excel 2014 (Options tab in Excel 2010 and previous), click anyplace in the pivot table that you wish to delete, then select the Analyze tab > Actions group, click the small arrow next to the Select button, select Entire PivotTable, and then press Delete.

PART 4: FEATURES FOR ACCOUNTANTS

CHAPTER SIXTEEN

INTRODUCING QUICKBOOKS ACCOUNTANTS

Do you need assistance installing QuickBooks Online Accountant? Do you want to learn how to manage your clients with the Accountant Toolbox? We've got your back! This guide will assist you become acquainted with the unique7 features of QuickBooks Online Accountant.

Feel free to browse or skip to the relevant section:

1. Create your account
2. Explore the dashboard
   - ❖ Clients
   - ❖ Team
   - ❖ ProAdvisor
   - ❖ Work
3. Accountant's Toolbox
   - ❖ Transaction reclassification
   - ❖ Voided/deleted transactions
   - ❖ Journal entries
   - ❖ Reporting options
   - ❖ Workpapers
4. Subscription and billing management

Create your account

The first thing you'll need to do after signing up for QuickBooks Online Accountant is set up your account. Ant time you log in, you will be prompted to enter the following information:

1. Launch QuickBooks Online Accountant.
2. Enter your company name.

3. Enter your firm's postcode — this will assist potential clients locate you on our ProAdvisor portal.
4. Click Continue.

Navigate the QuickBooks online accountant dashboard

QuickBooks Online Accountant allows you to handle your work and clients in one location. By selecting the Go to client's QuickBooks dropdown menu, you may see a complete list of your clients and swap between their books and your practice.

Select the QB Accountant icon to return to your client dashboard/list.

Let's take a look at the various areas you can visit via the QuickBooks navigation:

Clients

The Clients page is where you may add, track, and manage all of your QuickBooks Online Account clients, including those who don't use QuickBooks.

The client list displays information about your clients, including who their head accountant is. Select the Bookkeeping tab to display the current month-end review status for a given client.

To read a client's details in greater depth, choose their name in the Client/Contact column to visit their profile. You can do the following once you're in their profile:

❖ Include notes and important client information. QuickBooks stamps each note made in the client file so you can keep track of it.
❖ Shared document upload and management - both you and your customer can add, view, and delete shared documents.

Add clients in Quickbooks online accountant

Are you ready to start adding clients? Great! Adding clients is critical to developing your practice, and you'll get 10 ProAdvisor points when you do. Learn how to add a new client to your list and manage your client list.

Team

The Teams area lists all of your team members, as well as their user details and access to client files. However, because not everyone on your team does the same responsibilities, you can monitor their roles and permissions and limit client access and administrative tasks.

You may add and manage team members in your accounting or bookkeeping firm from this dashboard. Alternatively, if you need to add, change, or remove team members, here's how to manage your firm's users.

ProAdvisor

With QuickBooks Online Accountant, you get free access to an unlimited amount of training materials, such as how-to videos, on-demand webinars, virtual conferences, certification examinations, and more, to help your business succeed.

You can earn points to obtain more perks, such as marketing tools and resources to help you build your practice, by becoming a certified QuickBooks ProAdvisor.

Pricing and plans

Learn how wholesale billing works so that you may pass on savings to your customers. If necessary, here's how to assess and manage existing clients in your plan, as well as move clients to your preferred price scheme.

Work

In the Work tab, get a bird's-eye perspective of upcoming or overdue assignments so you never miss a beat. Create projects and tasks to track all of your company's work from start to completion, all organized by due date.

Projects consolidates your team's work in a single location, allowing you to maintain a consistent workflow, complete projects on schedule, and engage with clients and your team. You can also develop bespoke templates to meet the demands of your company or client.

Select the From QuickBooks option to automatically display activities and actions to perform in your client's QuickBooks.

Accountant's toolbox

Have you ever yearned for tools to help you do your work more quickly? Save time by using the Accountant Toolbox, which contains some of the commonly used tools for working on your clients' books. You will actually save time and remain focused.

Let's look at some of the tools available in the Accountant Toolbox:

Reclassify transactions

The Reclassify tool allows you to locate transactions that have been incorrectly assigned to accounts, classes, or locations. Instead of manually altering these transactions, use this tool to reclassify the account, class, or VAT on a large number of them at once.

Voided or deleted transactions

Do you want to see an audit log report of deleted/voided transactions and make some changes? No worries. To filter the report by user, date, and events, select Voided/deleted transactions from the Accountant Toolbox.

Journal entries

When you need to make a journal entry for a special transaction, use the Journal entries tool. Assume you need to manually enter debits and credits, transfer money between income and spending accounts, or a transaction should have been divided into two separate ledger accounts. In any case, QuickBooks Online Accountant allows you to handle these transactions by creating general journal entries.

Reports Options

Do you want reports that are more useful to you and your company? Not a problem! If you want to receive your client reports in a month-to-date manner, you may customize reports and choose a default date range.

Workpapers

By organizing your workflow using Workpapers, you can save time and resources needed to gather formal reports and financial statements at the end of the year.

From a single dashboard, you may evaluate client accounts, update journal entries, and perform year-end engagements or period-end activities.

Manage your billing and subscriptions

You can edit subscription billing information and firm details in QuickBooks Online Accountant at any time.

Is your client looking for more from QuickBooks Online? Or is their current product sufficient? You can change your clients' QuickBooks Online subscription level to provide them with additional (or fewer) accounting capabilities.

Adding Clients To Quickbooks Online Accountant

Discover the best ways to grow your business.

A new client is wonderful. Using QuickBooks to connect with clients makes keeping track of their books much simpler. To get their information, add them to your company. If a client asks you to be their accountant, you can equally make direct changes to their accounts.

Adding clients who already use QuickBooks Online or Self-Employed is explained here. You will also see how to add clients that have never used QuickBooks before.

Add existing QuickBooks customers

Tell your client to accept you as their accountant if they already use QuickBooks Online or Self-Employed:

1. Request that your client send the invitation to your QuickBooks Online Accountant firm's email address.
2. Click the Accept Invitation link in the invitation email after opening it.
3. Enter your user ID and password to log in.
4. Choose the QuickBooks Online Accounting company you want to connect your client with if you have multiple.

QuickBooks links their accounts to your business and adds them to your customer list when you accept the invitation. Now that their books are out for evaluation and revision.

Don't worry if find it difficult to connect. If you are unable to accept their invitation, follow these steps.

Sending clients with existing quickbooks subscription to your Proadvisor Preferred Pricing Plan

These methods can be used to transfer a client's membership if they already pay for their subscription but want to join your ProAdvisor Preferred Pricing plan.

Remember that you cannot add the following products to your ProAdvisor Preferred Pricing plan if your customer has recently canceled or has recently canceled the following products related to their QuickBooks Online subscription:

❖ QuickBooks Time
❖ QuickBooks Live Bookkeeping

- ❖ QuickBooks Online Contractor Direct Deposit
- ❖ FormFly

Add newly acquired clients to QuickBooks

Include more customers in the ProAdvisor Preferred Pricing package.

You can sign up clients for QuickBooks and add them to your ProAdvisor Preferred Pricing plan. This enables you to choose the products that meet their demands the best.

1. To add your client to the ProAdvisor Preferred Pricing plan, click the ProAdvisor discount option in the QuickBooks area.
2. Examine the payroll and QuickBooks products that are offered in each subsection. Important: Your ProAdvisor Preferred Pricing plan must include payroll products if your client wants them. They are unable to independently acquire and pay for their payroll plan.
3. Decide which goods you want your client to subscribe to.
4. Click the Make me the Primary Admin checkbox if you also intend to handle administrative tasks for your customer.
5. When you are ready, choose Save.

Include customers who desire to cover their own QuickBooks subscription costs.

You can also directly discount customers and let them manage their own membership and billing.

1. Choose Direct discount under QuickBooks. This offers your client a discount, but they are still responsible for paying for their QuickBooks subscription.
2. Check the Make me the Primary Admin box if you also intend to handle administrative tasks for your customer.
3. When you are prepared, choose Save.

Their accounts are linked by QuickBooks, and they are added to your client list. Now that their books are out for evaluation and revision.

Add customers who do not use QuickBooks

Add your client to your company even if they don't use QuickBooks so that all of their information is in one place:

1. In the Clients menu of QuickBooks Online Accountant, click.
2. Select Client Add.
3. Decide between Business and Individual.
4. Enter the client's information.
5. Choose No subscription under the Products section.
6. Click Save when you're done.

Working With The Client List

Learn how to keep track of your clients and keep your client list up to date. Your client list is constantly expanding. It's simple to keep your client list up to date in QuickBooks Online Accountant. Here's how to update client information.

Add clients

For you to add clients to your QuickBooks Online Accountant firm, follow these steps.

Important: the present system can only handle about 2000 clients per QBOA firm. For larger firms with 2000 or more clients, it is recommended to consolidating the client list and establishing a new QBOA firm for clients who exceed the limit.

See your clients

Navigate to the Clients menu in QuickBooks Online Accountant.

The client list displays information about your clients, including who their head accountant is. You'll also be able to view the status of projects such as Prep for Taxes and tax returns.

Select a client's name to see additional information. The profile tabs show you what QuickBooks products they have, papers you've emailed them, and tax return information.

Note: To manage clients on your ProAdvisor Preferred Pricing plan, go to Settings > Subscriptions and Billing. Accountant-billed subscriptions should be selected.

Update or change a client's information
1. Navigate to Clients menu in QuickBooks Online Accountant.
2. Locate the client.
3. In the Actions column, click Edit client.
4. Make the necessary modifications.
5. When you're finished, click Save.

Refresh the web browser if you don't see the changes right away.

Making a client inactive
If you have seasonal clients or clients with whom you don't work frequently, make their profiles dormant. Inactive clients will not appear on your client list, but QuickBooks will keep all of their information.

It is important to note that deactivating a client does not cancel their subscription. It also does not deactivate your ProAdvisor Preferred Pricing plan.

1. Navigate to Clients menu in QuickBooks Online Accountant.
2. Locate the client.
3. Choose Make inactive from the Edit client dropdown.

To view your inactive clients, go to:

1. Navigate to Clients menu in QuickBooks Online Accountant.
2. Right at the top of the list, click the Settings icon.
3. Check the option that says Include inactive customers.

To reactivate a client and resume where you left off:

1. Navigate to the Clients menu in QuickBooks Online Accountant.
2. Locate the client.
3. In the Actions column, select Make active.

Delete a client permanently

You can permanently delete clients if you are the primary admin for your QuickBooks Online Accountant firm. You lose access to their firm and any work in features such as Tax Prep.

It is critical to note that deleting a client does not terminate their QuickBooks Online membership. If they need to terminate their QuickBooks Online subscription, here's how.

If you know you need to delete a client, do the following:

1. If you are currently the primary administrator for your client's firm, ensure that your customer appoints a new primary administrator.
2. Remove the client from your ProAdvisor discount plan if they are a member. After updating their billing information, your client gains full access to their accounts.
3. Log in as an administrator to QuickBooks Online Accountant.
4. Clients should be chosen.
5. Select the name of the client you want to delete.
6. Select Delete permanently from the Edit client dropdown menu.
7. To confirm, click Yes.

Please keep in mind that deleting a client who is already connected through ProConnect Tax Online simply deletes their QuickBooks profile. It has no effect on their ProConnect profile.

Proadvisor Preferred Pricing Versus Pro Advisor Revenue Share

Proadvisor preferred pricing

As a ProAdvisor, you have access to the simplified discount program known as ProAdvisor Preferred Pricing, which can help you expand your business and that of your clients. Customers that are new to QuickBooks Online can receive special savings.

The wholesale discount program is replaced by ProAdvisor Preferred Pricing for new subscriptions added on or after July 15, 2021.

How ProAdvisor Preferred Pricing works

ProAdvisor Preferred Pricing was developed to offer best-in-class discounts with the flexibility needed to match the way you handle client subscriptions based on feedback from accounting professionals like you. The ProAdvisor Preferred Pricing program incorporates QuickBooks Online, QuickBooks Online Payroll, and QuickBooks Time in an effort to provide a more straightforward pricing structure throughout our ecosystem.

You can cover the cost of a client's subscription through the ProAdvisor Preferred Pricing program or let them pay on their own. In either case, joining the ProAdvisor Preferred Pricing program enables you to offer price breaks to your customers.

With the ProAdvisor discount, you cover the cost of your client's subscription and can continue to give them savings off the going rate with the flexibility to stop at any moment. You receive an itemized view of all subscriptions your firm bills you for each month to make managing subscriptions for clients straightforward.

You may offer your customers a temporary Direct discount on their subscription if they choose to be invoiced directly.

ProAdvisor Preferred Pricing Benefits

1. **Flexibility:** ProAdvisor Preferred Pricing grants your company freedom in what it may provide. You can either incorporate the cost of QuickBooks Online as part of your company's services or charge consumers a particular discounted rate when using the ProAdvisor discount. You can choose the Direct discount if you want your client to pay. It is up to your company.

2. **Long-term savings options:** ProAdvisor Preferred Pricing offers your company and clients the finest long-term savings option, including sole continuous discount. Only through this program are accounting professionals like you able to take advantage of this ongoing QuickBooks Online discount. The ProAdvisor Preferred Pricing is based on the subscription's current list price and is subject to change.

3. **Peace of mind:** With the ProAdvisor discount, you take care of everything for your customers, so they don't have to worry about subscriptions or fees.

How to sign up customers for ProAdvisor Preferred Pricing savings

1. Open QuickBooks Online Accountant and log in.
2. In the Add client screen, enter your client's information.
3. Choose the team members whose accounts you want to be accessible.
4. Choose between the ProAdvisor discount (we bill your company) and the Direct discount (we bill your client).
5. Choose the item(s) you suggest for your client, then click Save.

Proadvisor Revenue share

To reward accountants who assist their small business clients in using QuickBooks Online, Intuit today unveiled the QuickBooks ProAdvisor Preferred Pricing Revenue Share program.

The brand-new, still-in-beta program acknowledges the labor accountants do to suggest, set-up, and onboard new clients onto QuickBooks. On new QuickBooks Online or Payroll subscriptions, accountants will receive 30% of the monthly invoiced amount that their customer pays.

Key advantages of the new revenue split program include:

- ❖ **Discounts for Clients:** ProAdvisors will receive a percentage of the revenue, while clients will enjoy their first month free as well as a 50% discount for the following three months.
- ❖ **Revenue Growth:** For a period of 12 months, accountants will be paid a basic charge of 30% and a 15% employee fee for QuickBooks Online Payroll.
- ❖ **Time Savings:** Clients will be invoiced immediately, which will free up accountants' time to manage subscriptions.

How it works

The new QuickBooks ProAdvisor Preferred Pricing Revenue Share program is currently in beta testing. Here is a summary of how it functions. Noteworthy is the fact that clients are not informed when a company joins the revenue share scheme.

- ❖ **Enrolling:** When it becomes available, accountants can sign up for the income sharing program through your dashboard by choosing the gear icon. It must be finished by the principal admin or business owner of your company, and it must start with your company's tax ID.
- ❖ **Adding a client:** When adding a client, choose "Add Client" from QuickBooks Online Accountant's menu, followed by "Revenue Share" under the "Bill my client" section. After that, choose the appropriate product (such as Payroll or QuickBooks Online), enter your client's information, and then save. With this, the client will begin a 30-day free trial, and Intuit will provide them directions on how to access the new accountant. A customer must provide

payment information prior to the trial's expiration in order to activate the subscription and get the very first three months of service for 50% off.

❖ **Calculating revenue share:** When you sign up for revenue share, you'll start being paid each month for all subscriptions from qualifying clients. After a subscription is created, payouts won't start coming in for a few of months. Because your customer starts with a 30-day free trial and the payout is only determined once your client begins a paying subscription, this is the case.

CHAPTER SEVENTEEN

MANAGING YOUR CLIENTS BOOKS

Opening A Clients Company

To ensure that everything is set up correctly for your customer, you should probably verify the company setup information for their QuickBooks Online (QBO) companies. You can benefit from the Client Overview, which offers, well, an overview of the client's QBO company's current situation. You should also check the QBO firms owned by each client's settings, Chart of Accounts, and lists.

The client overview page

You can use this website to gain a sense of the situation at your client's QBO company. Open the client's QBO company using the Go to Client's QuickBooks list box on the QuickBooks Online Accountant (QBOA) toolbar to see the Client Overview. Next, select Overview from the Navigation bar's tabs. You may see details about the client's subscriptions and associated apps at the top of the Client Overview page (see figure).

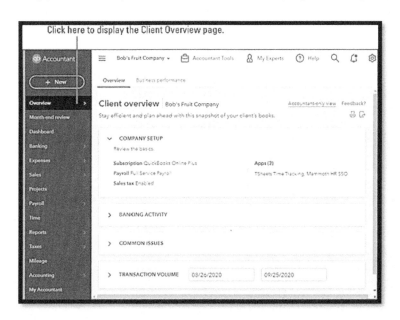

Information about the client's subscriptions and associated apps is displayed at the top of the Client Overview page.

The information on the client's financial activity is displayed in the second area of the Client Overview page, which is depicted in the accompanying picture. The accounts in the list are either set up as bank accounts or as credit card accounts.

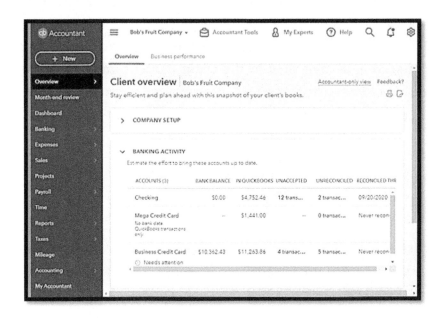

The banking activity section of the client overview page

The third section of the Client Overview page provides you with leads on information you might need to check out in the Client QBO company by displaying the state of the Client QBO company in relation to problems you frequently encounter in Client QBO companies (see the accompanying picture).

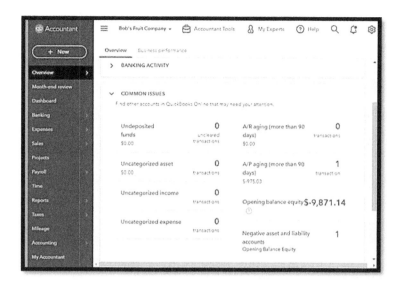

The Client Overview page's Common Issues section

The transaction volume for a specified date range is displayed in the client overview page's last section. It's intended to assist you in estimating how much time you'll need to spend on a specific client's books, as you can see in the following image.

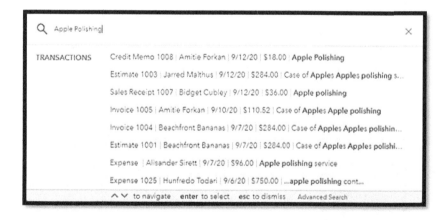

Transactions section contains information about transactions.

Be aware that there are no links on the Client Overview page other than the View Chart of Accounts link at the bottom of the Client Issues section.

However, you might wish to first check the material on company setup before clicking on that link.

Company setup information

To ensure that the customer QBO company employs the proper accounting technique, employer EIN, and legal business organization, you evaluate company setup information. You can also choose whether to utilize account numbers in the Chart of Accounts (you can choose to do so, but we've never met an accountant who wished to do so). Reviewing company settings involves the following steps:

1. Check out the client QBO firm by opening it. On the Clients page of QBOA, you can either utilize the list of clients on the QBOA toolbar under Go to QuickBooks, or you can click the QuickBooks logo to the left of the client's name there.
2. To access the Gear menu, click the Gear button on the right side of the QBOA toolbar.

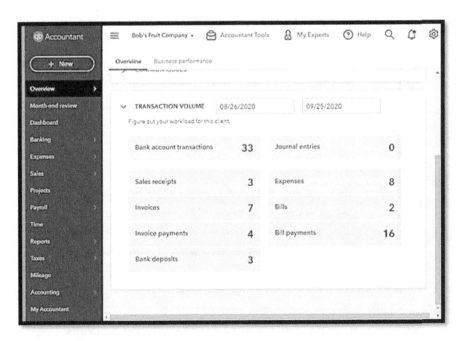

The Gear section

3. Click Account and Settings with in Your Company group of the Gear menu's left side. The Account and Settings dialog box's left side will reveal the Company tab when clicked.

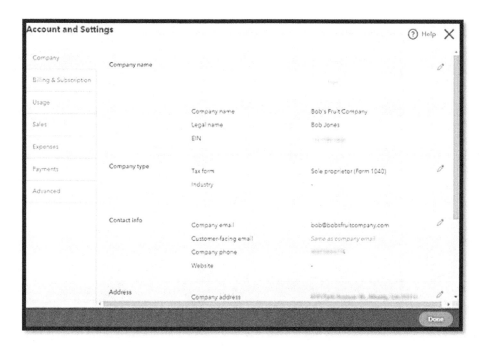

Account and Settings   ⑦ Help ✕

Company   Company name   ✎

Billing & Subscription

Usage
                            Company name   Bob's Fruit Company
Sales   Legal name   Bob Jones
                            EIN
Expenses

Payments   Company type   Tax form   Sole proprietor (Form 1040) ✎
                                Industry   .
Advanced

                Contact info   Company email   bob@bobsfruitcompany.com   ✎
                                Customer-facing email Same as company email
                                Company phone
                                Website   .

                Address   Company address   ✎

                                                                      Done

A client QBO company's Account & Settings dialog box

Note: When you create a company for a client, QBO shows the Company Profile dialog box and asks you to provide the company's email, address, city, state, and zip. Although the dialog box must be displayed, you can close it by clicking the X in the top-right corner of the form.

4. Look at the options. Set or correct the Company Name, Legal Name, and Employer ID in specific (EIN). Click any setting or the pencil that appears in the top-right corner of the settings area to make changes. The setting options are made available by QBO; make your selections and then click Save.

5. On the left side of the Account and Settings dialog box, click Usage. You can review how the client QBO subscription fits within the

usage limits Intuit applies to the selected subscription on QBO's Usage Limits tab, which is displayed.

6. On the left side of the Account and Settings dialog box, click Advanced. The Account and Settings dialog box's Advanced page settings become visible.

Examine the settings on the Advanced tab of the Account and Settings dialog box and alter them as necessary.

7. Look at the options. Set or make the following corrections in particular:

❖ The options in the Accounting section, which detail the fiscal and tax years and specify the accounting technique used by the QBO company

❖ The tax form setting for the Company Type section reads:

❖ You may manage how numbers are used in the Chart of Accounts by adjusting the parameters in this area.

❖ The options in the Other Preferences section, which is hidden but contains warnings when duplicate check numbers and bill numbers are used, include warnings being displayed.

346

8. Examine any further options you believe may want your attention on any of the pages in the Account and Settings dialog box.
9. To save your changes, click Done. The top of the screen in QBO shows a notice stating that your modifications have been saved.

The charts of Accounts

You should probably inspect your client's Chart of Accounts to make sure it displays the way you want it in addition to checking the company settings. To access your client's Chart of Accounts, click the link at the bottom of the Client Overview page. Alternately, you can use the Navigation bar: Click Accounting > Chart of Accounts in the client QBO firm Navigation bar. The page for the Chart of Accounts appears.

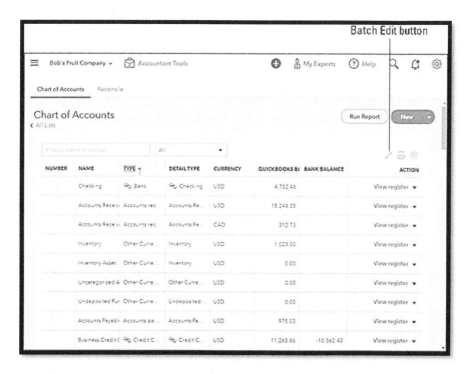

You can add and modify accounts from Chart of Accounts page.

Note: The Accountant Tools option also allows you to access the Chart of Accounts. Every path leads to Rome.

The Chart of Accounts page displays a column for account numbers at the left edge of the page and the Batch Edit button in the upper-right corner—it looks like a pencil—if you decided to allow the option to utilize account numbers while you were evaluating company settings. The Batch Edit button can be used to add account numbers.

Importing a chart of Accounts

The Chart of Accounts that QBO thinks you'll need is automatically set up when you form a new firm. You don't have to utilize it, though. If your client's business requires sub-accounts, you can import a Chart of Accounts that you've drawn up in Excel or as a CSV file that can include both the sub-accounts and their parent accounts.

Use the Account, Subaccount convention when importing subaccounts, which calls for listing the parent account first, followed by a colon, and the subaccount. You can download a sample file to familiarize yourself with the layout before setting up your file because the file you import must adhere to a specific format. Click the arrow next to the New button on the Chart of Accounts screen, then select Import. The Import Accounts page is displayed by QBO. To see the format your file should adhere to, click on the Download a Sample File link and then open the sample file in Excel.

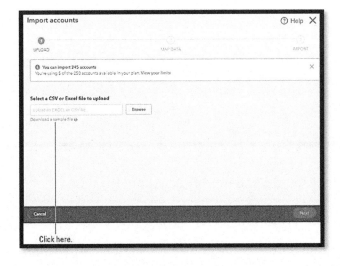

The page for Import Accounts

Returning to the Import Accounts page after setting up your Chart of Accounts file, click the Browse button to choose your file, then click Next in the lower-right corner of the page. You select your field names from the list boxes in the Your Field column of the table on the page that appears, as shown in the following figure, and then click Next to map the headings in your file to the fields in QBO.

Converting fields in QBO to their equivalents in your file

If everything appears to be in order, click Import, and QBO imports your Chart of Accounts. QBO displays the accounts it anticipates to import.

Editing or adding accounts

If there is need to alter an account, you can do it via the Account window by changing the account's name or Category Type.

Note: There is a far simpler method, which was demonstrate in the section below titled "Adding account numbers," that you may use if you prefer to add account numbers to the Chart of Accounts rather than doing so in the Account window.

Click the down arrow in the Action column to the right of the account, and then select Edit from the pop-up menu to open the Account window.

Click on the down arrow in the Action column to edit an account.

Alternately, you can click the New button above the list if you need to establish a new account. Similar to the window you usually see when editing an existing account, the window you see when creating a new account has the same layout.

Note: Any Asset, Liability, or Equity account's register can be viewed by clicking View Register next to it. The exception is retained earnings, which operates similarly to the income and expense accounts. To get a Quick Report for the account, click Run Report to the right of the Income or Expense account.

Adding account numbers

First, make sure the setting is enabled in Chart of Accounts section of the Settings dialog box's Advanced tab.

Then, to display the page depicted, click the Batch Edit button (the one that resembles a pencil and is located on the right side of the table above the table heads) on the Chart of Accounts page.

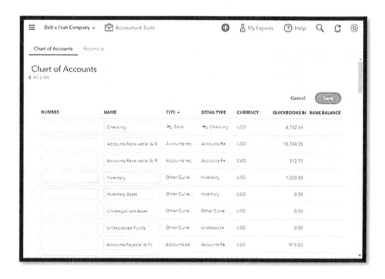

Account numbers for the Chart of Accounts can be configured on this page.

Fill out the Number column with account numbers. After you have finished entering the account numbers, click one of the save buttons that are located in the top-right and bottom-right corners of the page, respectively (you cannot see the bottom of the page).

Note: You might wish to save frequently as you enter account numbers because a QBOA session times out automatically by default after 60 minutes of inactivity. This is in case something unforeseen takes you away from your work. By selecting Number in the column headers on the Chart of Accounts page after adding account numbers, you can sort the Chart of Accounts in account-number order.

List information

You can also look at the list's details. You can obtain a summary of information about clients, partners, and workers by clicking on the links in the Navigation bar. Click Sales in the Navigation bar (it might also say Invoicing, depending on the selections made when the company was created), then click Customers to display customers as shown.

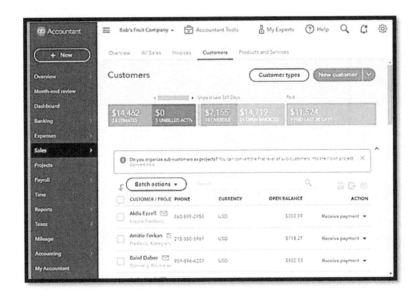

The Clients page

Select Expenses in the Navigation bar, followed by Vendors, to access vendor details. Click Workers in the Navigation bar, followed by Employees, to access employee data. The 1099 suppliers that the client has set up are displayed by QBO when you click Workers > Contractors.

The status bar located at the top of the page can be used on any of these pages, with the exception of the Contractors page (where payroll must be configured before you can use it), to show activity over the previous year. If you click one of the elements on the status bar, QBO filters the list so that you can view that specific subset of the list. To view just clients with past-due invoices or only customers with unbilled activity, for instance, you can filter the list of customers on the Customers page. Additionally, you

352

can execute batch activities using the Batch Actions button (located directly above the table), such as sending a batch of emails to customers.

If your list is lengthy, you can actually search for a specific list entry using the text box next to the Batch Actions button. Click the appropriate heading under the Batch Actions button to sort the list by name or open balance. Be aware that a people list can import names.

Click the Gear button in the QBOA toolbar to view additional listings. You can choose to examine any of three typical lists in the Lists area of the Gear menu that opens (the Products and Services list, the Recurring Transactions list, or the Attachments list). Alternately, you can utilize the Lists page that is displayed when you select All Lists at the top of the Lists section to access any list other than a people-oriented list.

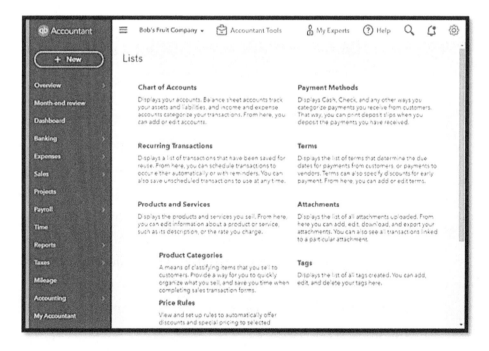

Use this particular page to open any list other than the customers, vendors or Employees list.

Export and import bank feed rules

You can assist in making sure that transactions post correctly when your client uses bank feeds to download transactions from the bank to his QBO company. In many circumstances, the rules utilized by one client can also be applied by another, thus export the rules from one client and import them into the other instead of generating new rules.

All of the rules in the client's company are exported by QBO when you export rules. The Import Rules wizard then allows you to import rules only those you choose.

Open the client firm to which you want to export rules, then carry out the following actions:

1. Rules under Banking can be found in the Navigation bar. QBO shows a Rules page.
2. Next to the New Rule button, click the down arrow.
3. Select Export Rules by using the down arrow close to the New Rule button. The rules are created by QBO, which saves them in an Excel file in your Downloads folder. Click Close in the QBO message. The file name contains the name of the client whose rules you exported together with the words "Bank Feed Rules."
4. Change to the organization you want to import these rules into.
5. Replicate Steps 1 through 3; at Step 3, select Import Rules. QBO launches a wizard to assist you in importing the rules.
6. Select the file you created in Step 3 and click Next on the Import Rules wizard's opening screen.
7. Choose the rules you want to import on the second wizard screen and press Next.
8. You can choose categories for the rules that match the client's Chart of Accounts on the third wizard screen. Make any necessary adjustments, and then click Import when you are done. How many rules were successfully imported is disclosed by QBO.

9. To finish, click. You can check that the rules you wanted to import are present on the Rules page for the client you opened in Step 4 after QBO has re-displayed it.

You can export rules from one client and import them into another client using this page.

Discovering Quickbooks Online Accountant Tools

You also receive accountant-specific tools to improve your bookkeeping in addition to your ProAdvisor perks. These tools improve the efficiency of evaluating your QuickBooks Online clients' accounts. They enable you to accomplish more in less time.

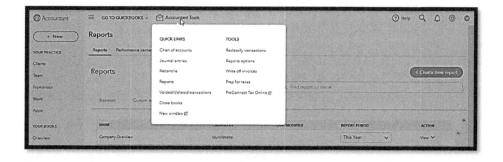

Reclassify transactions

Do you need to alter numerous transactions or transfer them to another account? You don't have to modify them one at a time with QuickBooks Online Accountant. Save time by applying the same adjustment to several transactions at once by using the reclassification tool.

Reclassify and move transactions

Be aware of the transactions you wish to reclassify first. You can discover this information in a few reports, such as a profit and loss statement. Use the reclassification tool to shift transactions to related accounts or alter their classes once you've located those transactions.

1. Launch the QuickBooks Online company for your client.
2. Select Reclassify Transactions under Accountant Tools.
3. To view revenue and expense accounts, choose Profit and Loss from the Account types dropdown box. To view your asset, liability, and equity accounts, choose Balance sheet.
4. Choose account that contains the transactions you want to alter from the Account list.
5. To filter the list, use the type, class, customer/supplier, and modify filters. Alternatively, you can choose Cash to only show paid transactions or Accrual to display both paid and unpaid transactions.
6. Choose Find transactions
7. For each transaction you want to alter, check the box.

A word of caution: you might need to set up locations for your account if you don't see Change location to.

Make sure there is a client or supplier before moving transactions to Accounts Receivable or Accounts Payable. Please fill out all of these fields.

8. Choose Reclassify.
9. From the Change account to menu, choose a new account or class to which to transfer the transactions.
10. When ready, choose Apply.

Reclassify by location

Use may change the classification of transaction locations. Make sure your client's locations are turned on first.

1. Launch the QuickBooks Online company for your client.
2. Click Account and Settings from the Settings menu.
3. Choosing the Advanced tab
4. Select Edit from the Categories section.
5. Activate Track locations.
6. Choose Save.

Write off invoice

Can't you pay the invoices at your company? Use the Write Off Invoices tool rather than managing them manually. Bad invoices that are automatically zeroed out by QuickBooks are discounted before being posted to your write-off account. Your cost and accounts payable are balanced as a result.

Tip: Encourage your clients to manually write out any incorrect invoices.

1. Select Write off invoices from Accountant Tools.
2. To locate the invoice, set the Invoice Age, To Date, and Balance Less Than filters. Next, choose Find invoices.
3. Check the customer name in the column.
4. Check the boxes close to the invoices you want to deduct.
5. Choose Write off.
6. Choose your bad debt account from the Account drop-down menu.
7. Click Apply.

Invoices dated prior to your closing date can be written off without entering your closing date password.

Undo reconciliations

For your clients, learn how to reverse reconciliations. Only accountants who use QuickBooks Online Accountant have access to this. You have a unique option for reconciliation if your company uses QuickBooks Online Accountant. In some cases, it's advisable to start over from beginning when one of your clients wishes to modify or undo a number of transactions on an earlier reconciliation. You can start over by undoing their entire reconciliation.

Additionally, whenever necessary, your clients can edit specific transactions on a reconciliation.

Undo a whole reconciliation

Download any attachments related to the reconciliation before you begin. A reconciliation can be undone to remove any attachments.

Editing earlier reconciliations should be done with caution. A reconciliation cannot be undone without also undoing all subsequent reconciliations. For instance, if you reverse the reconciliation from January in May, you will also reverse the reconciliation from March and April. This may lead to mistakes. Move backward starting with the most recent reconciliation.

1. Launch QuickBooks Online Accountant and log in.
2. Locate and open the QuickBooks Online company for your client.

When you are examining their company file:

1. Select Accounting from the menu.
2. Choose the Reconcile tab
3. Select Account History.
4. From the dropdowns, choose the account and time period you want to reconcile.
5. On the list, locate the reconciliation.
6. To view the reconciliation report, choose View report

7. Go over any errors and modifications that your client requests.
8. When you're ready, choose Undo from the dropdown menu in the Action column.
9. To confirm, choose Yes and then Undo.

Make sure you've opened your client's company file from QuickBooks Online Accountant if you don't see Undo.

Reporting tool

You can choose a default date range in QuickBooks Online Accountant to view your clients' accounting data. Reviewing particular time periods, including year-end and reconciliations, is a little bit simpler as a result. QuickBooks automatically sets reports and tools to the default date range when you open their company file. This doesn't affect how your client views things; it just alters your perspective.

Set a default date range

Tell your client to invite you to be their accountant if you haven't already. When you're prepared to provide a time frame for a particular client:

1. Click GO TO QUICKBOOKS in QuickBooks Online Accountant, then choose your client's company file.
2. Choose Accountant Tools, followed by Reports.
3. Choose a date range in the From and To fields and a time period in the Date field. In the Basis field, you can additionally specify the accounting technique.

Now, this date range is the default for all reports and tools for your customer.

Understanding the prep for Taxes page

QuickBooks Online has a function for tax preparation. You can review a client's accounts using Accountant from a single dashboard. It resembles a trial balance greatly. Any clients who utilize QuickBooks Online are eligible to use it. Prep for taxes automatically exports accounts to the correct lines on tax forms after you have reviewed your client's accounts. To get an early start on your clients' tax returns, you can export the mapped tax forms to ProConnect Tax Online (or as a CSV).

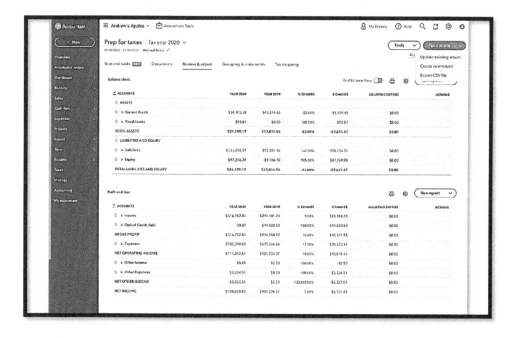

Note: Here's how to begin a brand new tax return for your customer from QuickBooks Online Accountant if you don't want to map and export their information.

Step 1: Open Prep for taxes

Each client has a personalized page just for tax preparation. To prepare for taxes, there are two ways:

If you're an accountant using QuickBooks Online:

1. Select the Clients tab.
2. Locate your client and choose Tax Preparation in the Actions column.

In the event that you are utilizing a client's QuickBooks Online account:

1. Choose Accountant Tools from the dropdown.
2. Click on Tax Prep.

Step 2: Review your client's accounts

Enter the Review & Adjust tab to begin working. You can quickly compare the annual balance sheet and profit and loss report for your client by looking at them side by side. Additionally, you'll see any adjusting entries you've made, account disparities, and totals from the previous year.

To explore a particular account:

1. Expand the list of accounts..
2. Choose the account total for the current year from the column.
3. Examine the account's transactions.

Step 3: Make adjusting journal entries

It is simple to record modifying journal entries if necessary when preparing for taxes. These enable you to change transaction totals while keeping the original record intact. While you are on the Review & adjust tab, you can make an adjusting journal entry as follows:

1. Expand the list of accounts..
2. Locate the account you wish to modify.
3. Click Make change in the Actions column.

When necessary, you can attach notes and documents to individual accounts to track work:

1. Click the little arrow icon in the Actions column.
2. Choose Add note or Add attachment.

For quick access, icons are displayed next to each account.

Enhance your review

The accounting method view can be modified.

For ease of review, you can switch between accounting method views. The settings or view for your client in QuickBooks Online won't be impacted by this.

1. Click on the pencil symbol up top.
2. Change the basis of calculation between cash and accrual.

Examine the Changes List.

An audit log can be found in the Change List under the Review & Adjust tab. This list is updated each time a change is made to Prepare for Taxes. Select Accept changes to accept these changes so QuickBooks may implement them.

Step 4: Map accounts to tax forms

You will assign your clients to particular lines on tax forms after evaluating their finances.

1. Select the Tax Mapping tab.
2. Click Edit under the form's name.
3. Decide which tax form is best for your customer.

Note that changes made to one form do not affect other forms. Changing forms in the middle of mapping accounts necessitates redoing any adjustments on the new form.

Most accounts are automatically categorized as tax lines as part of tax preparation. The "We identified unmapped accounts" section displays any unassigned accounts. Move them to the appropriate tax line by selecting Assign tax line.

Examine every tax line. If a separate tax line needs to be assigned to an account:

1. On the tax form, locate the account.
2. To edit, choose Edit.
3. Select the appropriate tax line.

Step 5: Export the mapped tax forms

When you are prepared to export, choose the tax option from the dropdown menu. Afterward, choose one of the methods below to enter the data into ProConnect Tax Online:

❖ If you started a client's tax return in ProConnect Tax Online before beginning work on the preparation of taxes, choose Update existing return.

It's important to note that this will replace any information you previously entered into ProConnect.

❖ Choose Create new return if you completed your work in Prep for Taxes before beginning a tax return in ProConnect. In ProConnect, this results in a fresh return.

ProConnect populates tax return fields with data from the tax forms you've mapped. Verify that everything was exported properly. Finish your client's return in ProConnect after that.

Download a CSV for other tax preparation software

The CSV file is designed for use with Lacerte's tax preparation program. However, the CSV can be modified to work with different programs:

1. Choose Tax choices, then click Export CSV.

Examining voided and deleted transactions

The Audit Log can be seen by selecting Voided/Deleted Transactions from the Accountant Tools menu. The Audit Log's default view (shown in the accompanying picture) provides details about transactions that have been nullified or removed. However, you may establish a range of additional filters by selecting the Filter option in order to observe other types of transactions and events. View all types of activities in the QBO company by using the Audit Log.

Closing the book

The Advanced page of Account and Settings dialog box for the QBO company is displayed when you use the Close Books command from the Accountant Tools menu, as illustrated in the following picture. The Accounting section's fields, including the field for the books' closure date, can be edited by clicking anywhere inside that section.

Setting a close date

Setting a closing date gives you the option to either demand a password to enter changes before the closing date or to enable changes prior to the closing date once QBO offers a warning. To save your changes, click Done.

Taking a brief look at other accountant tools

A few other tools that simplify the work of accountants may be found in the Accountant Tools menu, like the Reconcile page, where you can choose to reconcile a selected account or check previous reconciliation reports. You can also choose Journal Entries or Chart of Accounts from the Accountant Tools menu to open the Journal Entry window or the Chart of Accounts window, respectively. To open a new window in QBOA rapidly, you can use use the New Window command.

The last option is ProConnect Tax Online, which opens a new browser window and takes you to the Tax Hub of ProConnect Tax Online where you can view the status of your clients' tax returns. This option can be found under the Accountant Tools menu. ProConnect Tax Online is a separate product with its own menus in the Navigation bar, though it connects to your QBOA account.

CHAPTER EIGHTEEN

PRACTICE MANAGEMENT

Look at the Work page in Navigation pane, which serves as a practice management tool, before getting started with using the QuickBooks Online Accountant (QBOA) capabilities accessible while you are working in a client's QBO company. The availability of the Work page in QBOA to every of the team members in your company makes it possible for you to centralize practice management by utilizing such a tool.

Introducing The Work Page

It's crucial to realize that while the Work page is only accessible through QBOA, only you and your team members have access to it. Additionally, only his clients—those to whom your team member has access—are mentioned in the information that every of the team member sees on the Work page. It is possible to keep track of what has to be done for both your clients and your own company on the Work page. And while though the Work page uses the term "projects," keep in mind that these projects are not the same as the ones your clients can create in Qucikbooks online.

The Grid view in QBOA

When you select Work from the Navigation bar, QBOA shows the page in its standard Grid view. Task cards are displayed in the Grid view in date ranges (Due Today, This Week, Next Week, and in the Next 30 days).

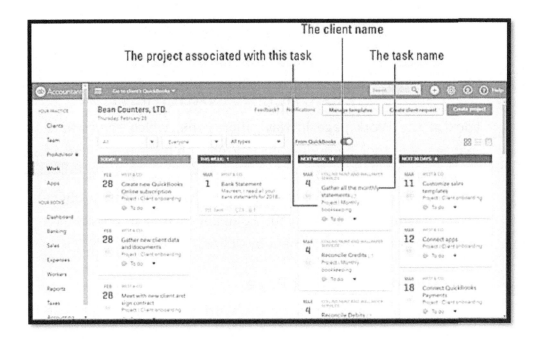

Work page in QBOA's Grid view.

Each task card for a specific project lists the project name and the client to whom the work must be completed (or your own firm if the project is not for a client). The task name can be found specifically on each task card.

Some of the things you see on the Work page's Grid view is under your control. About instance, you can filter the page to see information for your company, a certain client, or a member of your team. The Work function also uses information from client QBO companies to automatically provide due dates and tasks for you to complete, such as payroll due dates and related banking transaction reconciliation. You can select the From QuickBooks slider to hide this automatically generated data from view. The Work feature does not currently connect to rest products like ProConnect Tax Online and only automatically offers actions to take related to QBO.

You won't notice any sort of visual relationship between activities because the Grid view groups tasks by due date; in other words, no lines connecting tasks to one another appear because the Grid view isn't a flow chart. List view and Calendar view are other options on the Work page; you can learn more about these once I cover creating projects and tasks later in this chapter.

How to create tasks and projects

The Work page can be used to create customer requests. In practice management, you establish projects on Work page to represent tasks that need to be completed. You divide each project into tasks, which are smaller units of the project and give more specific instructions on what must be done to finish the project. You can assign several team members to various tasks on the same project after creating them as a part of it. Tasks list the exact actions you must take to finish a project, whereas projects are often generic undertakings that must be completed by a certain date.

You give a project a due date as you create it, and you give each task in the project a due date as well. You name the team member who is in charge of the project as well as the client with whom it is related. Alternatively, you may state that the initiative only has an impact on your company and none of your clients.

Project templates provided by QBOA make it simple to quickly construct tasks like client onboarding and monthly bookkeeping. Whenever you utilize one of these templates, QBOA creates both the project and its associated tasks. The project can then be modified as necessary.

Creating a project

Although you can or will create tasks when you create projects, we'll discuss project creation apart from task creation to make this information as straightforward as possible. Take the following actions to create a project:

1. In the Navigation pane, click Work. (Your firm's Work page is displayed by QBOA).

2. In the top right corner of the page, click Create Project. (To start a project, use the QBOA panel that shows on the right side of the page).

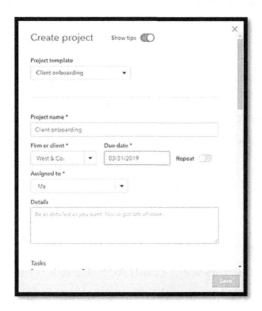

Using a template to create a project.

3. Choose the template right from the Project Template list box if your project fits into one of the established template categories, such as Bi-weekly Payroll, Client Onboard, Monthly Bookkeeping, or Yearly Taxes.

   The tasks related to the project template are added to the project, and each work is given a due date of "tomorrow."

4. Give the project a title.

   If you chose a project template, QBOA uses the name of the project template to fill in the project name.

5. Choose the QBO client that is linked to the project from the Firm or Client list box.

Choose My Firm if the project only affects your company and no clients.

6. Designate a project deadline.

    The project due date you choose is a restriction; if you add tasks, you won't be able to set due dates for the tasks that happen after the project's conclusion.

7. Assign the project to a member of your team using the Assigned To list box.

    If you would like, you can add project specifics.

For tasks that need to repeat frequently, like reconciling a bank statement, click the Repeat slider to specify how often QBOA should carry out the operation.

Working with tasks

You can now work with the project's tasks after creating the project. You can make a change the due dates that QBOA gives to the tasks, add and remove tasks, and rearrange the sequence of tasks in a project.

1. Click the Add a Task button at the down side of the list of tasks to add a task to a project.

    A form for task information is shown by QBOA (see the next figure).

Give the job a name, specify a deadline, and assign it to a company team member.

2. Provide the task's name, deadline, recipient on the team, and any other relevant information, like the QBO commands required to complete the assignment.

   You are free to create as many tasks as you want.

3. Click Collapse in the task card's lower right corner to make the task you're working on disappear so you can go on to another.

   Instead of saving individual tasks, you should save the project, which also stores the details of each job.

4. Click the task to delete it or modify its details.

   The task's details are shown via QBOA.

Drag a task to reorder it or click it to change or delete it.

- ❖ To modify the task, just provide the updated data.
- ❖ Select the Remove link to remove the job.
5. Collapse a task, then drag the square icon at the right border of the task up or down to reposition it within the project.

    The symbol that you drag to rearrange a task is visible.

6. To save the project and associated tasks, click Save.

    The new projects and tasks are displayed on the Work page as QBOA updates it.

Updating task status in Quickbooks Online Accountant

Right from the Grid view of the Work page, you may immediately update a task's status as you make work on it. To alter a task card's status, click the downward pointing arrow.

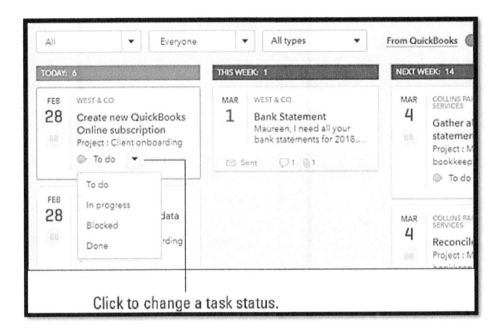

Click to change a task status.

To view the available statuses for a job or project, use the down arrow on the card.

The states of tasks include To Do, In Progress, Blocked, and Done. When something prevents you from finishing a task, you use the Blocked status.

How to delete and edit project information

All projects and tasks can be edited, with the exception of those generated automatically from a Quickbooks Online firm, which can only be hidden or displayed using the From QuickBooks slider. No matter what view you have selected on the Work page, click any task within a project to edit the project. After that, QBOA displays information about the task you clicked and opens the Edit Project panel on the right side of the screen.

By modifying the top section of the Edit Project window, you can modify the project's details. By selecting the trash can symbol in the lower left corner of the Edit Project window, you can actually delete any project from there (see the following figure).

374

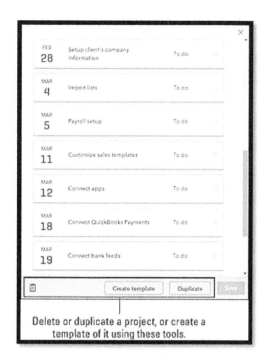

Delete or duplicate a project, or create a
template of it using these tools.

Delete, copy, or make a template from a project.

Since many projects you make are interchangeable, you should clone previous project to create a new one to save time. Additionally, you can use previous project as a model for future initiatives of a similar nature. Duplicate the project by selecting it in the Edit Project panel and then picking the Duplicate button. Click Generate Template to create a template from the project.

It is possible to edit project and task information, but you cannot convert one into the other. Click the X in the top-right corner of the Edit Project panel to close it.

How to operate in List view

Due to the cards' large screen footprint, the Work page's Grid view is restricted in what it can display. Click the List View button in the top right corner of the Work page to view the projects and tasks in List view, as illustrated above (below the Create Project button).

The List view of the Work page.

You can access additional filters from this view. You have the option to filter by status and choose a date range of interest in addition to selecting a customer, a team member, and the type of work (project, task, or client request). Additionally, you may still change any project or task by clicking anywhere on its line to bring up the Edit Project window that was previously displayed.

Working with the Calendar view

The tasks that are due on any given date are shown in the Calendar view. You can see how many tasks are due on each date on the calendar. When you select a date, QBOA displays the tasks that are due on that day using the right side of the Calendar view.

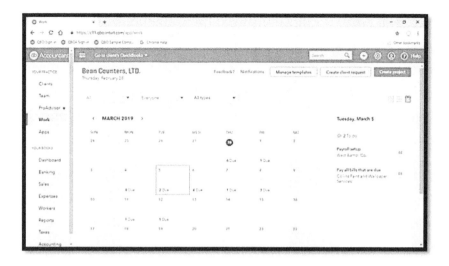

Project tasks are shown in calendar view according to due dates.

Communicating With Team Members About Work

The importance of communication in a team setting cannot be overstated, at the risk of sounding obvious. With QBOA, you may send email notifications for a range of events connected to the tasks and projects that are displayed on the Work page. Click the Notifications link at the top of the Work page to open Notifications tab of the Company Settings dialog box and specify the notifications you want QBOA to deliver to your team.

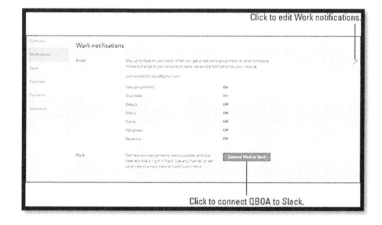

Set up email alerts for team members to get work-related information.

377

To toggle email notifications for different actions that happen on the Work page, select the pencil in the upper right corner of the Email section. When finished, click Save before selecting Done to fo back to QBOA. Each team member has the ability to manage his notifications. Each team member automatically receives notifications of new assignments and due dates, but you can customize the other notifications by having each member log into his or her individual QBOA account.

You may introduce Slack with QBOA if your company utilizes it. Slack is a collaboration tool that fosters team communication. By selecting Connect Now on the Work page, you may add the app to QBOA. Select the Connect Work to Slack button on the Notifications tab of the Company Settings dialog box if you previously hidden the Slack advertisement. Small teams interested in trying out Slack can use the free version, however it has some restrictions. Standard and Plus are the two "paid" versions that Slack also offers; the price of these versions is determined by how many Slack users are active each month.

CHAPTER NINTEEN

AUTOMATING QUICKBOOKS ANALYSIS WITH POWER QUERY

An application for preparing and transforming data is called Power Query. With Power Query, you may perform transformations to data obtained from sources using a Power Query Editor and a graphical user interface. You may import data from a variety of sources, clean it up, convert it, and then reshape it to suit your needs using Power Query, a business intelligence tool provided by Microsoft Excel. Doing so, you can actually create a query once and use it again by simply refreshing.

Top Power Query Benefits And Uses

1. Data Transformation

Data transformation is Power Query's main objective. This include changing the organization, fixing typos, and overall improving the data's suitability for analysis.

In Power Query, common data transformations are carried out as follows:

- Pivot / Unpivot
- Splitting / Merging Columns
- Filtering Data
- Creating custom columns
- Deleting header / blank / error rows
- Changing data types
- Fill down values

Example: In this case, the user needs to compute each store's monthly performance. The data in their text file presents a challenge because it looks like this (below).

Users of Excel will be quite familiar with this type of data because they are aware of the effort required to reformat data to meet their analysis needs.

The file's top rows are unnecessary, and there are columns of empty values, values to fill in lower on the page, and dates to unpivot.

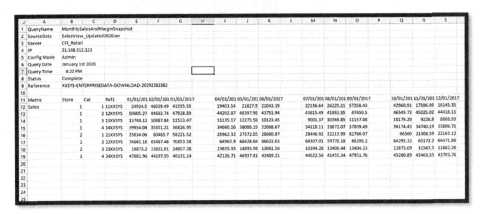

Power Query enables the user to convert the data into the format shown below in just a few easy steps. And perhaps most significantly, the procedure was finished in just a minute.

	Store	Cat	Date	Sales
1				
2	1	1	1/1/2017	24924.5
3	1	1	2/1/2017	46039.49
4	1	1	3/1/2017	41595.55
5	1	1	4/1/2017	19403.54
6	1	1	5/1/2017	21827.9
7	1	1	6/1/2017	21043.39
8	1	1	7/1/2017	22136.64
9	1	1	8/1/2017	26229.21
10	1	1	9/1/2017	57258.43
11	1	1	10/1/2017	42960.91
12	1	1	11/1/2017	17596.96
13	1	1	12/1/2017	16145.35
14	1	2	1/1/2017	50605.27
15	1	2	2/1/2017	44682.74
16	1	2	3/1/2017	47928.89
17	1	2	4/1/2017	44292.87
18	1	2	5/1/2017	48397.98
19	1	2	6/1/2017	43751.94
20	1	2	7/1/2017	43615.49
21	1	2	8/1/2017	41892.55
22	1	2	9/1/2017	47450.5
23	1	2	10/1/2017	46549.73
24	1	2	11/1/2017	45025.02
25	1	2	12/1/2017	44418.11

2. Repetitive Processes

If the aforementioned illustration wasn't sufficient, Power Query also keeps track of each step that was taken to alter the data. As a result, model inputs can be refreshed instantly whenever reports are updated or modifications are made, eliminating the need to start the entire process over.

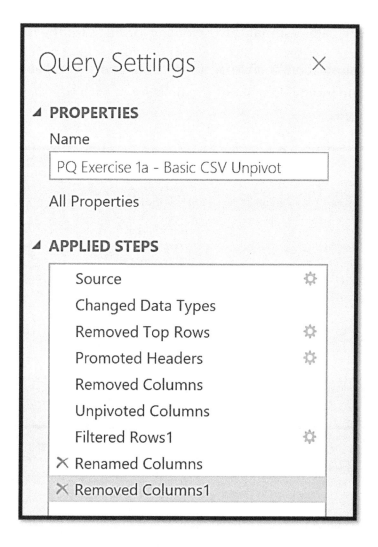

Example: The steps that were used to process this dataset are shown in the image. The procedures are used, and the results are updated, each time we refresh the data source.

3. Merging Different Tables

We can aggregate data from various connected tables using Power Query. Lookup formulas could be used by Excel users to complete the same operation. They would be limited to 1 million rows and discover that when more formulas were included, their models got slower and slower.

Instead, Power Query quickly and efficiently combines the tables using matching fields without the use of any formulas for the full dataset.

In this illustration, a table of transactions is displayed at the top. We have some supporting data about the delivery of each transaction in the second table below.

1²₃ Transaction ID	ABC 123 Order Date	ABC 123 Brand	ABC 123 ValueAtCost
1	2018-01-01	Belvedere	2483.711219
2	2018-01-01	Absolut	361.2076989
3	2018-01-01	Balvenie	5016.09073
4	2018-01-01	Abelour	543.8890102
5	2018-01-01	Hendricks	8672.912697
6	2018-01-01	Highclere Castle	26.16586063
7	2018-01-01	Tanqueray	8714.192278
8	2018-01-01	Mission Hill White	4892.822733
9	2018-01-01	Mission Hill Red	4076.722736
10	2018-01-01	Coke	7520.47324
11	2018-01-01	Fever Tree Tonic	5983.6566
12	2018-01-01	Belvedere	4593.162078
13	2018-01-01	Absolut	4708.591021
14	2018-01-01	Balvenie	5640.099104
15	2018-01-01	Abelour	7976.687715
16	2018-01-01	Patron	9251.192362
17	2018-01-01	Clase Azul	1833.512102
18	2018-01-01	Mission Hill White	5737.202795

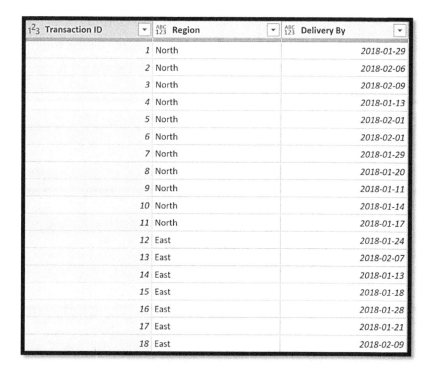

1^2_3 Transaction ID	ABC 123 Region	ABC 123 Delivery By
1	North	2018-01-29
2	North	2018-02-06
3	North	2018-02-09
4	North	2018-01-13
5	North	2018-02-01
6	North	2018-02-01
7	North	2018-01-29
8	North	2018-01-20
9	North	2018-01-11
10	North	2018-01-14
11	North	2018-01-17
12	East	2018-01-24
13	East	2018-02-07
14	East	2018-01-13
15	East	2018-01-18
16	East	2018-01-28
17	East	2018-01-21
18	East	2018-02-09

With just a few clicks in Power Query, we can merge the two data and add the delivery information to the original table by using the matching fields.

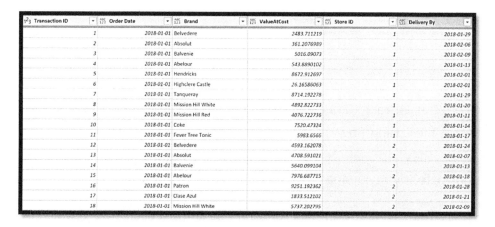

Transaction ID	Order Date	Brand	ValueAtCost	Store ID	Delivery By
1	2018-01-01	Belvedere	2483.711219	1	2018-01-29
2	2018-01-01	Absolut	361.2076989	1	2018-02-06
3	2018-01-01	Balvenie	5016.09073	1	2018-02-09
4	2018-01-01	Abelour	543.8890102	1	2018-01-13
5	2018-01-01	Hendricks	8672.912697	1	2018-02-01
6	2018-01-01	Highclere Castle	26.16586063	1	2018-02-01
7	2018-01-01	Tanqueray	8714.192278	1	2018-01-29
8	2018-01-01	Mission Hill White	4892.822733	1	2018-01-20
9	2018-01-01	Mission Hill Red	4076.722736	1	2018-01-11
10	2018-01-01	Coke	7520.47324	1	2018-01-14
11	2018-01-01	Fever Tree Tonic	5983.6566	1	2018-01-17
12	2018-01-01	Belvedere	4593.162078	2	2018-01-24
13	2018-01-01	Absolut	4708.591021	2	2018-02-07
14	2018-01-01	Balvenie	5640.099104	2	2018-01-13
15	2018-01-01	Abelour	7976.687715	2	2018-01-18
16	2018-01-01	Patron	9251.192362	2	2018-01-28
17	2018-01-01	Clase Azul	1833.512102	2	2018-01-21
18	2018-01-01	Mission Hill White	5737.202795	2	2018-02-09

4. Merging Several Files

Data from several related files can be effortlessly combined using Power Query's capabilities.

Consider this scenario: We have three comparable files, each of which contains sales information for our businesses for a specific month. A single file with a consolidated list of transactions is necessary for our model.

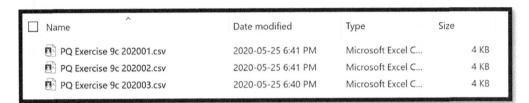

	Name	Date modified	Type	Size
☐	PQ Exercise 9c 202001.csv	2020-05-25 6:41 PM	Microsoft Excel C...	4 KB
	PQ Exercise 9c 202002.csv	2020-05-25 6:41 PM	Microsoft Excel C...	4 KB
	PQ Exercise 9c 202003.csv	2020-05-25 6:40 PM	Microsoft Excel C...	4 KB

We can quickly create a single table as shown below by combining the aforementioned files using Power Query. This can help analysts save a ton of time and reduce the chance of manual error.

	Month	$1^2{}_3$ Store	1.2 Value
1	2020-01-01	1	5418118.589
2	2020-02-01	1	5067778.57
3	2020-03-01	1	5418118.589
4	2020-01-01	2	7448728.793
5	2020-02-01	2	6966412.639
6	2020-03-01	2	7448728.793

5. Access to Main Data Sources

You can extract data from SQL databases, websites, cloud storage, and local files using Power Query's numerous connections. Analysts can make sure they are all operating from the same version of the truth by consistently reviewing centralized sources of data.

It is simple to tailor queries to obtain data from each sort of data source by using the Get Data menu.

Please see the Microsoft Power Query Connections documentation for a complete list of the Power Query connectors that are offered.

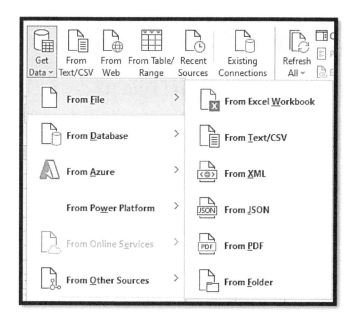

Who Should Can Use Power Query?

1. Analysts working in Excel

By using Power Query, Excel users will see a significant improvement in their capacity to handle and manage data. Analysts can now automate inputs and concentrate on their work instead of using manual updating models once a week or once a month.

2. Analysts with a business intelligence interest

The business intelligence process includes a crucial stage called data transformation for projects (see below). For any analyst that is Excel-based and interested in business intelligence, Power Query is a wonderful place to start. It utilizes the comfortable Excel environment, offers skills that can be applied to Power BI, and is exceedingly simple to use.

3. Anyone who handles data

Power Query is ideal for experimenting with data or quickly integrating files for different projects, even if Excel or Power BI are not your preferred

BI tools. Use a worksheet to load the outputs and use it to quickly prototype a clean data BI solution.

Power Query: Where Can I Find It?

Both Microsoft Excel and Microsoft Power BI support Power Query.

Excel's Power Query

Power Query is now natively available in Excel 2016 and later. You might need to download it as an add-in if you use an earlier version of Excel.

The Get & Transform Data area of Excel's Data tab now contains a number of buttons that can be used to access Power Query.

Power BI's Power Query

The market-leading dashboarding tool from Microsoft, Power BI, enables users to ingest and modify data, build a data model, and produce interactive dashboards.

The same Power Query technology is used by Power BI to carry out the necessary data transformations. The Home tab's Data and Queries area is where you may find it.

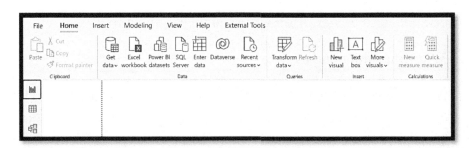

PART 5: THE PART OF SHORTCUTS

QuickBooks Keyboard Shortcuts

General	Key
To start QuickBooks without a company file	Ctrl + double-click
To suppress the desktop windows (at Open Company window)	Alt (while opening)
Display information about QuickBooks	F2
Cancel	Esc
Record (when black border is around OK, Next or Previous button)	↵ (Enter key)
Record (always)	Ctrl + ↵ (Enter key)

Dates	Key
Next day	+ (plus key)
Previous day	- (minus key)
Today	T
First day of the Week	W
Last day of the weeK	K
First day of the Month	M
Last day of the montH	H
First day of the Year	Y
Last day of the yeaR	R
Date calendar	Alt + down arrow

Editing	Key
Edit transaction selected in register	Ctrl + E
Delete character to right of insertion point	Del
Delete character to left of insertion point	Backspace
Delete line from detail area	Ctrl + Del
Insert line in detail area	Ctrl + Ins
Cut selected characters	Ctrl + X
Copy selected characters	Ctrl + C
Paste cut or copied characters	Ctrl + V
Copy line in an invoice	Ctrl + Alt + Y
Paste copied line in an invoice	Ctrl + Alt + V
Increase selected check or other from number by one	+ (plus key)
Decrease selected check or other form number by one	- (minus key)
Undo changes made in field	Ctrl + Z

Help window	Key
Display Help in context	F1
Select next option or topic	Tab
Select previous option or topic	Shift + Tab
Display selected topic	↵ (Enter key)
Close Help window	Alt + F4

Activity	Key
Display the Chart of Accounts list	Ctrl + A
Display the Write Checks window	Ctrl + W
Copy a transaction in a register	Ctrl + O
Display the Customer:Job list	Ctrl + J
Delete a check, invoice, transaction, or item from a list	Ctrl + D
Edit lists or registers	Ctrl + E
QuickFill and Recall (type first few letters of name and press Tab, name fills in)	abc Tab
Find a transaction	Ctrl + F
Go to register of transfer account	Ctrl + G
Display the Help in context	F1
History of A/R or A/P transaction	Ctrl + H
Create an Invoice	Ctrl + I
Display the List for the current field	Ctrl + L
Memorize transaction or report	Ctrl + M
Display the Memorized transaction list	Ctrl + T
New invoice, bill, check or list item	Ctrl + N
Paste copied transaction in register	Ctrl + V
Print	Ctrl + P
QuickZoom on report	↵ (enter key)
QuickReport on transaction or list item	Ctrl + Q
Display the Use Register window	Ctrl + R
Show list	Ctrl + S
Use list item	Ctrl + U
Display the Transaction Journal	Ctrl + Y

Moving around a window	Key
Next field	Tab
Previous field	Shift + Tab
Report column to the right	Right arrow
Report column to the left	Left arrow
Beginning of current field	Home
End of current field	End
Line below in detail area or on report	Down arrow
Line above in detail area or on report	Up arrow
Down one screen	Page Down
Up one screen	Page Up
Next word in field	Ctrl + →
Previous word in field	Ctrl + ←
First item on list or previous month in register	Ctrl + PgUp
Last item on list or next month in register	Ctrl + PgDn
Close active window	Esc

CHAPTER TWENTY

BROWSERS SHORTCUTS AND EXCEL KEYBOARD SHORTCUTS

Browsers Shortcuts

Use keyboard shortcuts to haste up navigation within QBO is easy. These shortcuts listed below will work in the following browsers:

❖ Firefox
❖ Internet Explorer
❖ Chrome Keyboard shortcuts available in QuickBooks Online

How to open a second window

❖ For Internet Explorer: Press Ctrl + N.
❖ For Firefox: Press Ctrl + N.
❖ For Chrome: Press Ctrl + N.

Searching for text in a window

❖ CTRL + F
❖ A Find toolbar appears on your screen when Firefox is launched.
❖ A search box will appear in Chrome at the top right of the screen.

Entering dates

❖ Next day + (plus key)
❖ Previous day - (minus key)
❖ Today: T
❖ First day of the Week: W
❖ Last day of the week: K
❖ First day of the Month: M
❖ Last day of the month: H
❖ First day of the Year: Y
❖ Last day of the year: R

❖ Press Alt+down arrow to access the pop-up calendar icon to the right of a date field.

Calculating amounts and rates

In any of the Amount or Rate field, just enter a calculation. When you press Tab, QBO calculates the result.

- ❖ Add + 1256.94+356.50
- ❖ Subtract - 48.95-15
- ❖ Multiply * 108*1.085
- ❖ Divide / 89.95/.33
- ❖ Group ( ) 13.95+(25.95*.75)

How to move around fields on most forms

- ❖ Use the Tab key to go forward.
- ❖ Use Shift+Tab to go back.
- ❖ Use the Space Bar to check a check box field.

How to save forms

- ❖ From any form, just press Alt + S instead of clicking on Save.
- ❖ In Firefox and Chrome, you must use Alt + Shift + S. For Mac users it is Option + Control + S.

How to respond to messages

- ❖ Hold down the Alt key. If the button names have underlined letters, you can keep the Alt key held down and type the letter to select the button you want.

How to select a transaction type in an account register

- ❖ Press Shift + Tab to pick the transaction type field in a fresh, yellow transaction row.
- ❖ To access the list, press Alt and the down arrow.
- ❖ You can scroll through the list by pressing the up or down arrows, or you can type the first letter of the transaction type you desire. Type the letter twice to choose the second transaction type if there

are two that share the same initial. For instance, type C once to choose Cheque and C again to choose Cash Purchase.

❖ To advance to the next field and choose the transaction type, press Tab. As soon as you are comfortable with the possible transaction kinds, you can tab to the field and just input the first letter without having to open the list.

How to save or edit selected transaction

❖ To save, press Alt + S. Shift + Alt + S (for Firefox and Chrome).

❖ To edit a saved transaction, press Alt + E. The transaction form is then shown.

How to navigate through the register's transactions while picking the date field at each stop

❖ To choose the transaction above, press the up arrow.

❖ To choose the transaction below, press the down arrow.

Changing print alignment

❖ To raise or lower the number, select the Vertical or Horizontal field and then press "+" or "-".

❖ The numeric keypad's keys must be used.

Keyboard Shortcuts for QuickBooks Online

In Chrome or Firefox:

❖ Press Ctrl+Alt+I = Invoice

❖ Press Ctrl+Alt+A = Accounts

❖ Press Ctrl+Alt+C = Customers

❖ Press Ctrl+Alt+V = Vendors

❖ Press Ctrl+Alt+F = Search transactions

❖ Press Ctrl+Alt+W = Write Checks

❖ Press Ctrl+Alt+X = Expense

❖ Press Ctrl+Alt+R = Receive Payment

❖ Press Ctrl+Alt+E = Estimate

- ❖ Press Ctrl+Alt+L = Lists
- ❖ Press Ctrl+Alt+H = Help

On Transaction Pages (Invoice, expense, etc.)

- ❖ Press Ctrl+Alt+D = Save & Close
- ❖ Press Ctrl+alt+M = Save & Send
- ❖ Press Ctrl+Alt+X = Exit transaction
- ❖ Press Ctrl+Alt+C = Cancel
- ❖ Press Ctrl+Alt+S = Save & New

Spreadsheet Management Tips And Tricks For Microsoft Excel

Microsoft Excel is a crucial tool for business. Some people enjoy Excel's features and find it to be a helpful tool that makes managing, reporting on, and illuminating data tables simple. Others, though, find it tiresome and are unable to see how Excel may help them beyond maintaining orderly columns and rows of data. Microsoft Excel management can give you the technological edge you need to complete the task, whether you're analyzing massive amounts of data or battling timesheet designs.

Are you the one who has trouble understanding it? It's alright. With the help of these Excel tips, you can work with this database multi-tool much more efficiently and effectively. Along the process, you might even enjoy learning a few Excel functions.

Excel trick 1: Select all cells in a spreadsheet

Do you need to reformat your Excel workbook's font or make any other significant changes? To select every cell in the workbook, click the square in the top left corner. Where the tops of the rows and columns converge is where you'll find it. All of the cells in the document, including empty cells, will be highlighted when this box is clicked.

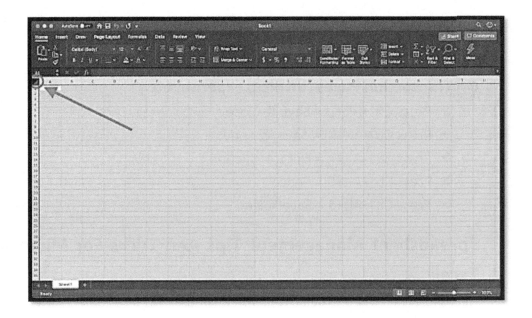

If you'd rather use keyboard shortcuts, you can also select every cell by simultaneously pressing the Ctrl and A keys (Ctrl + A). This is a fantastic way to format multiple cells at once. Do you want to change a lot of the cell rules or do you have a formula that is incorrect? Making all of these adjustments at once using the Select All function will save you a lot of time.

Note: Use conditional formatting, a pro Excel tip. Depending on the provided cell value, conditional formatting in Excel enables you to highlight cells of a certain color. This is a fantastic choice for people who want an ordered perspective into their data sets but may not require the structure of a VLOOKUP.

Excel trick 2: Copy a worksheet from one workbook to another

Have you ever needed to duplicate one or more sizable data sets while working in an Excel file? Manually entering this data if you have a lot of formatting is a hassle.

This is when copying a worksheet (a group of many pages) from one workbook to another comes in.

1. Enter your "source" workbook first (the one with the data you want to copy).
2. Open the workbook you want to use (the one you want to copy to). This could be a brand-new or used workbook.
3. Locate the name of the sheet you want to replicate in the lower left-hand corner of your source worksheet. The worksheet should have a name like "Sheet1" unless you've altered it.
4. Use the right mouse button to choose the sheet you want to copy. If you're using a single-button mouse on a Mac, you might need to hold down the Command key as you click.
5. Go to the menu and choose "Move or Copy...".

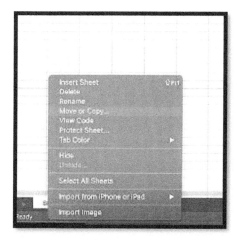

6. Choose the location from the list to which you wish to move or duplicate the sheet. To view other open workbooks, use the dropdown menu at the top.
7. Select the workbook to copy it to and the position in the existing worksheets' order that you want it to be in.

As an alternative, you can drag the worksheet with your mouse from one workbook to another. To be safe, copy it instead, at least until you feel more confident with Excel.

Try the copying method if you ever need to validate a lot of data and want to prevent making a mistake with a calculation. Making a backup workbook in this manner can be simple and quick.

Excel trick 3: **Add multiple rows or columns at once**

It's possible that you'll need to add several rows and columns at once. Let's imagine, for illustration, that you wish to insert two rows into the middle of a set of data. You'll require:

1. Beginning with the row just beneath where you want the new rows to appear, choose two rows. (You can select whichever many rows you require. In this illustration, we're only employing two.)
2. Click with the right mouse button (PC) or command button (Mac) and choose Insert from the drop-down menu.
3. Your new rows will be displayed above the row you chose in step one.

Excel will insert the highlighted number because it recognizes that you wish to insert rows as a result of the rows you've highlighted. Two rows are highlighted in this example, therefore when you choose Insert, two blank rows will be displayed. This approach also functions if you highlight columns.

Excel trick 4: Filter data

To give each column a clickable dropdown menu, pick Filter from the Data tab at the top of the page. Every cell in the first row will have the menu. Choose one, and a range of data sorting options are available.

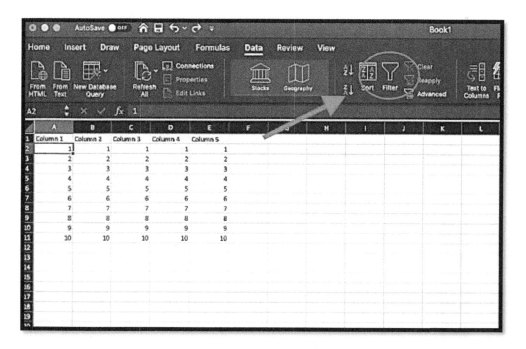

You have the option to select specific values or names from the list that shows. Simply click on the names you desire, then click Select All to deselect all. The dropdown option will vanish after you click OK, revealing only the names you've chosen.

The values you selected have now been added to the list after it was truncated. The other data, however, has not been destroyed, as seen by the circled row numbers. In this view, it is merely "hidden."

	A	B	C	D	E	
1	Column 1	Column 2	Column 3	Column 4	Column 5	
3	2	2	2	2	2	
4	3	3	3	3	3	
5	4	4	4	4	4	
6	5	5	5	5	5	
12						
13						

By selecting Select All once more from the Filter menu at the top, you can quickly reverse any sorting that has been done.

Excel trick 5: Copy figures from one worksheet to another in the same workbook

Without copying and pasting, you can utilize a figure from one worksheet's cell in another worksheet's cell. This is particularly useful for calculations where a number may change from month to month but you have one worksheet that totals everything up for the entire year.

The workbook's first tab, which displays year-to-date sales, spending, and revenue totals, is illustrated in the sample below.

JAN and FEB are the labels for the second and third tabs, respectively. You must type the formula =SUM(JAN!B3+FEB!B3) in the desired cell to find the sum. Without quotation marks, the formula is "WorksheetName!WorksheetCell."

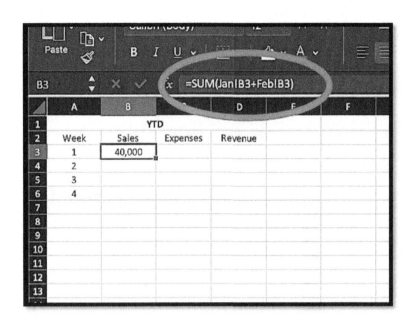

Excel trick 6: Copy a formula across rows or down columns

Using your mouse, you can copy any formula across a number of cells. As an illustration, the prior formula only needs to be entered once, in the B2 cell. Select the cell after entering the information, then click on the tiny box that appears in the bottom right corner. You can then drag it across the desired range of cells to fill it with the same formula.

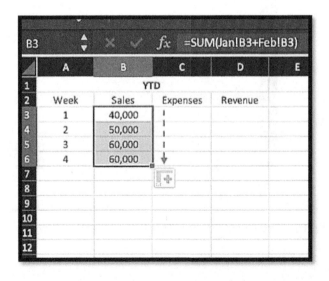

This duplicates the formula across the cells, but it modifies the values in accordance with the location of the new cell. For instance, the formula will appear without quotes in the B3 cell as "=SUM(JAN!B3+FEB!B3)". The formula will appear in the C3 cell as "=SUM(JAN!C3+FEB!C3)" and so on.

If you drag the box downward rather than across, you may accomplish the same task. The formula is then duplicated in the column. The formula for the B3 column will therefore read "=SUM(JAN!B3+FEB!B3)," "=SUM(JAN!B4+FEB!B4)," and so on.

Excel trick 7: Transpose columns and rows

Don't give up if you need to shift existing data from columns to rows or vice versa.

Copy the data you've chosen to transpose (Ctrl C).

- ❖ To use the dropdown menu, right-click on the cell you wish to insert the data into. You should choose Paste Special from that option.
- ❖ Select the Transpose checkbox in the lower right-hand corner of the Paste Special menu, then click OK. The following screenshot will appear if you're using a Mac.
- ❖ Rows will become columns and columns will become rows as the data flips.

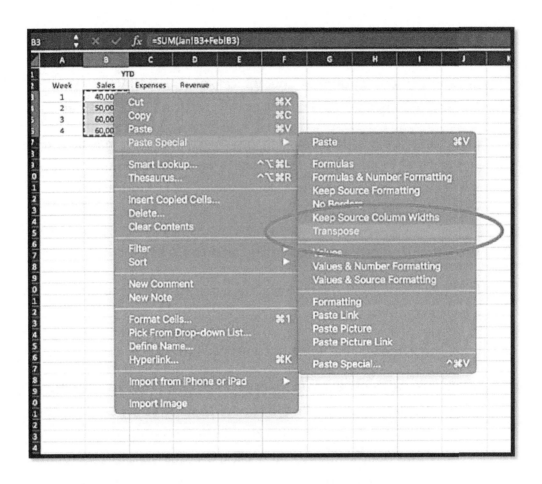

Excel trick 8: **Continue a series down a column or across a row**

There is a quick way to enter a numbered list in Excel without having to number every row.

- ❖ Start your number sequence.
- ❖ Select the first cell in the list after that, then drag down on the tiny box in the bottom right corner (similar to trick 6). Excel will automatically fill the cells with the information it thinks you want. (It is possible to use common sense and determine if it is a numbered list, a list of dates, etc.) However, as you can see in the example below, it simply duplicated a 1 into each cell of the column, which is not what we want. Therefore, we'll need to make some adjustments.

❖ If you right-click, the second choice on the pop-up menu will be "Fill Series." You can modify the settings by clicking there.

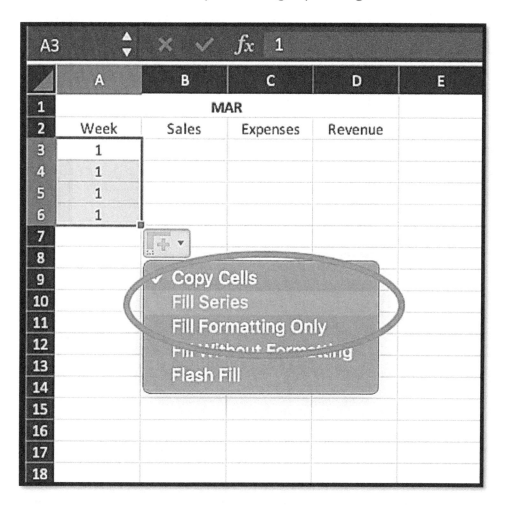

By doing this, the cell values will be changed to a numbered series. The program will adjust for however many of the cells you have highlighted, as shown below. Therefore, select 100 cells if you want it to be numbered from 1 to 100.

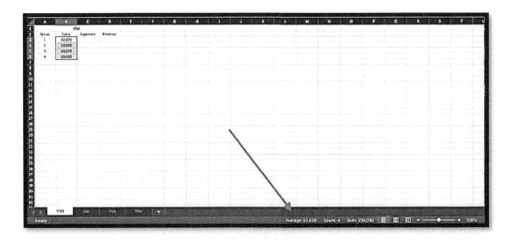

	A	B	C	D	E
1			MAR		
2	Week	Sales	Expenses	Revenue	
3	1				
4	2				
5	3				
6	4				
7					
8					
9					
10					
11					
12					
13					
14					
15					

Excel trick 9: Highlight a list of numbers to see basic information

Many Excel experts love this trick since it's straightforward and quite useful, especially when working with numbers and budgets.

The lower right-hand corner of Excel will show some information about the highlighted collection of numbers. You can see the number of highlighted cells, the sum of all the cells, and the average value across all the cells.

If you're searching for a quick total or average without having to type a formula, this Excel spreadsheet trick is really helpful.

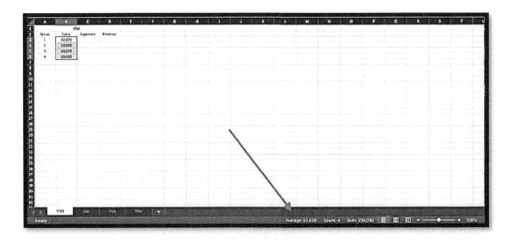

Excel trick 10: Essential shortcut keys and tips

The best Excel advice is to become familiar with shortcuts. Here are a few opportunistic shortcuts you might not have known about. Even though some of these are common to many Microsoft Office programs (such as Word, PowerPoint, etc.), they are still highly useful while using Excel.

- ❖ Pressing Ctrl Z will reverse the previous action you made on the worksheet. In the upper left-hand corner of the Excel window, above the navigation menu, you can use the backward arrow or the shortcut key Ctrl Z.
- ❖ Ctrl Shift up or down arrow: Selects all cells that are immediately above (up arrow) or below (down arrow) the currently selected cell. This won't choose empty cells because it only selects cells above and below that have data.
- ❖ Shift F11: Adds a new worksheet named "Macro1" to your existing workbook. The insert tab shortcut is another name for this short cut. The Fn key might be necessary in Mac OS for this shortcut to function.
- ❖ Ctrl Home: Navigates to cell A1.
- ❖ Ctrl End: Navigates to the last cell that contains data.
- ❖ Format Painter: Select the cell whose format you want to copy. Then click on Format Painter (the little paintbrush) in the upper toolbar on the Home tab. Alternatively, you can click on the paintbrush in the pop-up format menu that appears when right clicking, then select the cell you want to format.
- ❖ Pivot table: You can track and analyze data patterns by using a pivot table, which is a condensed summary of your input data packaged in a visually appealing graphic. Excel's pivot tables are incredibly helpful features that efficiently produce an accurate and comprehensive summary of thousands of rows and columns of disorganized data. You may arrange massive amounts of data into a consumable spreadsheet by utilizing pivot tables. To quickly construct a pivot table in Excel, press Alt+N+V.

QuickBooks Online And QuickBooks Online Accountant Shortcuts On The Keyboard

Time-saving keyboard shortcuts are available. When entering data into QBO or QBOA, you can keep your hands on the keyboard by using keyboard shortcuts. Users of Macs should change Alt to Option in the following tables.

To	Press
To open the Check window	Ctrl+Alt+W
To open the Expense window	Ctrl+Alt+X
To open the Estimate window	Ctrl+Alt+E
To open the Invoice Transaction window	Ctrl+Alt+I
To open the Receive Payment window	Ctrl+Alt+R
To Display Help	Ctrl+Alt+H
To Display the Lists page	Ctrl+Alt+L
To Display the Customers page	Ctrl+Alt+C
To Display the Vendors page	Ctrl+Alt+V
To Display the Chart of Accounts page	Ctrl+Alt+A
To Display the Search Transactions page	Ctrl+Alt+F
To Display keyboard shortcuts	Ctrl+Alt+/

While working in a transaction window, use the following keyboard shortcuts:

To	Press
Save the transaction and starts a new one	Ctrl+Alt+S
Save the transaction and close the transaction window	Ctrl+Alt+D
Save and send the transaction	Ctrl+Alt+M
Print the transaction	Ctrl+Alt+P

If you've made modifications, a notification will ask you to confirm that you wish to close the window without saving your changes before you may shut the transaction window.	Ctrl+Alt+X or Ctrl+Alt+C

INDEX

Made in the USA
Coppell, TX
09 May 2023

16632871R00234